BRITISH POETRY, 1900–50

British Poetry, 1900–50

Aspects of Tradition

Edited by

GARY DAY

and

BRIAN DOCHERTY

St. Martin's Press

First published in Great Britain 1995 by
MACMILLAN PRESS LTD
Houndmills, Basingstoke, Hampshire RG21 2XS
and London
Companies and representatives
throughout the world

A catalogue record for this book is available
from the British Library.

ISBN 0–333–53278–3 hardcover
ISBN 0–333–53279–1 paperback

10 9 8 7 6 5 4 3 2 1
04 03 02 01 00 99 98 97 96 95

Printed in Great Britain by
Ipswich Book Co Ltd
Ipswich, Suffolk

First published in the United States of America 1995 by
Scholarly and Reference Division,
ST. MARTIN'S PRESS, INC.,
175 Fifth Avenue,
New York, N.Y. 10010

ISBN 0–312–12406–6

Library of Congress Cataloging-in-Publication Data
British poetry, 1900–50 : aspects of tradition / edited by Gary Day
and Brian Docherty.
p. cm.
ISBN 0–312–12406–6
1. English poetry—20th century—History and criticism.
2. Influence (Literary, artistic, etc.) I. Day, Gary, 1956–
II. Docherty, Brian.
PR601.B75   1995
821'.91209—dc20
                                                94–33036
                                                CIP

Contents

Acknowledgements

The editors would like to thank Charmian Hearne for her valuable support in seeing this book through to its completion, Clive Bloom and Christopher Norris for their suggestions, and special thanks to Elena Bonelli for her time and comments on Chapter 5.

The editors and publishers wish to thank Faber and Faber Ltd, for permission to reproduce the extract from *The Collected Poems of W. H. Auden*, edited by Edward Mendelson.

Notes on the Contributors

Ian A. Bell is a Lecturer in English at the University College of Wales at Aberystwyth.

Clive Bloom is General Editor of the **Insights** series and has written widely on literary theory and popular culture.

Steven Connor is a Reader in Modern English Literature at Birkbeck College, University of London, and is the author of several books and numerous articles on critical and cultural theory.

Alistair Davies is a Lecturer in English at the University of Sussex.

Gary Day is a Lecturer in English Literature at the University of Wales College of Cardiff. He is a member of the **Insights** series Editorial Board and one of the General Editors of the Longman **Literature and Culture in Modern Britain** series.

Martin Gray is a Lecturer in English at the University of Stirling.

Alasdair D. F. Macrae is a Senior Lecturer in English at the University of Stirling.

John Pikoulis is a Senior Lecturer in English at the Department for Continuing Education, University of Wales College of Cardiff, and has published widely in the fields of nineteenth- and twentieth-century English and American literature.

Neil Roberts is a Lecturer in English at the University of Sheffield.

Stan Smith is Professor of English at the University of Dundee. He has published widely on twentieth-century poetry.

Jeffrey Walsh is Subject Leader of English at Manchester Metropolitan University.

George Walter is a teaching fellow in the Department of English at Saint David's University College, University of Wales.

Gina Wisker is a Lecturer at Anglia College, Norwich. She has published a number of articles with the **Insights** series, and edited *Black Women's Writing* for the series.

1

Introduction: Poetry, Society and Tradition

GARY DAY

The aim of this collection is to encourage the reader to think about two related questions: first, what is the relation of poetry to society, and secondly, what is the role of a poetic tradition? As each essay raises one or both of these issues in its own way it is not the purpose of this introduction to pre-empt them by summary, rather it is to provide a general context in which the various arguments may be understood.

One such context is suggested by the work of Pierre Bourdieu. Simplifying drastically, he argues that the literary work needs to be understood in relation to what he calls the literary producers, the literary field and the dominant power relations of society. Each of these can be subdivided, with each new subdivision having to be articulated with subdivisions in its own and other fields before any attempt can be made to synthesise them.[1] Although Bourdieu's proposals are too intricate and extensive to be practically implemented, they are a salutary reminder that literature – and therefore poetry – cannot be separated off from the society of which it is a part.

The name of F. R. Leavis cannot be ignored in considering the relation of poetry to society. Indeed, *New Bearings in English Poetry* was specifically addressed to this very question.[2] But while Leavis acknowledged that poetry needs to be situated in its social, economic and political contexts, he nevertheless argued that these were marginal when it came to giving an account of the value of a particular poem. Only the discourse of literary criticism could do that.[3] Thus the project of analysing the complex relations between poetry and society is transformed into the problem of how to evaluate individual poems. This could, however, be seen as a concern with the very specificity of poetry which anticipates those arguments about the autonomy of the cultural realm to be found in the work of Althusser and Macherey.[4]

One of Leavis's central claims is that the poetry of his age is more or less determined by the 'pre-conceptions of the poetical and its corresponding habits, conventions and techniques' (*NB*, p. 12) Leavis claims the poetical is the product of social and economic conditions and, though these may alter, 'the poetical' will persist. When this happens poetry is cut off from 'life' and its words are 'rootless' (ibid.): they conform to ideas of 'the poetical' rather than confront experience.

There are a number of problems here. First, how can 'the poetical' be both determined and determining? It arises as a result of social and economic conditions, thus producing poetry which reflects them. Yet, because 'the poetical' persists after those conditions have been displaced, it also produces a transcendent poetry. 'The poetical' thus generates a concept of poetry which both mirrors and does not mirror society. Leavis's logic seems to suggest that he prefers the former and his argument shows little awareness that the gap between society and 'the poetical' could be exploited to critique both terms, their imbalance introducing a faultline into the otherwise smooth continuity that Leavis envisages as the ideal relation between poetry and society.

The notion of 'genius' offers Leavis an escape from the problems of 'the poetical' but at the cost of society disappearing from his argument altogether. Leavis's 'genius' is reminiscent of the Nietzschean superman, the being who escapes all social determination. Leavis cites Eliot as an example of 'genius' and there is a certain irony in this, given that Eliot was American and one of Leavis's major concerns in *New Bearings* is to bring out the *Englishness* of English poetry. But, as he shows, this can only be achieved by the importation of what is foreign. The irony intensifies when it is remembered that, for Leavis, America and Americans represented the very worst aspects of modern culture, which needed to be vigorously resisted if it was not to become totally degenerate.

Leavis applies the term 'genius' to those poets who are more sensitive, aware and sincere than their contemporaries. These qualities are manifest in their verse to the extent that it breaks with 'the poetical', and Leavis understands this break in terms of technique. Technique 'is inseparable from the rare adequacy of mind, sensibility and spirit that it vouches for' (*NB*, p. 14). It sharpens awareness of 'ways of feeling, so making these communicable' for the 'essential' qualification of a poet is 'the need to communicate something of his own' (*NB*, pp. 17 and 15).[5] The poet is also 'the most conscious point of the race in his time' and 'his interest in experience is not separable from his interest in words' (*NB*, pp. 16–17). Technique is identified with consciousness in these comments and consciousness itself is associated with self-knowledge since the poet scrutinises his or her own experience so as to be able to communicate it. This self-knowledge is expressed through 'wit' and the 'play of intelligence' and it is preferred to the sensuousness of someone like Browning (*NB*, p. 21).

The emphasis on intellect and its clear separation from the flesh suggests that Leavis's knowing subject is one who has transcended the body. And yet the text reveals an obsessive concern with the body through its continual promotion of the concrete – 'my main concern is with the concrete' – and the particular above the abstract – above, that is, the intellect (*NB*, p. 9). But perhaps the text's pre-occupation with the body is most evident in the discussion of rhythm.

Rhythm is one of the main characteristics of technique but, ironically, whereas technique is directed to the refinement of consciousness, rhythm acts upon it like a drug. Rhythm is related to technology for, as Leavis, citing Eliot, notes, 'the modern's perception of rhythm has been affected by the internal combustion engine' (*NB*, p. 24). The cumulative effect of the references to rhythm in his argument suggests that it is a principle of movement. It is not articulate but a pulse and, as such, calls into question all Leavis has been saying about the relationship between technique and heightened consciousness. Rhythm, as technique, is the very opposite of consciousness. It points, indeed, to the unconscious, thereby undermining the claim that the poet is one who knows himself. Furthermore, in pointing towards the unconscious, rhythm is associated with desire and therefore with the return of the body, which Leavis has tried to banish by his emphasis on wit and intellect.

Leavis's endeavour to understand the relationship between poetry and society, then, results in a concentration of the former at the expense of the latter. Society, like the body, apparently vanishes from his text and, in the complex economy of Leavis's argument, knowledge of self is substituted for knowledge of the relation between poetry and society. However, this self-knowledge is based on repression of the body, which, as rhythm, returns to disrupt claims about the necessity and importance of consciousness. Moreover, the association of rhythm and technology brings together the body and society, both of which are then opposed to the individual

consciousness and poetry.[6] Thus, despite asserting that the best
poetry 'belongs to the world [the poet] lives in', Leavis ends by
saying the opposite, that the best poetry is based on a repression
of body and society if not, indeed, the world (*NB*, p. 21).

T. W. Adorno's article 'Lyric Poetry and Society' is also an attempt to explore the complex set of interrelations between verse
and the world.[7] Adorno argues that the importance of poetry lies in
the way that it brings 'to light things undistorted, ungrasped, things
not yet subsumed – and thus [it] anticipates, in an abstract way, a
condition in which no mere generalities can bind and chain what is
human' (*LPS*, p. 156). The key notion here is that poetry points to
utopian possibilities. It does this by deploying language in a way
which subverts its normal use for instrumental and administrative
purposes. For this reason Adorno describes lyric poetry as a 'sphere
of expression whose very essence lies in defying the power of social
organisation' (*LPS*, p. 155).

Poetry is thus opposed to society, it is subjective and society is
objective. This separation between subjective and objective is an opposition which Adorno wants to overcome. He claims that the two
poles can be reconciled in lyric poetry, which fuses the objective
part of language, dealing with concepts and ideas – hence relating
it to social reality – with the subjective, 'feeling' part of language to
create a new condition that is both subjective and objective. This
gives language a force which propels it 'beyond a restricted and
restricting social condition to a more humane one' (*LPS*, p. 160).

Adorno's account of this process is far from satisfactory. He claims
that it is brought about by the poet abandoning himself or herself
to language, which means he or she is objectified as the language
is subjectified. But what does this mean? This claim remains at the
level of abstraction and so partakes of that rationalistic discourse
which Adorno is trying to overturn. Terms like subject and object
also need to be historically contextualised before they can yield the
kind of insights Adorno is claiming for them. Adorno's failure to
clarify these and other points means that, when he turns to the
criticism of actual poems, he, like Leavis, lapses into simple evalu-
ative language.

And, as with Leavis, this language reveals concerns other than
those to which it is ostensibly addressed. This is evident in Adorno's
metaphors which suggest banished desires. Poems are seen 'echo-
ing as a memory' (*LPS*, p. 166) or as 'a buried condition of the soul'
(*LPS*. p. 169). What Adorno had earlier identified as a longing to

reconcile subject and object has now become 'the speaker's insatiable erotic longing' (LPS, ibid.). That this longing is given neither name nor object is perhaps consistent with those metaphors of foreign languages and borders which accumulate in the course of the essay. They suggest the enigma of desire rendered in a language stubbornly resistant to the reconciling powers which Adorno finds in lyric poetry. These metaphors speak of a desire which escapes rapprochement and future direction and which therefore exceeds the logic of Adorno's argument. Once again the attempt to theorise poetry and society has resulted in the emergence of desire.

Antony Easthope places desire at the heart of his study of poetry. In *Poetry and Phantasy* he argues that '[t]here is now no alternative to reading literature in some relation to psychoanalysis'.[8] The Thatcherite echoes are disquieting but Easthope's case is that psychoanalysis offers a better understanding of literary texts than traditional literary criticism and for the following reasons. One, its theoretical vocabulary makes it more consistent; two, it shows the subject as an effect of language rather than a source of it; and three, it is able to offer a critique of identity and sexuality which traditional literary criticism takes for granted (*PP*, pp. 8–9).

Easthope deploys psychoanalysis to uncover the operations of phantasy in poetry. He is careful to argue that phantasy should not be understood in a purely private sense, for 'phantasy in poetry is always already socialised' (*PP*, p. 14) and '*cannot be separated* from the ideologically determined meanings in which it is set' (*PP*, p. 17, italics in original). Poetry is thus identified with ideology. Easthope then considers the problem of the relation between ideology and the unconscious, but he concludes that 'no synthesis can be found to integrate [them] within a single theoretically coherent framework' (*PP*, p. 23).

Easthope's argument is not always clear and this is because he has four terms, ideology, the unconscious, poetry and phantasy, which he uses interchangeably without always clarifying the relation between them. For example, ideology signifies poetry as well as the dominant beliefs which govern Western society. Indeed, it could even be said that Easthope runs all his concepts together, in that he uses psychoanalysis to conceptualise poetry as phantasy thus conflating it with ideology and the unconscious. Psychoanalysis is thus Easthope's solution to the problem of how to relate poetry and society. Phantasy makes them simultaneous.

But this simultaneity, which Easthope declares is the only way of

understanding ideology and the unconsicous (*PP*, p. 43), contradicts something which he wrote earlier when he was advocating
the advantages of adopting Althusser's view of the social formation
as a decentred structure. Easthope uses this concept to try and for-
mulate the relation between ideology and the unconscious. Since
'there is', he glosses, 'no general principle govern[ing] all [its] levels
and times, there is no need to suppose that the time of the unconscious coheres with that of ideology' (*PP*, p. 32). Easthope goes on
to argue that this temporal difference is crucial if their respective
autonomy is to be preserved, an autonomy he later disregards in
his concept of simultaneity.

Another problem with Easthope's account is his claim that psychoanalytic criticism 'breaks with all reflexive accounts of aesthetic
texts' (*PP*, p. 22), which is at odds with his conclusions that show
that poetry does represent or reflect certain phantasies, phantasies
which have persisted in poetry from the Renaissance to Pound.
Easthope sums these up in the following way

> what has been demonstrated is that the transcendent ego is a
> masculine ego, constantly maintaining its dominance by equat-
> ing masculinity with knowledge, activity, looking and mastery,
> and femininity with sexuality, passivity and being looked at. In
> some the 'I' of this subject depends on a hypostasised idea of The
> Woman as its subordinate Other.   (*PP*, p. 193)

This seems a somewhat reductive claim. Can poetry from the Renaissance to Pound be summed up, indeed *mastered*, like this? Isn't
such a statement itself evidence of the phantasy it claims to detect
in poetry? Easthope locates the oppression of women in male
phantasy without acknowledging, except in the most general way,
how that phantasy is social. Of course Easthope could claim the
principle of simultaneity, that the poetic phantasy merely reflects
the social reality, but again this contradicts what he said earlier
about ideology and the unconscious each having their own separate, temporal spheres.

Easthope's analysis, while acknowledging that desire plays a
part in the relation between poetry and society, is ultimately unsat-
isfactory. The history of poetry is reduced to the male phantasy of
mastery, which reflects the oppression of women in society. On this
scheme, poetry and society reinforce one another rather than relate

to one another. Is society caused by the male phantasy or the male phantasy by society? Easthope gives no answers.

Furthermore, his conflation of different terms suppresses their complexities and tensions as well as the relations between them. For example, Easthope's view that poetry is 'a shared symbolic expression which has meaning for others' is far too sweeping (*PP*, p. 43). There is no awareness that the social is structured by class as well as gender and that 'shared meanings' are not uniformly shared by different classes.

In addition, the use of phantasy as the simultaneity of poetry and society allows no possibility of using poetry to oppose society. Desire emerges as a conservative force in Easthope's argument since it is nothing more than an expression of the social order, and this makes his analysis less radical than that of Leavis or Adorno, where desire disturbs any attempt to relate poetry and society.

Leavis, Adorno and Easthope all fail to relate poetry and society, perhaps because their attempts to do so involve a reconciliation which belies the very framing of the problem, since it stresses their oppositional nature. It may therefore be more useful to foreground this opposition rather than endeavour to overcome it. The problem lies in defining that opposition. One possible approach is to articulate it in terms of verse structure, which is what Antony Easthope does in his book *Poetry as Discourse*.[9]

Easthope's case is that modernist poetry represents a radical opportunity for the creation of new subjectivities in that it breaks with the constraints of the iambic pentameter. Easthope argues that the iambic, by effacing the signifying elements of poetry, helped to create the illusion of a speaking voice with which the subject could identify. Thus the iambic fulfilled a conservative function by offering subject positions consistent with the ones demanded by bourgeois society. Easthope claims that modernist poetry, by promoting the signified at the expense of the signified, undermined the illusion of the speaker's presence, thereby making it harder for the reader to identify with him or her. In addition, this foregrounding of the signifier is held by Easthope to disrupt the phantasy of male mastery. In its place are a variety of phantasies proclaiming 'the value of the body, pleasure and satisfaction . . . against the canonical appeal of narcissism, mastery and phantasy' (*PP*, p. 194).

This is a powerful argument but it overlooks the fact that the movement away from the iambic need not necessarily lead to the dissolution of traditional subject positions. For instance, the reader of modernist poetry is placed in a transcendent position vis-à-vis the text, since he or she is required to make connections between its disparate moments. This reinforces the subject's mastery, it does not undermine it. Furthermore, Easthope ignores the way in which free verse can be used to bolster traditional subject positions as well as interrogate them. D. H. Lawrence uses free verse but in a manner consistent with the concerns of traditional notions of subjectivity. Lawrence may question the contents of that subjectivity but, despite his fluctuating line lengths, the structure of that subjectivity remains intact.[10]

The real flaw in Easthope's argument is, however, his failure to note that free verse elides the distinction between poetry and prose. This issue is explored by Graham Hough, who notes that in metrical verse there are two rhythms, the metrical norm and the syntactical structure, and powerful effects can be obtained by playing one off against the other.[11] But free verse, like prose, is organised only in terms of syntactic units, whereas in traditional verse the line had length and shape independent of syntax.

This merging of poetry and prose through the development of free verse has a number of consequences. The most important, according to Hough, is that the disappearance of metrical verse entails the disappearance of those public and permanent themes which found their expression in traditional verse structure.[12] By implication this means that free verse has to content itself with – or is more suited to – slighter, more fugitive, ephemeral themes. As such, it is more perfectly integrated into a society where the trivial and the cliché are presented as superlatives. Formulaic films are advertised as being 'beyond your wildest imagination.'[13] Read in this way, free verse is not oppositional at all and Easthope's analysis therefore needs rethinking.

But how did free verse arise? T. S. Eliot noted that the task of poetry in the early part of the century was the development of a poetic idiom related to the living speech of the day, not to conceptions of what poetic language ought to be.[14] This living speech, however, is a myth. What has happened in this century is the hijacking of language by popular newspapers, magazines, radio and television. This view is not to be taken as an expression of nostalgia for a lost speech of true presence but as an observation that language has become more and more institutionalised so that any deviation from the norm of simple transparency, which reinforces the status quo, is instantly dismissed as bizarre or nonsensical. The mass media organise the experience of living in Western society by varying the simple narrative of consumerism. People are addressed primarily as shoppers and their lives are propelled along that trajectory.

It is at this point that poetry becomes important, for, as an oppositional force, it should help to subvert the institutionalised narratives of capitalism. Of course, as soon as that word 'should' enters the argument analysis starts to shift towards evaluation, hence repeating the slippages noted in both Leavis and Adorno. Bearing that in mind, I still have to assert that one of the tasks of poetry – whether intended or not – is to map out a space in which other traditions of constructing, organising, analysing and evaluating experience can be brought to bear on late twentieth-century life other than those that are offered, for example, in the television sit-com.

An understanding and appreciation of the role of tradition is important here. At its simplest, tradition is a means of describing a literary sequence, thus the Georgians come before the modernists, who in turn are superseded by the political poets of the 1930s. But tradition is more than chronology, it is also a narrative that tells one particular story of literary development out of a number of possible others. This then raises the question of why this narrative rather than another should come to predominate. One likely answer is that it articulates more clearly and persuasively the ruling ideas and beliefs of society. Moreover, by identifying the language in which those beliefs are expressed as literature, those ideas and beliefs are then endowed with the qualities traditionally associated with literature: beauty, truth and permanence. Brian Doyle has argued that this conception of tradition serves the interests of capitalism since it answers the central problem of political economy, namely, how to ensure the popular acceptance of exchange value, which it does precisely by constructing culture as a 'repositor[y] of value prior to exchange'.[15]

If tradition can be regarded as the attempt to universalise the particular interests of the ruling group in society, then it is imperative that it be contested. This is where feminism has been so effective. It has recovered a number of female writers who had previously been neglected, reflecting thereby the patriarchal bias of tradition.

But, while political considerations are an essential part of contesting tradition, it is important to remember that tradition is not just *reducible* to history or politics even though it is unimaginable without them. Here we are entering very dangerous territory, for the implication is that tradition somehow transcends history and struggle, articulating a human essence that is true for all time. But this betrays the kind of binary thinking that Derrida has taught us to distrust. To say that tradition is not reducible to history does not mean that it transcends it.

The problem with seeing tradition as purely historical is that it ties it completely to the past. Perhaps it's time to look at tradition not as a reflection of the past but as a resource against the present. Political considerations are important here but so too are aesthetic ones. The two must not be conflated. The problem of how to maintain the specificity of each yet keep in view the complex relations between them cannot be entered into here, where my main point is that tradition is a nuanced vocabulary, a language finely tuned for the purpose of analysis and evaluation, hence making it possible to discuss notions of worth and value. Again, these are highly contentious issues which are unfortunately difficult even to raise in the current intellectual climate, dominated as it is by theory, which tends to cloak complex problems in objective sounding jargon.

One critic who has taken on the challenge is Steven Connor, who attempts the Herculean task of thinking value in both its absolutist and relativist modes simultaneously, through what he calls 'the imperative of value'.[16] Its absolutist character is evident in its 'irreducible orientation towards the better', or in its urge to 'continue evaluating in the face of every stable and encompassing value in particular'.[17] Its relativist mode, on the other hand, is manifest in its self-reflexivity, which is 'an imperative to continue evaluating the imperative to value'.[18] Connor's exploration of value is conducted within the parameters of cultural theory but he is not over reliant on theoretical vocabulary. As such, his work can be seen as an attempt to close the gap between specialist discourses and 'spontaneous lived experience'. And it is able to do this precisely because it moves from the particular to the general, always using one to modify the other. The absolutist perspective holds relativism in check while the detailed study of historically situated values guards against the tendency to absolutism.

The effort to bring theory and 'experience' together without conflating them is analogous to literature, at least in one of its modes, whereby it can be seen as a continuation and refinement of ordinary language, defamiliarising it not to the point of incomprehensibility, but enough to raise questions about its deployment in politics, advertising and administration. Constant exposure to the blandishments and soundbites of institutionalised discourse dulls awareness of language, but literature can revive it. The role of tradition is important here because it is a storehouse of poetic discourses whose variety constitutes alternative ways of constructing and rendering 'experience'. Tradition needs to promote this diversity and to find ever new ways of linking literature and life.

At the same time that it can intervene in the present, tradition is also a mark of what is past. This is important for two reasons. First, as a construct, tradition is a reminder that the meaning of history is not fixed and thus can be applied to the present, encouraging us to see it as orientated towards the future instead of as the inevitable outcome of what has gone before. Also, as an index of the past, tradition helps to maintain an historical perspective which is atro- phying in a culture of 'an eternal present'.[19] The second reason why the *pastness* of tradition matters is that it is a record – always a provisional one – of what has been deemed worthy of preservation, and this constitutes a reproach to a society based on planned obso- lescence. In this, tradition respects one of the impulses of poetry, which is to conserve an experience or event and so invest it with significance. A discussion of this significance needs to form a part of tradition since it represents a mode of valuing quite different from the exchange value which predominates in our society.

Another part of tradition concerns the means whereby certain poems are included in 'the canon' and others are not. Again, this process can never be final, but without some form of selection the history of poetry has neither shape nor meaning. There are many different ways of discriminating between poems, to do so politically is to make them 'speak' in one way, to do so aesthetically is to make them 'speak' in another; but without some form of discrimination, without establishing some form of relation between them, poems simply cannot signify. Whatever the discriminatory nature of tradi- tion – and the attempt should always be to maximise it – it acts as a kind of grammar which gives poetry a meaning in the culture. In the process it also keeps before us the problem of valuation, what kind of criteria to use and why, and that is no bad thing in a society of reflex judgements and packaged responses.

Obviously, it is impossible to cover all aspects of the question of the relation between poetry and society in so short a space, and the above should therefore be regarded as a ground-clearing exercise on which the Introduction to the following volume (Macmillan, forthcoming) will attempt to build. Many of the issues raised here are taken up by the contributors in respect of individual poets and movements spanning the period from the Georgians to just after the Second World War, but, it should be noted, the 'traditions' discussed here are indicative rather than inclusive. The aim of this volume, as it is for next volume, is to give some sense of the variety of poetry that was being produced and thus to resist the idea of a single, representative tradition. Inevitably, this results more in a sketch than in a finished picture, but that is precisely the point, for a sketch can always be revised and can, by its very incompleteness, stimulate new lines of thought, whereas the finished picture only invites passive contemplation.

Notes

1. For a good introduction to the range of Bourdieu's writing on culture, see Pierre Bourdieu, *The Field of Cultural Production: Essays on Art and Literature*, ed. and introduced by R. Johnson (Cambridge: Polity Press, 1993).
2. F. R. Leavis, *New Bearings in English Poetry* (Harmondsworth: Penguin, 1972); hereafter referred to as *NB* with page references given in the text.
3. For a full discussion of this point, see F. R. Leavis, 'Marxism and Cultural Continuity', 'Under which King, Bezonian?', 'Marxism and Cultural Continuity' and 'Restatement for Critics', all in F. R. Leavis, *Valuation in Criticism and Other Essays*, ed. G. Singh (Cambridge: Cambridge University Press, 1986) pp. 31–7, 38–45, 46–53.
4. See, for example, L. Althusser, *For Marx*, trans. Ben Brewster (London: New Left Books, 1965) and *Lenin and Philosophy*, trans. Ben Brewster (London: New Left Books, 1971), and P. Macherey, *A Theory of Literary Production*, trans. G. Wall (London: Routledge and Kegan Paul, 1978).
5. Leavis invariably refers to poets as 'he'. He has little, if anything, to say about women poets. I discuss the implications of this for his reading of poetry in my forthcoming book *Leavis and Poststructuralism* (London: Macmillan).
6. For a discussion of the erotics of technology in the body, see M. Seltzer, *Bodies and Machines* (New York and London: Routledge, 1992) especially pp. 18–12 and 160–72.
7. T. W. Adorno, 'Lyric Poetry and Society', in *Critical Theory and Society: A Reader*, ed. and with an introduction by S. Bronner and D. Kellner (New York and London: Routledge, 1989) pp. 155–71; hereafter referred to as *LPS* with page references given in the text.
8. A. Easthope, *Poetry and Phantasy* (Cambridge: Cambridge University

Press, 1989); hereafter referred to as *PP* with page references given in the text.

9. A. Easthope, *Poetry as Discourse* (London and New York: Methuen, 1983).

10. See, for example, D. H. Lawrence's poems 'To Women, As Far As I'm Concerned' and 'No! Mr. Lawrence', which play with poetic form and rhythm but without once relinquishing the commanding, transcendent persona, both in *D. H. Lawrence Selected Poems*, ed. and with an introduction by K. Sagar (Harmondsworth: Penguin, 1972) pp. 205–206.

11. Graham Hough, 'Free Verse', in *Twentieth-Century Poetry: Critical Essays and Documents*, ed. Graham Martin and P. N. Furbank (Milton Keynes: Open University Press, 1975) pp. 105–25.

12. Ibid., p. 109.

13. A poster advertising Disney's *Aladdin* used this very phrase.

14. See T. S. Eliot, *The Music of Poetry* (W. P. Ker Memorial Lecture, Glasgow, 1942) p. 27.

15. Brian Doyle, *English and Englishness* (London and New York: Routledge, 1989) p. 13.

16. Steven Connor, *Theory and Cultural Value* (Oxford: Blackwell, 1992) p. 2.

17. Ibid., p. 3.

18. Ibid.

19. For a discussion of this notion, see Gary Day, 'Popular Culture: The Conditions of Control', in Gary Day (ed.), *Readings in Popular Culture: Trivial Pursuits?* (London: Macmillan, 1990) pp. 1–12, esp. pp. 6–8.

2

Loose Women and Lonely Lambs: The Rise and Fall of Georgian Poetry

GEORGE WALTER

The Georgian poets, a sadly pedestrian rabble, flocked along the roads their fathers had built, pointing out to each other beauty spots and ostentatiously drinking small-beer in a desperate attempt to prove their virility. The winds blew, the floods came: for a moment a few of them showed on the crest of the seventh great wave; then they were rolled under and nothing marks their grave.[1]

No other group of twentieth-century poets has suffered so badly at the hands of subsequent critics as the Georgians. Although C. Day Lewis was writing in the 1930s, his remarks are typical of the kind of censorious response that this so-called 'sadly pedestrian rabble' provoke even today. The Georgians, we are told, were mere versifiers who were 'content to employ the conventions of diction and forms of verse favoured by almost all English poets from Wordsworth to Hardy'.[2] We also learn that they were 'cut off from the major emotions of their age', that they 'withdrew themselves into worlds of birds and flowers',[3] and that this 'effete pastoralism . . . represented an attempt to escape from the realities of modern urban and industrial life'.[4] Add to this the charge that they cultivated a 'false simplicity'[5] and it soon becomes apparent why they became 'a stagnant creek far from the main current of English poetry'.[6] Nor is it just the content of these accusations that is similar; more often than not, they share Day Lewis's patronising, mocking tone. John Middleton Murry's declaration that he found it 'impossible to be serious' about the Georgians[7] encapsulates perfectly the attitude expressed in most subsequent critical considerations of their work.

One effect of this consensus is that the term Georgian has ceased to be denotative and has instead become pejorative. Indeed, as John

Press notes, such are the negative connotations of the name that any poet of merit who might possibly be called Georgian is excluded from the categorisation on the grounds that there is no such thing as a good Georgian poet.[8] F. R. Leavis, for example, refused to regard Edmund Blunden as a Georgian because of his 'genuine talent' and wrote of Edward Thomas as 'an original poet of rare quality who has been associated with the Georgians by mischance'.[9] Similar claims have also been made for Robert Graves, Siegfried Sassoon, John Masefield and W. H. Davies, amongst others.[10] Not only does this approach deny these poets the categorisation placed upon them by themselves and their contemporaries, but it also means it is possible to argue that the notion of significant Georgian poets is untenable. It therefore naturally follows that anyone so labelled is automatically regarded as mediocre and talentless and therefore not worthy of further attention. By establishing the unspoken principle that 'if it is good it cannot be Georgian; if it is Georgian, it must, *ipso facto*, be feeble',[11] critics have thus ensured the almost complete marginalisation of Georgian poetry and its practitioners.[12]

So do the Georgians actually deserve their negative reputation? Robert H. Ross's assertion that 'no group of poets since the Pre-Raphaelites has suffered more, or more ignominiously, from the widespread acceptance of oversimplified stereotypes and critical half-truths' contains a great deal of truth. He goes on to argue that this is partly the result of 'ignorance', but also identifies 'pure critical spleen' as a significant cause of these responses.[13] Trying to identify the origins of this 'spleen' is not a particularly difficult task; as Myron Simon points out, the formulaic nature of much anti-Georgian criticism suggests they are a product of the perspective placed upon twentieth-century English poetry by the Modernist movement.[14] Georgian poetry, it seems, has been derided and ignored not because of its own failings but because critics have been content to examine it only through what C. K. Stead calls 'the spectacles provided . . . by the later, more vigorous movement led by Pound and Eliot'.[15] Stead's remarks are perhaps a little too generous – it would be more accurate to talk of the blinkers supplied by Modernism in this context – but whether bespectacled or blinkered, it is clear that any attempt to rescue the Georgians from their negative critical reputation cannot hope to succeed unless it tries to examine them from a less biased perspective. Only when the 'oversimplified stereotypes and critical half-truths' have been swept away by a more accurate examination of the nature of Georgian poetry and its true historical context can a fairer assessment of the movement and its adherents be arrived at.

Before we do this, however, we must first try to establish who the Georgians actually were. Critical confusion over the use of the label means that no valid defence of the movement can be undertaken until this has been achieved, and a useful starting point in this respect is to look at the close relationship between Georgian poetry as a movement and the five *Georgian Poetry* anthologies edited by Edward Marsh and published by Harold Monro at the Poetry Bookshop between 1912 and 1922.[16] To some extent, these volumes offer a convenient definition of who should be considered as a Georgian – Blunden, Graves, Sassoon, Masefield and Davies and qualify by this criterion[17] – but it is important to recognise the dangers of applying this definition too mechanically. The first two volumes in the series contained a great many members of the previous poetic generation – G. K. Chesterton and T. Sturge Moore, for example – whilst the later ones failed to include certain writers who seem to have had distinct Georgian tendencies, such as Wilfred Owen. Owen clearly thought of himself as a Georgian,[18] and he and Edward Thomas[19] serve to illustrate the fallibility of using Marsh's anthologies alone to define the Georgian movement. We should also include those poets who expressed an affinity with Georgianism, either through their work or in their letters and other writings, and whilst much of what follows uses the five *Georgian Poetry* volumes as a basis for argument, it should be noted that it is this wider definition of Georgian poetry that is being employed here.

Most of the 'half-truths' that Ross refers to stem from the erroneous belief that Georgian poetry is one single homogeneous mass, to be accepted or rejected in its totality. By refusing to make a distinction between the early Georgians and their later counterparts, critical opinion has been able to ensure that the baby is thrown out with the bath water. But no accurate analysis of Georgian poetry can be undertaken until such a distinction has been made. Contemporary critics tend to forget that, in its earliest incarnation, the movement was hailed as symbolising 'the new rebellion' in English poetry[20] and was seen as being something radical and almost dangerous; it was only later that it became infused with 'pleasantness'[21] and an 'indefinable odour of complacent sanctity'.[22] It was no coincidence that these later criticisms coincided with the rise of Modernism, seeking as it did to present itself as 'the new rebellion'. By lumping all Georgian poetry together and following the Modernist line that it was 'complacent' and reactionary, subsequent commentators have ensured that Modernism has maintained its place as the only convulsive shift in the history of early twentieth-century English poetry. However, if we recognise that there were two separate phases of Georgianism – Ross calls the first 'Georgian' and the second 'Neo-Georgian', to distinguish them[23] – and place each phase in its historical context, it soon becomes clear that dismissing its practitioners as 'a sadly pedestrian rabble' in their entirety does them a great disservice and ensures that their true achievement remains unrecognised.

The first phase of Georgianism – hereafter referred to as the Georgian phase – can be loosely said to cover the years 1912 to 1915, and began with the publication in 1912 of *Georgian Poetry 1911–1912*. Marsh, a prominent civil servant and poetry enthusiast, compiled the anthology in the belief that many of the younger poets of his day were being undeservedly neglected and that the best way to draw attention to them was to publish selections of their work in one volume. His introductory remarks to the volume make interesting reading:

> This volume is issued in the belief that English poetry is now once more putting on a new strength and beauty.
>
> Few readers have the leisure or the zeal to investigate each volume as it appears; and the process of recognition is often slow. This collection . . . may if it is fortunate help the lovers of poetry to realize that we are at the beginning of another 'Georgian period' which may take rank in due time with the several great poetic ages of the past.   (*GP I*, Prefatory Note[24])

It is important to note the absence of any theoretical agenda here. The terms 'strength and beauty' are both vague and subjective and Marsh makes it clear that his intention is not to promote any particular new poetic movement, but rather, to make available the best work of certain poets in a convenient and accessible form. Taking up the point of this lack of an ideological agenda at a later date, Harold Monro comments:

> in its infancy the 'Georgian Movement' was uncharacterised by evidence of design, that is, it did not, like other schools, preach or practice a special dogma of poetic art. It was fortuitous and informal.[25]

Guided only by his belief that a good poem should be intelligible, musical, 'racy' and preferably written on 'some formal principle',[26] Marsh made his selections on purely subjective grounds. The name Georgian was chosen for the collection precisely because it reflected this lack of an agenda, combining, as it did, neutrality with historical descriptiveness.

However, this 'fortuitous and informal' anthology and its successor *Georgian Poetry 1913–1915*, published in 1915, were widely regarded by contemporary critics as representing a premeditated challenge to the prevailing poetic orthodoxy. D. H. Lawrence, himself a contributor to both volumes, welcomed the initial collection as 'a big breath taken when we are waking up after a night of oppressive dreams';[27] a less favourable reviewer, Arthur Waugh, went further, arguing that an 'atmosphere of empirical rebellion' permeated both books.[28] These responses are understandable, given the condition of English poetry at this time. The excesses of the Aesthetic movement of the 1890s, and the absence of any poets of the stature of the great Victorians, had led to a poetical climate characterised by both political and artistic conservatism. Dominated by writers of such questionable calibre as William Watson, Alfred Austin and Henry Newbolt, poetry had come to mean ornate public pronouncements of a particularly nationalistic kind expressed in a style which recalls the more superficial aspects of Victorian verse. Take the opening of Newbolt's 'The Vigil' for example:

> England! where the sacred flame
>   Burns before the inmost shrine,
> Where lips that love thy name
>   Consecrate their hopes and thine,
> Where banners of thy dead
> Weave their shadows overhead,
> Water beside thine arms to-night,
> Pray that God defend the Right.[29]

The function of such poetry was to deny individualism and thus exclude the possibility of personal response. Instead, the virtues of national identity and moral responsibility became predominant themes, with the result that the definition of a great poet in this period was, as Stead notes, 'a man who expressed a sound philosophy in verse'.[30]

Although selected on a purely casual basis, the Georgian anthologies emphasised poetry of a distinctly different nature. The organising principle behind them was Marsh's own personal taste, but this contrasted sharply with that of his contemporaries and this division of opinion is reflected in his selections. The majority of the poets he favoured, such as Rupert Brooke, Wilfrid Gibson, W. H. Davies and Lascelles Abercrombie, were notable for the way in which they consciously reacted against the excesses of much of the verse of their age. Compare the opening of W. H. Davies's 'Thunderstorms' with that of Newbolt's 'The Vigil':

> My mind has thunderstorms,
>   That brood for heavy hours:
> Until they rain me words,
>   My thoughts are drooping flowers
> And sulking, silent birds.
>
> *(GP II*, p. 65)

Here there is no outworn poetic rhetoric, no great moral or nationalistic sentiments, no sense that this is a public pronouncement. Instead, Davies writes straightforwardly and directly about the workings of his own sensibility in an intimate, casual manner. The tone of authority present in Newbolt's poem is absent, and in its place is a subjective, individual response to a wholly personal concern. Davies's approach was shared by many of the contributors to *Georgian Poetry*, and although their coming together was not intended to signal the arrival of a new literary movement intent on overthrowing the established poetical practices of their time, the early anthologies soon came to be regarded in this light.

Robert Graves provides a useful summary of what these writers had in common:

The Georgians' general recommendations were the discarding of archaistic diction such as 'thee' and 'thou' and 'flowerer' and 'whene'er' and of poetical constructions such as 'winter drear' and 'host on armed host' and of pomposities generally. It was also understood that, in reaction to Victorianism, their verse should avoid all formally religious, philosophic or improving themes; and all sad, wicked, cafe-table themes in reaction to the 'nineties. Georgian poetry was to be English but not aggressively imperialistic; pantheistic rather than atheistic; and as simple as a child's reading book.[31]

Encapsulated like this, Georgianism looks more like a process of avoidance than any kind of definite attempt to do something new; indeed, Graves continues: 'These recommendations resulted in a poetry which could be praised rather for what it was not than for what it was.' Undoubtedly, a large part of the 'Georgian revolt'[32] did consist of a reaction against the excesses of their contemporaries, and while this helps to explain why they wrote in the way that they did, it offers little that can be used to defend them against the accusations of subsequent critics. It could be argued that to call the Georgians' technique 'traditional' is somewhat misleading; as we can see, they deliberately avoided 'the roads their fathers had built' and instead chose to follow the lead set a century earlier by Wordsworth. Their preference of straightforward and casual language directly parallels his decision to write in 'the real language of men'[33] as a conscious rejection of the 'sickly and. . . . extravagant' style favoured by his fellow-poets.[34] However, this still leaves us with the allegations of escapism – what Simon calls 'non-recognition'[35] – and 'false simplicity' to deal with. What becomes clear in the process of doing this is that far from merely reacting against accepted poetic practices, the Georgians were in fact attempting to introduce a number of key innovations into English poetry.

Perhaps the most damaging allegation is that Georgian poetry 'withdrew from reality, not to an ivory tower, but to an oasthouse'.[36] In other words, the Georgians deliberately refused to recognise the times in which they lived, preferring instead to produce safe, escapist poetry that had little connection with the real world. As criticisms go, this is seemingly damning. Yet it is based on an incomplete reading of the evidence, ignoring as it does poems such as Davies's 'The Bird of Paradise', a graphic account of the death of a prostitute as told by another prostitute (*GP II*, p. 73). Another poem of his, 'The Head of Rags', might also be mentioned here:

> One night when I went down
> Thames' side, in London Town,
> A heap of rags saw I,
> And sat me down close by.
> That thing could shout and bawl,
> But showed no face at all;
>   (*GP I*, p. 62)

The 'thing' is a tramp, and Davies soon realises that he is beyond help; there have been 'Too many bitter fears / To make a pearl from tears'. W. W. Gibson's 'Geraniums' reveals similar concerns, dealing as it does with 'a poor old weary woman' whose only source of income is flower-selling (*GP I*, p. 106). In each of these cases, there is not only an awareness of the brutal realities of life but also a desire to make the poetry-reading public aware of these realities. Described as 'Broken with lust and drink, blear-eyed and ill', Gibson's flower-seller represents the unpleasant truth underlying Newbolt's patriotic rantings. The unpleasant face of British society had no place in the kind of poetry written by Newbolt and the like; to them, England was the 'Mother of happy homes and Empire vast'[37] and their mission was to maintain this image. The Georgians, on the other hand, were willing to draw attention to the existence of another aspect of society.

Whilst recognising its significance in terms of rescuing them from allegations of a lack of social awareness, it is important to note that this concentration upon such unacceptable figures as prostitutes and tramps is in fact part of a wider tendency towards brutality and coarseness in the poetry of the Georgians. This so-called 'Georgian realism'[38] is a central feature of the early anthologies, and is perhaps best defined as conscious anti-romanticism expressed in the most direct way possible. 'The Bird of Paradise', for example, pulls no punches in its opening stanzas:

> Here comes Kate Summers, who, for gold,
>   Takes any man to bed:
> 'You knew my friend, Nell Barnes,' she said;
>   'You knew Nell Barnes – she's dead.
>
> 'Nell Barnes was bad on all you men,
>   Unclean, a thief as well;
> Yet all my life I have not found
>   A better friend than Nell.'
>   (*GP II*, p. 73)

Contemporary critics were not slow to pick up on this 'self-conscious brutality';[39] Edmund Gosse, for example, noted the way that contributors to *Georgian Poetry 1911–1912* sought to 'exchange the romantic, the sentimental, the fictive conceptions of literature, for an ingenuousness, sometimes a violence, almost a rawness in the approach to life itself'.[40] Particularly singled out for attention were two longer works, Lascelles Abercrombie's 'The Sale of St. Thomas', with its descriptions of 'roasting living men / In queer huge kilns' (*GP I*, p. 9) and other tortures, and Gordon Bottomley's 'King Lear's Wife', summarised by Arthur Waugh in his review thus:

> We are given a sort of prelude to Shakespeare's tragedy . . . which serves . . . to explain the inhuman treatment meted out to their father by Goneril and Regan at a later stage of their history. The Lear of this fragment is still a man in his prime, lusty and lustful, with a sickly dying wife who has long since ceased to satisfy his uxurious demands. Goneril is just emerging into womanhood – a huntress maid; Cordelia is a prattling nursery child; Regan hangs about the kitchen for scraps. Upon Goneril falls the horror of revelation, for, as her mother lies dying on the great bed, she sees her father toying in the shadow with her mother's maid, who is already destined by the doting Lear to be the moribund wife's successor, while all the time the wanton is carrying on an intrigue with a younger man in the king's retinue. The honour of the house is in Goneril's hand, and she stabs her father's paramour to death, returning with the blood on her hands . . .[41]

As if this were not raw enough, the drama ends with the body of Lear's wife being washed. As they work, the servants sing:

> A louse crept out of my lady's shift –
> Ahumm, Ahumm, Ahee –
> Crying 'Oi! Oi! We are turned adrift;
> The lady's bosom is cold and stiffed,
> And her arm-pit's cold for me.'
>
> (*GP II*, p. 41)

There follows a brief scene of corpse-robbing and some further verses of the song, which contains such choice lines as the observation that the dead woman's 'savour is neither warm nor sweet' (*GP II*, p. 42). Bottomley's coarse anti-romanticism may not seem particularly shocking now, but some idea of contemporary opinions of the strength of his 'realism' can be gathered from the fact that when 'King Lear's Wife' was performed by the Birmingham Repertory Company in September 1915, the censor refused to allow the corpse-washers song to be performed.[42]

Clearly, accusations that the Georgians 'withdrew from reality' are somewhat ill-founded. Moreover, it can be argued that their concentration upon the less pleasant aspects of life represents a deliberate attempt to respond to the increasing sophistication of their age. Rupert Brooke, a central figure in the first phase of Georgian poetry,[43] provides an instructive explanation of the reasoning behind this overt realism:

> There are common and sordid things – situations and details – that suddenly bring all tragedy, or at least the brutality of actual emotions to you. I grasp rather relievedly at them, after I've beaten vain hands in the rosy mists of poets' experiences.[44]

Aware that poetry was failing to engage with actuality, preferring, as it did, to present a picture of the world as camouflaged by 'rosy mists', the Georgians sought to make poetry more relevant by making it a closer reflection of reality. Gosse was right to recognise that this 'rawness in the approach to life itself' was a direct challenge to the romantic and sentimental nature of much of their contemporaries' verse; it was a challenge that sprang from the early Georgians' awareness that their age demanded poetry that reflected rather than avoided real experiences. Brooke's belief that 'common and sordid things' were somehow a conduit for 'actual emotions' relates to this awareness; if they revealed their significance to the poet, then conveying them as precisely and honestly as possible would mean that the reader too could share in that significance. In poems such as Gibson's 'Geraniums' or Brooke's 'Menelaus and Helen', with its emphasis upon the less pleasant features of these classical personalities in their old age,[45] the Georgians were attempting to communicate a sense of real life in all its coarseness and, in the process, express the emotional reality that such subjects revealed.

But what of the Georgians' much-vaunted obsession with nature and the rural world? Surely this represents an attempt to escape from the horrors of modern civilisation? Again, it is instructive to look at the contents of the first two Georgian anthologies before responding to these accusations. What is immediately noticeable is how infrequently nature is merely praised for its own sake; more often than not it is used to explore other issues. In D. H. Lawrence's 'Snapdragon', for example, the flower is the starting point for an exploration of the 'dark deeps' of sexuality (*GP I*, p. 116), whilst his 'Cruelty and Love' (*GP II*, pp. 154–8) uses the symbol of the snared rabbit to suggest the way that desire is formed from the ambiguous relationship between terror and erotic passion. Ralph Hodgson's

'The Bull' looks, at first sight, to be a straightforward account of 'an old unhappy bull / Sick in soul and body both' (*GP II*, p. 137), but a closer reading reveals that it is in fact an examination of the fears and regrets that accompany the coming of death. Other examples of this technique abound – Gibson's 'The Hare' (*GP I*, pp. 93–105) deserves a mention in this context – and what soon becomes evident is that, by and large, nature functions in the same way as realism does in these poems: it is used as a means of communication rather than as an end in itself. What is being conveyed is, in Brooke's words, 'the brutality of actual emotions' and the Georgians' emphasis upon these represents a deliberate response to the dehumanising nature of the modern age. Writing in a period of increased complexity and emotional dislocation, they were attempting not merely to reassert the importance of human experience, but also to explore it in all its intricacy.

Innovative as all this realism and emphasis upon emotional response is, it must be seen in the wider context of the Georgians' struggle to restore the individual to a position of importance in poetry. Not only was their age dehumanising in a social sense, but also in an artistic sense. The effusions of Newbolt and his like-minded cohorts all stress the importance of community – in this case, the nationalist, morally-correct community of imperial England – and there is no place in their work for either the individual or any kind of personal, subjective response. Throwing themselves into their self-appointed roles as 'great poets', they express these sentiments in the kind of public, authoritative tones that leave no room for either idiosyncrasy or intimacy. The Georgians, on the other hand, stressed the importance of the individual by concerning themselves almost wholly with personal experience, whether it be actual, emotional or spiritual. By ignoring self-consciously improving moral or political ideas as subjects for poetry and instead confining it 'within the limits of what had actually been experienced',[46] they sought to make their verse an entirely subjective utterance, a personal and private communication between writer and reader. Their interest in emotional states in particular – Walter de la Mare's 'cloudlike dread' in 'The Sleeper' (*GP I*, p. 68) or John Drinkwater's profound yearning for 'yesterday reborn' in 'Of Greatham' (*GP II*, p. 91) for example – shows this in action; whilst the average readers might find authoritarian pronouncements about 'happy homes and Empire vast' less than accessible, they would have no difficulty at all in relating to poems that explore such shared human experiences.

Writing in a casual, direct style that eschewed the post-Victorian rhetoric of their contemporaries, they were able to engage directly with their readership, giving them a subjective response to wholly idiosyncratic experiences in an easily understandable form. Viewed in the light of this, accusations that the Georgians favoured 'false simplicity' seem somewhat inaccurate; their simplicity was in fact a crucial element in their mission to make poetry accessible and thus make the relationship between poet and public a direct, shared experience.

Some idea of how successful the Georgians were in their attempt to communicate directly with their public can be gathered from the sales of *Georgian Poetry* – the first volume sold 15,000 copies, the second 19,000, the third 16,000, the fourth 15,000 and the last a disappointing 8,000.[47] Whilst this popularity goes a long way in justifying their consciously egalitarian approach to poetry, it was not greeted with approval from all quarters. Arthur Waugh's argument that the Georgians' 'poetic liberty and licence' threatened to 'hand over the sensitive art of verse to a general process of literary democratisation'[48] is an interesting one; although he accurately isolates the Georgians' mission to make poetry accessible and relevant to the ordinary reader, he makes it quite clear that this is a negative achievement. Reading between the lines, it seems that Waugh, in common with many of his literary and critical contemporaries, believed that 'the sensitive art of verse' should remain a specialised, remote discourse for the pleasure of the educated classes alone. As Stead notes, the Georgians belonged to the 'new liberal intellectual group . . . perhaps best illustrated by the Schlegel sisters in E. M. Forster's *Howard's End'*[49] and, like Forster, their response to the social uncertainties of their age was 'only connect'.[50] Such a philosophy, with all its implications of tumbling class barriers and rampant egalitarianism, clearly horrified Waugh and his ilk but it remains one of Georgian poetry's most significant strengths, and its realisation represents the true achievement of Georgianism. That its importance has not been consequently recognised is due largely to the way in which Modernist-inspired criticism has echoed Waugh's belief. As Gary Day points out, Modernism's insistence that art should be complex and inaccessible and thus 'the preserve of an intellectual elite'[51] has meant that any form of writing easily understood by a mass audience has been either marginalised or, as we have seen in the case of the Georgians, set up as a critical Aunt Sally.

If placing the first phase of Georgianism in its proper historical context thus allows us to see its true achievements, the same unfortunately cannot be said for its second phase. The Neo-Georgians, as Ross calls them, do largely fulfil the negative expectations associated with the Georgian movement as a whole, but they nevertheless deserve consideration, if only on the grounds that they have regrettably come to represent Georgianism for most critics. Again, historical context plays a major part in the growth of their poor reputation, but it is important to recognise that much of the blame in this case can be also be laid at the doors of the Neo-Georgian poets themselves. The last three volumes of *Georgian Poetry*, published in 1917, 1919 and 1922 respectively, are of a distinctly different nature from that of their predecessors; the popularity of the Georgians had led to imitation, but these imitators misunderstood the poetic credo of their idols and instead only seized upon the superficial aspects of their work. Thus simplicity, ruralism and subjectivity ceased to be used as means to an end and became instead an end in themselves. Marsh, still making his selections on the same casual grounds, was suddenly faced with a flood of poems that appealed to him for the same reasons that the original Georgians had, and he thus not unnaturally included them *en masse* in his anthologies. The result was the publication of such poems as John Freeman's 'Stone Trees', with its pointless checklist of cows, sheep, 'conies' and rooks (*GP III*, p. 132), and William Kerr's 'Counting Sheep':

> Half-awake I walked
> A dimly-seen sweet hawthorn lane
> Until sleep came;
> I lingered at a gate and talked
> A little with a lonely lamb . . .
> . . . And then I saw, hard by,
> a shepherd lad with shining eyes,
> And round him, gathered one by one
> Countless sheep, snow-white;
> More and more they crowded
> With tender cries,
> Till all the field was full
> Of voices and of coming sheep.
>
> (*GP V*, p. 112)

Kerr is the archetypal Neo-Georgian: simplistic, superficial, deeply in love with nature and a keen utiliser of the 'rosy mists' that Brooke railed against. Gone is the sense that some kind of personal and profound emotional experience is being communicated to us, to be replaced by an embarrassing 'prettiness' – the 'snow-white' sheep, the 'shepherd lad with shining eyes' and so on. The process of what Harold Monro described as the 'narrowing and hardening' of the Georgian ethos[52] at the hands of the Neo-Georgians resulted in a poetry that has almost nothing in common with its progenitor.

Contextualising the Neo-Georgians historically does little to alter the facts in their case. It is true that the perspective supplied by Modernism denies the radical nature of the early Georgians, but it must be recognised that these revolutionary intentions are completely absent in their followers, leaving little room for critical manoeuvre. The earliest phase of Georgian poetry was a deliberate revolt against the poetic establishment of its age; five years later, the Neo-Georgians were the establishment and Modernism was the revolutionary force. Whereas it is possible to argue that the Georgians represent a decisive shift in the history of English poetry, the Neo-Georgians represent the eventual debasement and entrenchment of that shift into poetic orthodoxy. Comparing the poetry produced by the first phase of Georgianism with that of its later development only underlines the extent of the decline that took place; comparing the work of the Neo-Georgians with that of their Modernist contemporaries brings an even greater shock. Georgian poetry, once a determined response to the complexities of its age, evolved into a lightweight, escapist kind of lyricism and nowhere is its irrelevance more clearly proved than in the immediate post-war period; it is T. S. Eliot's *The Waste Land* and not Kerr's 'Counting Sheep' that expresses fully the dislocations and anxieties of the time.

The Neo-Georgians' response to the First World War is similarly disappointing. True, it does make its appearance in poems such as J. C. Squire's excruciatingly maudlin 'To A Bulldog', in which the narrator attempts to explain to a dead soldier's faithful dog why 'We shan't see Willy any more' (*GP III*, p. 27), and John Freeman's 'Ten O'Clock No More', a threnody for a fallen tree, which ends:

> 'Ten O'clock's gone!'
> Said sadly everyone.
> And mothers looking thought

Of sons and husbands far away that fought: –
And looked again.

(*GP IV*, p. 64)

Freeman is clearly trying to convey something of the emotional trauma that wartime separation brings, but any impact that this final stanza might have is nullified by the preceding eight, which concentrate on the 'Ten O'Clock' of the title – a tree. Emphasising how the wind 'raught / Her ageing boughs' (*GP IV*, p. 63) and how 'pewits round the tree would dip and cry' (*GP IV*, p. 64), he shows a typical Neo-Georgian obsession with superficial natural description, with the result that the ending seems like an afterthought; it is the tree that Freeman is interested in, not the emotional experience. James Reeves argues that this concentration upon 'country cottages, old furniture, moss-covered barns, rose-scented lanes, apple and cherry orchards, village inns and village cricket' actually represents a direct response to wartime trauma because it expresses 'the nostalgia of the soldier on active service',[53] but, tempting as this view is, it still looks like special pleading. Whilst it is undoubtedly true that the wartime volumes of *Georgian Poetry* were immensely popular because they offered a somewhat idealised evocation of the Britain being fought for, it nevertheless remains a fact that the Neo-Georgians seem to be either avoiding or retreating from the situation, rather than engaging with it.

Survivors from the first phase of Georgianism were still finding their way into Marsh's anthologies during this period. Some, like W. H. Davies and John Drinkwater, succumbed to the influence of the Neo-Georgians and turned in light, undemanding lyrics; others, such as Lascelles Abercrombie and Walter de la Mare, remained true to their original intentions and continued to write in the manner of their earlier contributions. Authentic Georgianism was also kept alive by a group of newcomers to the series – Robert Graves, Siegfried Sassoon and, to a lesser extend, Robert Nichols – and, interestingly enough, it is their poetry which represents the only profound reaction to the war to be found in *Georgian Poetry*. More usually categorised today as war poets, these writers nevertheless deserve recognition as true Georgians; as Stead notes, their poems all share 'the characteristics which mark off the Georgians from their immediate predecessors':

a rejection of large themes and of the language and rhetoric that accompanied them in the nineteenth century; and an attempt to

come to terms with immediate experience, sensuous or imaginative, in a language close to common speech.[54]

Nowhere is this more vividly illustrated than in Sassoon's 'They':

> The Bishop tells us: 'When the boys come back
> They will not be the same; for they'll have fought
> In a just cause: they lead the last attack
> On Anti-Christ; their comrades' blood has bought
> New right to breed an honourable race.
> They have challenged Death and dared him face to face.'
>
> 'We're none of us the same!' the boys reply.
> For George lost both his legs; and Bill's stone blind;
> Poor Jim's shot through the lungs and like to die;
> And Bert's gone syphilitic; you'll not find
> A chap who's served that hasn't had *some* change.'
> And the Bishop said: 'The ways of God are strange!'
>
> (GP III, p. 45)

Sassoon's poem fits all of Stead's criteria. Its casual realism echoes
that of W. H. Davies's 'The Bird of Paradise', and its theme – the
distance between civilian wartime rhetoric and the actuality of war
– directly parallels the early Georgians' attempts to get beyond the
poetic rhetoric of their age to express its true nature. Similarly,
whilst Robert Nichols's other poems display distinct Neo-Georgian
tendencies, 'The Assault' maintains an authentic Georgian approach
and shows how the notion of using ordinary language to convey an
immediate experience can be developed:

> Over the parapet!
> I'm up. Go on.
> Something meets us.
> Head down into the storm that greets us.
> A wail.
> Lights. Blurr.
> Gone.
> On, on. Lead. Leăd. Hail.
> Spatter. Whirr! Whirr!
> 'Toward that patch of brown;
> Direction left.' Bullets a stream.

Devouring thought crying in a dream.

(*GP III*, p. 61)

Striving to broaden traditional Georgian techniques to suit an extreme situation, Nichols here actually creates a form of poetry that echoes the experimental approach of Modernism. In so doing, he suggests one way in which Georgian poetry could have developed for the better.

Wilfred Owen was another poet who developed the techniques of early Georgianism to cope with profound experiences, and his later war poetry shows again and again how the traditional Georgian approach could be used with remarkable sophistication. Take the opening of 'Exposure' for example:

Our brains ache, in the merciless iced east winds that knive
     us . . .
Wearied we keep awake because the night is silent . . .
Low, drooping flares confuse our memory of the salient . . .
Worried by silence, sentries whisper, curious, nervous,
     But nothing happens.[55]

Owen's determination to communicate the reality of trench life in all its intensity to the reader is self-evident, and he utilises 'a language close to common speech' to do this. However, he manages to make his realisation of experience all the more effective by using this in conjunction with a skilful combination of pararhyme, alliteration, onomatopoeia and assonance. Although language and diction are here being pushed to innovative extremes, there is no sense of artificiality or self-consciousness; instead, the reader is able to engage directly with what is being described in an immediate, intense fashion. Owen's brand of Georgianism manages to both remain true to the early poetic ideals of the movement and yet also develop them to cope with the demands of challenging new experiences.

Had he not been killed in the last week of the war, Owen might have been able to revive the flagging peacetime fortunes of Georgianism. However, a combination of factors served to ensure that the movement was all but dead by 1922. Declining sales and the obvious hostility of the Modernists towards the Neo-Georgians convinced Marsh that a sixth volume of *Georgian Poetry* would not be well received.[56] He must have also been aware that events had, to a large extent, run their course; what had begun as a personal crusade to popularise 'a new strength and beauty' in English poetry had evolved first into a revolutionary challenge to accepted poetic practices and then into an entrenched, reactionary literary establishment. The remains of the Neo-Georgians limped on for a while, marshalled in the pages of the *London Mercury* under the watchful eye of its editor, J. C. Squire;[57] attempting to revive past glories, Squire assembled a number of Georgians and Neo-Georgians in a series of anthologies, but the defensive tone adopted by the Prefatory Note to the first of these, published when the movement was in its death-throes, suggests that he knew exactly which way the poetical wind was blowing:

> Several living poets of the highest repute have won their reputation solely on short poems, and there are, and have been, a very large number indeed who have written one or two good poems. ... Should our literary age be remembered by posterity solely as an age during which fifty men had written lyrics of some durability for their truth and beauty, it would not be remembered with contempt. It is in that conviction that I have compiled this anthology.[58]

Less than a decade earlier, Marsh had argued that the 'new strength and beauty' in poetry would ensure that his age would 'take rank in due time with the several other great poetic ages of the past'. Now Squire was reduced to fighting a rearguard action, hoping that 'short poems' about 'truth and beauty' would restore the image of Georgian poetry. But times had changed, and no amount of 'lyrics of some durability' could possibly compete with the output of the Modernist movement. Despite his conviction to the contrary, it was, as we have seen, 'with contempt' that the Georgians and Neo-Georgians came to be remembered.

Ironically enough, all three of Squire's anthologies contained poems by the one writer who might have been able to revitalise Georgianism in Wilfred Owen's absence. A self-confessed Georgian,[59] Ivor Gurney's war poetry suggests that he had learned the lessons of his poetical mentors well:

> He's gone, and all our plans
> Are useless indeed.
> We'll walk no more on Cotswold

Where the sheep feed
Quietly and take no heed.

His body that was so quick
Is not as you
Knew it, on Severn river
Under the blue
Driving our small boat through.

You would not know him now . . .
But still he died
Nobly, so cover him over
With violets of pride
Purple from Severn side.

Cover him, cover him soon!
And with thick-set
Masses of memoried flowers –
Hide that red wet
Thing I must somehow forget.[60]

Recognising the need for new forms of expression in the immediate post-war period, he turned to such diverse sources as Elizabethan poetry and Walt Whitman for inspiration. The result was a wholly new kind of Georgianism:

Smudgy dawn scarfed with military colours
Northward, and flowing wider like slow sea water,
Woke in lilac and elm and almost among garden flowers.
Birds a multitude; increasing as it made lighter.
Nothing but I moved by railings there; slept sweeter
Than kings the country folk in thatch or slate shade.[61]

Gurney's experiments with language and metre presented a wealth of opportunities to anyone bold enough to utilise them as he did, in the context of traditional Georgian concerns, but his was a lone voice crying in the poetical wilderness of Squire's collections. Plagued by mental instability for much of his adult life,[62] he was committed to an asylum in September 1922 and his achievement was, until recently, almost completely forgotten.[63] He died in 1937, and by that time Georgian poetry had become history, to be remembered, if at all, as the outpourings of 'a sadly pedestrian rabble' noted for their 'effete pastoralism' and 'false simplicity'. Whether or not Gurney could have saved the Georgians from this epitaph is debatable; as we have seen, it was the product of the kind of prejudice that refuses to recognise historical fact and, from the 1920s onwards, this prejudicial attitude was so firmly established that perhaps nothing could have dislodged it. To all intents and purposes, the Georgians had been consigned to their unmarked grave.

Notes

1. C. Day Lewis, *A Hope for Poetry* (Oxford: Basil Blackwell, 1934) p. 2.
2. John Press, *A Map of Modern English Verse* (London: Oxford University Press, 1969) p. 105.
3. Edith C. Batho and Bonamy Dobree, *The Victorians and After* (London: Cresset Press, 1950) p. 72.
4. John H. Johnston, *English Poetry of the First World War* (Princeton: Princeton University Press, 1964) p. 28.
5. John Middleton Murry, 'The Condition of English Poetry', *The Athenaeum*, 5 December 1919, pp. 1238–5; reprinted in *Georgian Poetry 1912–1922: The Critical Heritage*, ed. by Timothy Rogers (London: Routledge & Kegan Paul, 1977) pp. 231–7 (p. 232).
6. Press, op. cit., p. 107.
7. Murry, op. cit., p. 233.
8. Press, op. cit., p. 105.
9. F. R. Leavis, *New Bearings in English Poetry* (London: Chatto & Windus, 1932) p. 66.
10. For further details, see Rogers, op. cit., pp. 1–2.
11. Press, op. cit., p. 105.
12. The clearest indication of this marginalisation is the current unavailability of anthologies of Georgian poetry. Two previous collections – *Georgian Poets*, ed. by Alan Pryce-Jones (London: Edward Hulton, 1959) and *Georgian Poetry*, ed. by James Reeves (Harmondsworth: Penguin Books, 1962) – are now both out of print.
13. Robert H. Ross, *The Georgian Revolt: Rise and Fall of a Poetic Ideal* (London: Faber and Faber, 1965) p. 15.
14. Myron Simon, *The Georgian Poetic* (Berkeley: University of California Press, 1975) p. 1.
15. C. K. Stead, *The New Poetic: Yeats to Eliot* (London: Hutchinson, 1964) p. 81.
16. The most detailed account of the history of the *Georgian Poetry* series can be found in Ross, op. cit. For an account of Edward Marsh's life and times, see Christopher Hassall, *Edward Marsh: Patron of the Arts* (London: Longmans, 1959).

17. Supporters of Georgian poetry appear to be divided on this method of categorisation. Rogers, Simon and Ross limit their comments to those poets who appeared in *Georgian Poetry*, whilst Press, Pryce-Jones and Reeves also include poets who did not appear there but nevertheless show Georgian traits in their work.

18. See his letter of 8 January 1918 to Leslie Gunston: 'We Georgians are all so old.', in *Wilfred Owen: Collected Letters*, ed. by Harold Owen and John Bell (London: Oxford University Press, 1967) p. 526. Also of interest is his letter of 31 December 1917 to his mother: 'I am held peer by the Georgians; I am a poet's poet' (p. 521).

19. For a detailed and convincing explanation of why Thomas should be regarded as a Georgian, see Press, op. cit., pp. 114–16.

20. Arthur Waugh, 'The New Poetry', *Quarterly Review*, October 1916, pp. 365–86; reprinted in Rogers, op. cit., pp. 139–59 (p. 143).

21. T. S. Eliot, 'Verse Pleasant and Unpleasant', *The Egoist*, March 1918, pp. 43–4; summarised in detail, because of copyright complications, in Rogers, op. cit., pp. 213–15 (p. 215).

22. Murry, op. cit., p. 232.

23. Ross, op. cit., pp. 183–4.

24. Henceforth all quotations from the five volumes of *Georgian Poetry* will be referenced in the text using the following abbreviations: *Georgian Poetry 1911–1912*, (*GP I*); *Georgian Poetry 1913–1915*, (*GP II*); *Georgian Poetry 1916–1917*, (*GP III*); *Georgian Poetry 1918–1919*, (*GP IV*); *Georgian Poetry 1920–1922*, (*GP V*).

25. Harold Monro, *Some Contemporary Poets* (London: Leonard Parsons, 1920) p. 150.

26. See Ross, op. cit., p. 108.

27. D. H. Lawrence, 'The Georgian Renaissance', *Rhythm*, March 1913, pp. xvii–xx; reprinted in Rogers, op. cit., pp. 102–5 (p. 102).

28. Waugh, op. cit., p. 142.

29. Henry Newbolt, 'The Vigil', *Poems: New and Old*, 2nd edn (London: John Murray, 1919) pp. 97–8 (p. 97).

30. Stead, op, cit., p. 73.

31. Robert Graves, *The Common Asphodel: Collected Essays on Poetry 1922–1949* (London: Hamish Hamilton, 1949) pp. 112–13.

32. The term is borrowed from the title of Ross's book.

33. William Wordsworth, Preface, *Wordsworth and Coleridge: Lyrical Ballads*, ed. by R. L. Brett and A. R. Jones, 2nd edn (London: Routledge, 1991) p. 241.

34. Ibid., p. 249.

35. Simon, op. cit., p. 3.

36. William York Tyndall, *Forces in Modern British Literature* (New York: Vintage, 1947) pp. 372–3.

37. Alfred Austin, 'Why England is Conservative', *Lyrical Poems*, 2nd edn (London: Macmillan, 1896) pp. 116–17 (p. 116).

38. Simon, op. cit., p. 47.

39. Anon., 'Georgian Poetry', *Times Literary Supplement*, 27 February 1913, pp. 81–2; reprinted in Rogers, op. cit., pp. 77–84 (p. 81).

40. Edmund Gosse, 'Knocking at the Door', *Morning Post*, 27 January 1913, p. 3; reprinted in Rogers, op. cit., pp. 73–7 (p. 75).

41. Waugh, op. cit., p. 156.

42. See Ross, op. cit., pp. 151–2.

43. For details of Brooke's involvement, see Hassall, op. cit., pp. 180–221.

44. Rupert Brooke, letter to Edward Marsh, 22 December 1911; in *The Letters of Rupert Brooke*, ed. by Geoffrey Keynes (London: Faber and Faber, 1968) p. 328.

45. For example: 'Oft she weeps, gummy-eyed and impotent; / Her dry shanks twitch at Paris' mumbled name'; from 'Menelaus and Helen', *Collected Poems of Rupert Brooke: With a Memoir* (London: Sidgwick & Jackson, 1930) p. 69. 'A Channel Passage' (p. 85) reveals the use of the same technique.

46. Stead, op. cit., p. 82.

47. See Rogers, op. cit., p. 17.

48. Waugh, op. cit., p. 143.

49. Stead, op. cit., p. 85.

50. The epigraph to Forster's *Howard's End*, first published in 1910.

51. Gary Day, 'The Poets: Georgians, Imagists and Others', *Literature and Culture in Modern Britain*, ed. by C. Bloom (London and New York: Longman, 1993) pp. 30–54, see esp. p. 34.

52. Monro, op. cit., p. 151.

53. Reeves, op. cit., p. xv.

54. Stead, op. cit., p. 88.

55. Wilfred Owen, 'Exposure', *The Poems of Wilfred Owen*, ed. by Jon Stallworthy (London: Hogarth Press, 1985) p. 162.

56. For details, see Simon, op. cit., pp. 86–7, and Ross, op. cit., p. 233.

57. The most detailed account of Squire and his literary activities is Patrick Howarth, *Squire: 'Most Generous of Men'* (London: Hutchinson, 1963).

58. J. C. Squire, Prefatory Note, *Selections from Modern Poets*, ed. by J. C. Squire (London: Martin Secker, 1921) pp. v–vii. The other two anthologies were *Second Selections from Modern Poets*, ed. by J. C. Squire (London: Martin Secker, 1924) and *Younger Poets of To-Day*, ed. by J. C. Squire (London: Martin Secker, 1932).

59. See his letter of February 1915 to F. W. Harvey: 'Tonight I have been reading the *Georgian Poetry Book*. . . . Our young poets think very much as we'; in *Ivor Gurney: Collected Letters*, ed. by R. K. R. Thornton (Ashington and Manchester: Mid Northumberland Arts Group and Carcanet, 1991) p. 12. Although his attempts to get himself included in the final volume of *Georgian Poetry* were unsuccessful, it was, ironically enough, upon his recommendation that Marsh included Kerr; see ibid., p. 511, and Hassall, op. cit., p. 491. Both Pryce-Jones and Reeves print poems by Gurney in their anthologies; see Pryce-Jones, op. cit., p. 27, and Reeves, op. cit., pp. 113–14.

60. Ivor Gurney, 'To His Love', *War's Embers* (London: Sidgwick & Jackson, 1919) p. 45; reprinted in *Severn & Somme and War's Embers*, ed. by R. K. R. Thornton (Ashington and Manchester: Mid Northumberland Arts Group and Carcanet, 1987) p. 76.

61. Ivor Gurney, 'Smudgy Dawn', *Second Selections from Modern Poets*, op. cit., p. 221; reprinted in *Collected Poems of Ivor Gurney*, ed. by P. J. Kavanagh (Oxford: Oxford University Press, 1982) p. 143.

62. For details of Gurney's life and work, see Michael Hurd, *The Ordeal of Ivor Gurney* (Oxford: Oxford University Press, 1978).

63. Squire continued to print his poems in the *London Mercury*, but to little avail. Similarly, two posthumous collections of his verse – *Poems by Ivor Gurney*, ed. by Edmund Blunden (London: Hutchinson, 1954) and *Poems of Ivor Gurney 1890–1937*, ed. by Leonard Clark (London: Chatto & Windus, 1973) – were largely ignored upon their appearance. It is only since the publication of Hurd's biography and Kavanagh's edition of his poems that Gurney's unique qualities have been recognised.

3

The Falling House that Never Falls: Rupert Brooke and Literary Taste

CLIVE BLOOM

'Rupert Brooke's poetry remains a firm favourite with readers and listeners alike': such might be the opinion of the popular poetry radio programmes broadcast by BBC Radio 4 or, perhaps, the comments in the introduction to yet another anthology of the slim collected works (with a selection of letters added for good measure). Brooke's reputation, which is at stake here, has never rested on anything other than quicksand. The 'worth' or quality of his poetic ability becomes, as has rarely been the case with any but Dylan Thomas, subordinated to a quasi-biographical determinism in which the poetry itself plays little part. It is ironic yet it can be said that the value of Brooke's reputation is independent of the very work he did to secure that reputation.

As a 'firm favourite', Brooke is damned as a lower-grade Kiplingesque populist by the academic community whose fare consists of the modernists and those the modernists chose to applaud. Meanwhile Brooke is relegated to the outer corridors of fame, conversing posthumously with the likes of both Ella Wheeler Wilcox and Longfellow. In such a way, Brooke is left to those whose poetic taste is untrained except by personal predisposition and whose 'love' of poetry consists of enjoying a large chunk of meaning laced with a keen disregard for free verse. Brooke's Georgianism is damned both by those who dislike it (academics) and those who applaud it ('untrained' amateurs). To like Brooke is a form of eccentricity, peculiar to the English upper middle classes, akin to that dilettantism which would prefer an elderberry wine to a vintage claret.

Having safely relegated Brooke's poetry to the realm of amateur taste, professional opinion can comfortably exist on the acceptable fare of modernism and pre- or post-modernist tendencies. This, I contend, has little to do with the merit or otherwise of particular writers, it is much more to do with the history of academic predisposition.

What might a typical poetry course look like? Most poetry courses would include Yeats and Eliot in their survey, they could then chose other rankers: Auden, Spender, MacNeice, and then, perhaps Larkin, Hughes and Heaney. At this point a loss of nerve would set in. They might have some Hardy, as a token of changes in poetic taste, but Kipling could be added only for the sake of debunking. Owen would represent war (*all* war). Plath, whose poetic abilities are not as great as claimed, would be included for the sake of form, and because she also represents a type of obligatory tokenism in British poetry courses despite being an American. Finally, new writing, where it was possible to include it, would consist of 'fringe' writers, writers found outside the 'canon', in order to appease students who dislike upper-middle-class-white-male-Oxbridge-educated-types and who need a dose of proletarian consciousness. The lecturer might turn gratefully to the very anthologies that inevitably prove pretty conclusively that the best poetry written in Britain in the last hundred years came from the very poets whose gender and education are now so out of fashion.

Although the canon of the literary great among novelists has been radically challenged, such a challenge to the canon of acceptable poets has not. Recent tastes masquerade as valid professional judgements, and female poets who indulge in four-letter words are acceptable primarily because the establishment (from which they come, to which they belong, and against which they intend no harm) can provide the very *fake* radical oppositional voices that half-educated students think are relevant. This amounts to a case of the emperor's new clothes. Alternative traditions and attitudes are always acceptable but not ever at the expense of the *full* and complex *real* history of poetry in this country.

Georgianism is the expression of British poetry in the twentieth century and yet modernism, with its primarily American base (Amy Lowell, H. D., Eliot, Pound and company) has taken the Georgians' place and stepped across the shadow they throw in order to obscure them. Which is simply to say that before we look for alternative new voices we must *recuperate* what has been lost and re-evaluate its relevance. This is *not* a question of the quality of the poetry produced – such is not the point. What is at stake is the very idea of poetry as having a real lived material history which one must explore. The names on such a 'lost' list are Housman, Brooke, de la Mare, Masefield, Graves, Hughes, Thomas (Edward and Dylan) and many others. The influence extends through much of the poetry of the First World War and that of the Second World War as well as to Larkin and the so-called post-modernism attributed to those anthologised in the *Penguin Book of Contemporary Verse* edited by Blake Morrison and Andrew Motion in 1982.[1]

Let me repeat, this is not a question of the quality of the works produced but a simple form of justice to poetic history and its grounding in material history. The work of feminist publishing houses has recuperated much of the 'lost' in women's writing and this we must do for poetry. Most of the poets I have listed have never been out of print, so the books are readily available; what is missing is the breaking out from methods of constructing poetic histories which circle around T. S. Eliot, however massive his influence. The other still voice in the poetic history of Britain in the modern age is the voice exemplified in Brooke. And this voice, as we shall see, has much more in common with the modernism of Eliot than is usually accepted by those only concerned with Brooke's association with the Georgian anthologies. The equation lacks its constituent parts, for the work of Ezra Pound and T. S. Eliot must be seen in conjunction, in Britain, with the work of Rupert Brooke and Edward Marsh. Such was the complex parallelism of influence that lead to the 'English' modernism of Virginia Woolf and the horticultural design interests of her friend Vita Sackville-West. Indeed, hostility to Georgianism did not come from the major modernists, however much they wished to carve out a path for themselves. What existed was rather, on the one hand a techno-futuristic modernism whose interests were urban and functional, and on the other a ruralist modernism whose interests were countrified and decorative. The two strands were *not* incompatible in modernism's heyday but have been pronounced incompatible only retrospectively. The latter type of Georgianism has become out of fashion, stranded in a Laura Ashley whimsicality, whereas the former has gained strength as the *only* form of modernism acceptable.

What must be said is that Brooke's poetry, more than much of that of his contemporaries, *is* modern in the terms of either of these two types of modernistic approach. Why then does Brooke exist only as a 'reputation' and as a marker and yet Eliot exist as a full-blown poet whose work is studied?

Before looking for an answer to the question just set, we must

pause to answer a real problem in literary history. If we are to
recuperate historical writers who are rarely read, at what point do
we stop? The ideological inconsistency of the canon of fiction as the
Leavises (husband and wife) constructed it was undermined by
those whose egalitarianism mistook popular for better. If the canon
was to be taught, then so were Agatha Christie, Dorothy L. Sayers,
Baroness Orczy and Mills and Boon. This, all in the name of relevance. Relevance to what? If to an idea of quality, then the list just
given hardly dents even the shadow of the Leavises' Desert Island
selection. If relevant only to history, then the questions posed by art
and the formal conditions governing aesthetics would of necessity
collapse. What happened was that the barriers did collapse and
everything became acceptable; for the discovery of Kate Chopin or
Alice Walker we have paid with the study of such dross as feminist
science fiction and lesbian detective tales.

And yet this was not a real emancipation of lost, forgotten or
half-remembered relevant texts, but a partial recuperation of what
is now actually only fashionable but which disguises that fashion-
ableness with an appeal to an unwritten agenda that suggests some
texts are higher than others on the 'worthiness' scale. Any real recuperation, however, must also include the *unacceptable*, that which
is racist, sexist, imperialist, ageist, rightist and elitist, and this is a
hard pill to swallow. We long ago learned to turn away from the
anti-semitic, misogynistic and religious T. S. Eliot in order to
understand both his contribution to culture's understanding of itself (alienation) and his contribution to literary form (style). In some
ways we have stripped Eliot of content in order to salvage his
achievement.

It is the very opposite with Brooke – if only he'd not written
those war sonnets! Brooke's contribution to formal practice (style)
is relegated to a secondary position whilst stripped from a content
highlighted for its naivety and gross nationalist romance. In Eliot's
case we recuperate his verse and in Brooke's damn it with a classic
double standard.

Let me pull some arguments together after this long digression,
before returning to the question of Brooke's position in literary
history. First, 'academics' (except in a form of tokenism) have not
found an alternative poetic tradition to the one usually offered in
courses. However, within those courses a radical suppression has
occurred that has distorted poetic history by an act of omission.
In general literary courses the idea of the canon has only been

undermined by an inclusiveness so wide as to be meaningless. Hence two things have been lost: the first is a sense of what art is and what it does. These are formal questions reserved for the realm of aesthetic analysis. The second is a sense of real history at work in the formal properties of the text and from which the text emerges as a type of *dialogue* with its culture. By widening choice in courses, the Leavises are not answered on any of their points (however right or wrong), they are merely *overrun*. By avoiding the forces of real historical process, the questions proper to the study of art (its discipline) do not even get approached. Brooke is a particular victim.

One must acknowledge that the forces that allowed Brooke to become a brilliant and urbane stylist (his class background, education, expectations etc.) also made much of what he said difficult to swallow. What too many people do is chuck out the baby with the bathwater: we must have the poet as a totality if he is to be seen and understood as a poet *qua* poet and if his poetry is to have any independent value.

People rarely die on cue. Brooke's glory and his tragedy is that he died 'on cue' in 1915. Unlike Owen (a poet technically of a lesser stature but able to put into words the horror of the war), Brooke's 'final' words were patriotic and, apparently jingoistic. Owen's hatred of war quite correctly gained the limelight once the war had finished but, in doing so, distorted the importance of Brooke's artistic (formal) achievement, which was 'suppressed' in favour of works whose content spoke of suffering banality.

Once dead, Brooke as the golden boy became the mythic tool of those who need heroes and hero worship. Brooke stood for an attitude which canonised him, his generation and his era and at the same time delivered his poetry over to non-professional advocacy. Parellel with the canonisation of Brooke by imperialist conservatives such as Winston Churchill, was the suppression of Brooke by the rising oppositional forces within Cambridge academics.

It was now indeed that in Cambridge, modern English literature made its appearance as an object of study for those released from the rigours of war and disillusioned by establishment (classical?) values. I. A. Richards's *Principles of Literary Criticism* became the standard text for what one did when studying literature. Such study was required to be *seen to be* impersonal and scientific and rigorous: as a former psychologist, Richards saw literature as a branch of communication and the study of literature as a branch of communication study (a behavioural process originating in neurology). This

whole pseudo-scientific procedure was needed to give the fledge-
ling study of modern literature a real base, but its origin lay not in
the human sciences such as psychology or sociology but actually in
T. S. Eliot's essay 'Tradition and the Individual Talent'. This aesthetic base was predicated on the idea of impersonality and of art
as a cultural artefact. Richards's work is deeply indebted to Eliot's
functionalist approach, which, whatever else it did, would, through
the *pedagogy* of Richards, force all poetry to conform to modernist
canons of taste. Richards's version of scientific enquiry was ultimately a procedure based on an aesthetic of modernist taste. In
such a process the romantic personality cult of Brooke could only
fare badly at the hands of the professionals.

At the same time, the '*Scrutiny* Group' around F. R. and Q. D.
Leavis were in an embattled position not only against the establishment in Cambridge but also against the philistines of 'Golders Green'
(see Eliot's 'A Cooking Egg'). Although they were not interested in
Brooke *per se*, his reputation does badly under the attacks on the
reading habits of Cambridge dons (an attack led by Queenie Leavis).
Donnish taste, it seems, was in the same lamentable condition as
that of the philistine public. Brooke, it turned out, was liked by
both readerships. In Q. D. Leavis's 'The Case of Miss Dorothy Sayers'
she trounces Sayers and those academics whose lack of judgement
support the latter's way of writing. In the essay, Leavis identifies
those shelves kept for show in a don's house and those where the
books are actually read and enjoyed. On *these shelves* all that is
second-rate and 'easy' is collected, including the work of Brooke.

> Run your eyes over enough academic bookshelves – not those
> housing shop but those where they keep what they really choose
> to read – and you get accustomed to a certain association of
> authors representing an average taste which is at best negative:
> Edward Lear and Ernest Bramah's *Kai Lung* (delicious humour),
> Charles Morgan and C. E. Montague (stylists), Rupert Brooke (or
> Humbert Wolfe or some equivalent), . . . we can all supplement.[2]

While Leavis and his wife acted as the opposition to Richards,
Richards actually saw himself as a force for radical change in the
gentleman's club of Cambridge. Of course, *both* Richards and the
Leavis group felt themselves to be outside the establishment of
Cambridge. How implicated in the establishment appeared Brooke
and how loved by uninformed opinion! For Richards, whose work

relied on Eliot's aesthetics, Brooke was outside the pale, because he was apparently an unregenerated romantic whose work did not conform to the aesthetic paradigm (clinically exact) of T. S. Eliot. For F. R. Leavis and his wife, Brooke's work belonged to those who *think* they are educated but who fail the acid test of culture (as defined by them and based firmly in the aesthetic of Eliot's seminal essay).

In such a way, and devoid of professional advocacy, Brooke's work fell foul of the very academic prejudice needed to launch modern literary studies in the first place. A pre-eminent modern writer, Brooke became a nowhere figure stranded helplessly at ten to three one sunny afternoon in Grantchester in 1912. For generations of English students modernism *was* English literature and T. S. Eliot *was* English poetry. Indeed, somehow one couldn't even study Brooke 'objectively' for his very emotionalism got in the way of the intellectual force of the argument; T. S. Eliot had convinced academics to convince themselves that poetry was a branch of philosophy or politics or theology.

The attack on the establishment by Richards and Leavis was doubly compounded when the New Left alliance in the 1960s and 1970s attacked Richards and Leavis themselves for being the voice of conservatism. In this attack, Brooke, imperialism, conservatism, liberal-humanist consensus were all crudely lumped together.

Those who supported Leavis were branded 'Leavisites', and the discipline of English letters as it had existed from 1917 to the mid-seventies began to fall apart. In this, Brooke became a casualty yet again – this time through association with perceptions about Leavis's conservatism – that very conservatism that had attacked Brooke years before!

On the Left, another story emerged. For the Left, a proper Marxist aesthetic has always been a problem, and an answer that allows for art has never really been successful. While historical materialism very adequately answers questions of cultural production and reception, it has no proper answer to questions about 'quality', 'value' and 'importance'. In a very basic sense, for Marxism, because all literature reveals the contradictions in social forces, the very best literature simply papers over the contradictions with greater skill. To such a Marxist view, the one levelled at Brooke, the work of art is always *faulty*, its perfection a deceptive bourgeois device to hide the contradictory tensions latent in society. In this view all art is *failure*. To Leavisite humanism the Brookian poetic is a failure because it says nothing true about the eternality of human values, whereas to the Marxist it is a failure because it says too much. On one count Brooke fails the quality test, on the other the test of being too obviously historical: a product of an imperialist élitist establishment. Curiously, the Leavis approach is the 'properly' formal examination as the Marxist would have to invoke outside criteria and then apply a *moral* caveat.

Thus has Brooke's reputation fared in scholarly debate – our loss of nerve over the empire and over our role in the world contributed to a worried condemnation of Brooke as representative of all we wished *not* to remember in the last hundred or so years.

For poets this was otherwise. By the 1940s modernism had lost its hold in Britain, Eliot was discredited because of his return to the church, Auden had scurried off to the United States when war broke out, Pound was in Fascist Italy, Yeats was dead. British poets, under the pressure of the War (and later Suez, with the introspective period that followed), rediscovered the Georgianism 'lost' previously. Yet the Georgianism they discovered was not that of Brooke but rather an emotionalised romantic ruralist poetry that appealed to 'ordinary folk' and which avoided the harsh, cynical and urbane note struck by Brooke. Rather than Brooke, we get a version of the world by a latter-day Edward Thomas or W. H. Davies.

The 'parochiality' actively sought by Larkin or the later Liverpool poets is quite against the grain of a parochial/lyrical content in Brooke, which is always at a distance from the metropolitan–international voice he employs. Quite simply, Brooke has more in common with T. S. Eliot than with Larkin and has more the tone of e. e. cummings or Noel Coward than that of Dylan Thomas.

> It's the very first word that poor Juliet heard
>   From her Romeo over the Styx;
> And the Roman will tell Cleopatra in hell
>   When she starts her immortal old tricks;
> What Paris was tellin' for good-bye to Helen
>   When he bundled her into the train –
> Oh, it's not going to happen again, old girl,
>   It's not going to happen again.
>   ('It's not going to Happen Again')

Georgianism is not a movement, despite any argument to the contrary – rather it describes another current in the modern movement sometimes parallel to and sometimes intermixed with imagism, vorticism and futurism. Despite the fact that many see Georgian poetry as a tag-end Victorianism, it is (again, despite its adherence to rhyme, metre and traditional content) a full branch of *modern* poetry. Note here, indeed, how Eliot himself adheres to strict metres and traditional rhyme.

If the tag 'Georgian' is dropped for a moment, then Brooke emerges as a modern writer with the concerns, both aesthetic and historical, of those who are known as modernists. His work is at once dextrous, urbane, metropolitan, 'free', distanced and ironic; his subject matter, modern life and experience. As a modern, his work also reveals the prejudice and posturing of that group of people at that time, and this cannot be ignored.

I do not intend in this essay to explore the importance of Brooke to the British version of the modernist movement or to attempt to prove in detail the relationship between modernist theory and Brooke's techniques. It must suffice that Brooke needs to be read with the same critical apparatus as T. S. Eliot and judged accordingly. Here, I reiterate that the question of quality is a separate issue and that I am only concerned to show that if a certain procedure is followed then Eliot and Brooke emerge as stablemates.

As a modernist, Brooke's best work compares more than favourably with that of Ezra Pound, and his work with Edward Marsh is every bit as distinguished as Pound's achievement with *Poetry*. What Brooke adds is a dimension rarely present in the functionalist performances of the imagists. In *Grantchester* (whose influence in terms of 'tone' on *The Waste Land* is rarely acknowledged) Brooke proves himself both a highly serious modernist and a Hogarthian humourist. His wit is founded on an attitude both distanced and yet comfortable. Brooke is both alienated and dispossessed, yet the seriousness of the meditation is only possible via the satiric panorama he puts before us.

Humour is a rarity in the modernist movement yet it goes with the urbane and sophisticated tone we expect of some aspects of modernism: those of Noel Coward, P. G. Wodehouse, Irving Berlin or Cole Porter. 'Grantchester' is, in this sense, a supremely cool and controlled poem, with its roots in Alexander Pope rather than Wordsworth and with its message drawn from money, continental travel and speed. At every point that 'Grantchester' has a Browningesque nostalgia it is undercut by a satiric distaste for the object of that nostalgia. Parochial in its subject matter yet international in its style,

'Grantchester' is the 'other' of *The Waste Land* and should be read by the discerning as a prefiguring and a commentary on Eliot's work. Brooke's work is almost *the* epic of the English character, both comic and yet, because comic, also true.

Brooke's achievement in the war sonnets, '1914 Sonnets I–V', is to provide a language the totality of which transcends its literal meaning. His phrasing displays a control of language which does not allow the musicality of that phrasing to be reduced to the banal jingoism of passions which hardly can have been felt by Brooke! Eliot 'proved' that sincerity was an unnecessary criterion in poetic appreciation. Whilst Brooke's message appears 'hot' and sincere, his control is as cool as a modernist's martini. The clean lines of the functional swimmer predominate. If we are embarrassed by nationalism we need not be embarrassed by the skill of the maker.

This might be special pleading on behalf of Brooke, but the message of modernism is the message of internal coherence. Purpose (moral integrity) had been replaced by organisation (aesthetic integrity), and the sonnets measure up to this criterion. The *skill* of the artist must be seen as integral to the message and the message as integral to the aesthetic (poetic) strategy of the poet in his culture. In such a way, Brooke can be seen as working complex emotional issues through a control of literary technical skills against which the overt anti-war messages of Owen appear dull and repetitive.

Brooke's oeuvre is slight, his reputation problematic, his future doubtful, yet despite all this it is necessary that he take his place as an important writer, whose main contributions to the history of British poetry, though slim, are probably the equal of the best of Eliot or Yeats and whose work demands to be read through the criteria of modernism and not relegated to the trashcan marked 'Georgian'.

For its part, Georgianism, which Brooke did so much to aid, is to be seen as a type of modernism rather than an outworn, outmoded, Victorianism finally defeated by the harsh *reality* of war.

I have described how Brooke's reputation has been caught between the rock of professional enquiry and the hard place of amateur enthusiasm. It may be that, as I suspect, Brooke's world was irrecoverably lost and will always be irrecoverably lost somewhere in our own 'Edwardian' mental space, and the half-life he suffers will continue much as before. But in a world intent on recuperating the lost to challenge the accepted, it is time we revisited the half-forgotten not merely for the sake of the historical record but also because we must, in the end, care about the value of art. In both these areas, Brooke deserves more than a passing mention.

Notes

1. Blake Morrison and Andrew Motion (eds), *Contemporary British Poetry* (Harmondsworth: Penguin, 1982) p. 20.
2. Q. D. Leavis, 'The Case of Miss Dorothy Sayers', in F. R. Leavis, *A Selection from 'Scrutiny'*, vol. 1 (Cambridge: Cambridge University Press, 1968) p. 145.

4

Lyrics of the First World War: Some Comments

MARTIN GRAY

This chapter attempts to argue two main points: first, that the poetry of the First World War was perceived as a homogeneous poetic kind from very early on in its history, and that publication in anthologies was both cause and consequence of this way of perceiving it; and secondly, that the characteristic lyric forms which the trench poets utilised are a necessary aspect of their meaning.

At certain stages in the developing history of twentieth-century poetry specific anthologies have occupied the foreground in the literary landscape, whether thrust there by the glare of publicity, or because of an anthologist's critical expertise and taste. Indeed, anthologies have been a vital element in the creation of groups of poets, and of critical fashions and moods, both transitory and long-lasting; though ultimately some of them may be perceived more as successes in the history of publishing and promotion, others have forged essential links in the transmission of poetic culture. Robert Conquest's *New Lines* (1956) and Alvarez's *The New Poetry* (1962) are obvious examples of successful anthologies, though very different in the manner of their influence.

At no time has the anthology been more significantly part of the means by which poetry should arrive in the public domain than during the years immediately before, after, and during the First World War, when the Georgian and Imagist anthologies were appearing almost annually, as well the Sitwells' short-lived *Wheels*.[1] During this time the anthology seemed the natural vehicle for the new and modern, as it has done at various stages in the development of twentieth-century poetry (for example during the 1930s, as well as in the 1950s and 1960s). After the First World War Eliot's *The Waste Land* shattered this assumption, yet perhaps it is not too fanciful to see the collage of allusions in that poem as a back-handed concession to the intrinsic pluralism of the anthology, the collection of literary 'flowers' that has been a filter and lens for the literary canon from Palgrave to Norton. Eliot's critical pronouncements, in spite of his espousal of 'objectivity' and rejection of biographical approaches, tended to focus on individual writers as stars in the constellations of the great tradition.

A fundamental aspect of the way the poetry of the First World War has been understood and absorbed into literary culture is the fact that its poets have tended to be grouped together, associated by their common subject matter and attitude to the war. Anthologies of 'war poetry' played a vital part in the immediate and later perception of these writers. Amongst the first was *Song and Sonnets for England in War Time, being a collection of lyrics by various authors inspired by the Great War* (1914). Edward Thomas reviewed four such anthologies in his essay on 'War Poetry', written in December 1914.[2] From the earliest days of the war, poetry seemed to offer a natural vehicle for expression of attitudes to war, whether propagandist or disillusioned. Newspapers and journals (*The Bookman, The Cornhill, The Nation, Saturday Post, The Spectator, The Times, Westminster Gazette*, and so on) rushed first to publish patriotic verse, and then poems sent back from the Front by unknown participants – the work of these 'soldier-poets' was featured because of its subject matter, because it was 'war poetry' of a new kind, not because it was poetry by known writers. Publishers hastened to put before the public the new poetry about war and by the victims of war: just one example is the way *Marlborough and Other Poems*, by C. H. Sorley, killed at Loos in October 1915, appeared in 1916 and ran into three different editions in that one year, but such speed of production and reprint was by no means uncommon. Anthologies continued to appear during the war, with titles like *For those who Mourn* (1917), *The Muse in Arms* (1917), and *Soldier Poets: Songs of the Fighting Men* (1916 and 1917).

The consolidation of critical perceptions of the poetry of the First World War as a coherent phenomenon occurred two generations after the end of the war, and is also mappable by means of anthologies: these were *Up the Line to Death* (1964), by Brian Gardner, and *Men Who March Away* (1965), by I. M. Parsons, but two other works are vital in the cultural recuperation of the First World War in the 1960s, providing the pictures and songs that make it familiar, the first an illustrated history, A. J. P. Taylor's *The First World War*

(1963), and the other the Theatre Workshop's *Oh, What a Lovely War!* (1965), later to be made into a film, and reproduced by drama clubs thousands of times since then.

Extraordinary figures are advanced for the importance and popularity of poetry as a way of coming to terms with the experience of war. One historian of the war notes tantalisingly that 'it has been estimated that one and half million war poems were written in August 1914 – 50,000 a day'.[3] We may speculate that for many of the educated middle-class participants in the war, poetry was often perceived in terms of writing as well as reading. Much of this writing, of course, is lost, or preserved unread in family archives.

What differentiates anthologies of war poetry, whether compiled during the war or later, is that their organising principle is not a matter of technique, of 'newness' or explicit modernity, or political slant, or nationality, but of subject matter, and a subject matter with a certain obvious, arresting 'relevance', in the educational jargon of the sixties, unlike poems about animals or landscape. Classification was never much in doubt during the war, whether the poems collected together were jingoistically pro-war, for the encouragement of the troops and those seeing them off, or the poetry of cynical disillusionment, or later attempts to give a historical overview of war poetry.[4] By 'war poets' now, we tend to mean 'anti-war poets'.

'War poets', then and now, have usually been seen as a group phenomenon, and are often praised or criticised as a group in spite of their manifestly different styles and attitudes. This was true from remarkably early in the history of this strand of poetical writing, and also provides a consistent way of perceiving this kind of poetry at later times. Thus Newbolt, friend of Haig and author of 'Vitai Lampada' ('Play up! Play up! and play the game') in 1924, writes disparagingly of 'Owen and the rest of the broken men [who] rail at the Old Men who sent the young to die. They have suffered cruelly, but in the nerves and not the heart . . .'.[5] And thus also Yeats, in his extraordinary 1936 *Oxford Book of Modern Verse*, bundles together 'certain poems' and dismisses them *en bloc* in his preface. His famous comment is worth quoting at length as it formulates a critical perspective antipathetic to war poetry, and a set of assumptions about it that are revealing and often reproduced in different forms by later critics:

I have a distaste for certain poems written in the midst of the great war; they are in all anthologies, but I have substituted

Herbert Read's *End of a War* written long after. The writers of these poems were invariably officers of exceptional courage and capacity, one a man constantly selected for dangerous work, all, I think, had the Military Cross; their letters are vivid and humorous, they were not without joy – for all skill is joyful – but felt bound, in the words of the best known, to plead the sufferings of their men. In poems that had for a time considerable fame, written in the first person, they made that suffering their own. I have rejected these poems for the same reason that made Arnold withdraw his *Empedocles on Etna*; passive suffering is not a theme for poetry. In all the great tragedies, tragedy is a joy to the man who dies; in Greece the tragic chorus danced. When man has withdrawn into the quicksilver at the back of the mirror no great event becomes luminous in his mind; it is no longer possible to write *The Persians, Agincourt, Chevy Chase*: some blunderer has driven his car on to the wrong side of the road – that is all.

Yeats objects to war poetry on the grounds of the poets' relationship with their subject matter, their first-person non-tragic point of view, which he argues results in 'passive suffering' and lack of detachment. He does not discriminate between different writers, but deals with them as a homogeneous group.

The manner in which Newbolt and Yeats perceived war poets, and the way they are perceived now, as a group, is not that different from the manner in which they perceived themselves at the time. Their group identity is, to an extent, part of the myth that they themselves create. Both during and after the war the poets are drawn together into loose fellowships, united by their common desire to come to terms with the traumatic experience of the trenches. Edward Marsh, the compiler of the Georgian anthologies, befriended and corresponded with many soldier-poets, including Isaac Rosenberg. The short-lived Owen–Sassoon–Nichols–Graves friendship is a well-known example of the way in which some of those poets met each other during the course of the war, and encouraged each other in their writing. Such affiliations never amounted to a literary 'movement'. They were drawn together as writers who wished in different ways and to different degrees to call attention to the nature of the war and to the suffering of the soldiers. Matters of technique and desire for mutual criticism and understanding drew them together, but above all it was their sense of themselves as 'poets' in difficult and special circumstances that led to the forging of temporary bonds during the course of the war. As is shown by Graves's part in the incident of Sassoon's public letter refusing to serve further in the army, in July 1917,[6] which resulted in his stay at Craiglockhart hospital (where he met Owen), they took different attitudes to the poet's role in the public debate about war, but they still shared a concern for the nature of war as the subject of poetry. After the war, they return almost obsessively to their war experience and rework it into autobiographical accounts (Aldington, Blunden, Graves, Sassoon, *et al.*).

In contradistinction with the Second World War, the broad experience of the First World War – in effect, of trench warfare – was, for most participants, in many respects remarkably similar and homogeneous whatever their regiment, rank (up perhaps to Captain), and even nationality. The facts and images by which we know it – patriotic volunteers, trenches looking out on shattered landscapes, corpses in the mud – gain a power from the knowledge that these were common, general experiences. By contrast, the next war was to be one of movement and vast geographical scope, and diverse and multifarious military activity.

Examining the poetry of this trench warfare, it is quickly apparent that common methods of approach and common subject matters unite poets who are speaking with very different voices. This can be perceived in a general way through the anthologies, where it is reflected by the division of material, frequently according to the typical curve of war experience rather than simply by poet. Of course, the organisation in these anthologies is an artificial and retrospective construction, but it is still a significant aspect of the cultural transmission of war poetry. Two anthologists of the 1960s subdivide their chosen poems as follows:

> Prelude – Happy is England Now – Field Manoeuvres – Tipperary Days – to Unknown Lands – Home Front – Death's Kingdom – A Bitter Taste – Behind the Lines – O Jesus, Make it Stop – At Last, at Last! – Epilogue
> > Brian Gardner in *Up the Line to Death*

> Visions of Glory – The Bitter Truth – No More Jokes – The Pity of War – The Wounded – The Dead – Aftermath
> > I. M. Parsons in *Men Who March Away*

This gradation from valorous anticipation to a despairing and bruised cynicism is the typical parabola of war experience, here organised by selection long after the event, but verifiable in almost every history, journal, collection of letters, and memoir. The subject matter of the poetry is even more precisely shared and echoed than this atmospheric list of headings suggests.

In *The Great War and Modern Memory* (1975), Paul Fussell has written eloquently of literature's encounter with the warfare of the trenches. His method is to annotate the way in which certain modes of perceiving the war (most characteristically, irony) and certain individual topics constantly recur in the writings of the participants, in notebooks, and letters, as well as more formal statements, and to relate these to the particular nature of the war and its effects. One example (explained by Fussell in detail) is the 'peculiar significance' (David Jones's phrase) of the morning and evening military duty of the stand-to in what Fussell calls the 'troglodyte world' of the trenches:

It was a cruel reversal that sunrise and sunset, established by over a century of Romantic poetry and painting as the tokens of hope and peace and rural charm, should now be exactly the moments of heightened ritual anxiety. (p. 52)

This exploitation of moments of waxing and waning half-light is one of the distinct hallmarks of Great War rhetoric. (p. 57)

He discusses a large number of references, in poetry and prose of the war, to dawn and dusk, drawing out the ironies of this clash between idealised preconceptions and trench life, and following it through to show the distaste for the picturesque that characterises post-Great War literature (Eliot's 'patient etherised upon a table', amongst other examples). War poetry is indeed full of ironically perceived twilight. Here is a single and complete instance of this fact, not used by Fussell (who prefers less self-aware illustrations), Richard Aldington's Imagist 'Sunsets' (1916):

> The white body of the evening
> Is torn into scarlet,
> Slashed and gouged and seared
> Into crimson,
> And hung ironically
> With garland of mist.

> And the wind
> Blowing over London from Flanders
> Has a bitter taste.

This is fully explicit in its ironic conjunction of the poetically 'beautiful' with death, equally poeticised, but then referred to the war.

Perusal of war poetry reveals that the poems are very often constructed out of an image-hoard of common, shared perceptions, like
Fussell's list of references to dusk and dawn: glimpses of natural
beauty, birdsong, memories of home, whether comforting or embit-
tered, sudden and grotesque encounters with death, the bitter cold,
skyscapes, the sounds of warfare, long boredom, anecdotes expressing the indomitable spirit or hopeless pessimism of the soldiers.

It is not surprising in itself to find poets sharing subject matter
with such predictability. However, that the poetry of the First World
War should be constantly treated in this way *en bloc* is a significant
fact about the poetry itself. Both for writer and critic, the terrible
knowledge of what the war was like seems to overturn poetical
concerns such as technique and genre. As Owen's draft preface
rather bluntly put the matter, 'Above all I am not concerned with
Poetry. My subject is War and the pity of War.' Urgency of content
is allowed to overpower form, and the tendency to let this happen remains a salient feature of the discussion and criticism of war
poetry.

Though the shared subject matter of war poetry is not in itself
surprising, what is perhaps intrinsically odd is the fact that the lyric
should be so much its dominant form: a genre devoted to the exploration of feeling (and especially love) becomes the common mode
for the expression of ironic indignation at the sufferings imposed
by war, and for the description of the horrors of trench warfare.
Yeats's objection to the perceived lack of distance and detachment
in the war poets is an attack on their use of lyric. His list of successful poems dealing with war are narrative in form (a tragedy and
two ballads: *The Persians, Agincourt, Chevy Chase*), and his image of
withdrawing 'into the quicksilver at the back of the mirror' seems
to criticise lyrical subjectivity.

The lyric's concentration on moments of feeling expresses an implicit collection of attitudes that might be termed a 'hidden agenda',
though the lyric philosophy, if we can call it this, is neither as hidden nor as systematised as the phrase suggests. Lyrics are inher-
ently anti-narrative. They may include the beginnings of narrative,

but their shortness curtails development of these possibilities to the point at which they might meaningfully be termed narrative. Poets writing out of immediate experience of the trenches seem to have been distrustful or incapable of narrative except in journals and letters which avoid full organisation and direction. To build discourses that provided a context for the horrors and boredom of their day-to-day experience, and thereby embed it in frameworks of meaning and purpose and direction, would have been to deny the pervading sense of war's futility that their poetry so often expresses. Such discourses were left to the much-despised newspapers which arrived every day in the trenches, and the official historians like John Buchan, who were structuring the events of the war for propaganda purposes (and who also produced some of its first novels in *Greenmantle* (1916) and *Mr Standfast* (1919)).

In contrast, the lyric is anti-narrative, anti-historical, anti-political, anti-theoretical; it is almost bound, as a form, to be existential and humanist in its direction. Lyrics avoid large statements of meaning, and by placing value on feelings that are evanescent and fragmentary they suggest that meaning is itself evanescent, fragmentary, and unstable, perceived only by glimpses. Even when the lyric operates within an accepted structure of meaning, in the manner, for example, of religious verse, it still validates feeling rather than argument and the momentary perception rather than theology.

Similarly, the patriotic war verse characteristic of the days before the Somme depended on a framework of stable values outside itself – nationalism, the moral rightness of battle, the glory of military valour and sacrifice. These are conveyed through feeling rather than reason, but lacking roots in real experience they ring decidedly hollow.

Prose written close to the war (that was not part of the propaganda effort) tends towards lyric rather than discursive narrative patterns. C. E. Montague's *Disenchantment* (February 1922) is an example. It has an approximate essay-like collection of topics that it discusses, but it moves in a rhapsodical and haphazard manner; it generalises the war experience, and muses upon it, rather than marshalling a collection of memories into a stable story with purpose and direction. Barbusse's *Under Fire* (1917), written in hospital from diaries kept in the trenches, is a set of episodes loosely strung around character studies.

As the war recedes into memory, the poets turn to narrative to explore their experience. The detachment Yeats implies he found in

Read's *The End of a War* (1933) becomes available to the combatants. Autobiography, embedded like the lyric in personal experience, is the common vehicle for this retrospective examination. And many of them, like Graves's *Goodbye to All That* (1929), stress the public meaninglessness of the experience, whatever its traumatic personal effect, and seek to leave it behind. Other forms start to come to terms with the war at the distance of a decade, for example Sherriff's *Journey's End* (1928), Manning's *The Middle Parts of Fortune* (1929), and Remarque's *All Quiet on the Western Front* (1929). David Jones's epic *In Parenthesis* is the notable exception to the general rule that the lyric is the characteristic form of the poetry of the First World War, and interestingly it is one of the last poems to grow out of the war, being published in 1937.

The associations of the lyric form make it intrinsically an odd vehicle for the purported realism of the poets' accounts of war. The 'disenchantment' suffered by the combatants leads to a new realism in the depiction of warfare. Though the verse often contains ironic reference to 'poetic' attitudes to war, much of the poetry makes a complete break with the traditional treatment of war in English poetry, in which heroic and idealised action leads to glory. Such is the staple poetic vision of war provided by the few poets who touch upon it as a theme suitable for poetry, with few exceptions (one notable one is the description of the Russo-Turkish war in Canto VIII of Byron's *Don Juan*). The heroic vision still dominates verse written in anticipation of fighting in the First World War, and the propaganda which continued to be produced for the home market. Rupert Brooke's few war lyrics are among the best of the many examples of this, and his poem 'Peace' – 'Now, God be thanked Who has matched us with His hour' – is the *locus classicus* for the idealisation of war as a cleansing of the 'dirty songs' of ordinary life and its 'half-men' (though the poem gains its strength from the ironic acceptance that the body will be broken in death).

In 1914, for the first time in human history, huge, non-professional, literate armies went to war. There had been no major conflict between the great European powers since 1871, the year after Forster's Elementary Education Act had begun the process of creating an entirely new class of readers and writers, a fact of immense significance in forging new kinds of literary production from the 1890s onwards. Conscription began early in 1916. Most of those soldiers, however, who wrote the war into verse for publication were volunteers, and not conscripts, and officers rather than private soldiers. Yet, in the poetry sent back from the front, suddenly the language and experience of the foot-soldier bursts into the English lyric tradition, filtered and mediated though it may be by young officers like Sassoon and Owen. Since much of the soldier-poets' work is now so familiar to us, it is sometimes easy to forget that here, for the first time in English literature, the effects and sensations of war are described fully and exactly. There are many precedents for what happens in the poetry of the First World War: Kipling's *Barrack-Room Ballads* (1892), John Davidson's *In a Music Hall* (1891) and *Fleet-Street Ecloques* (1893), and the hospital poems of W. E. Henley (1898), are examples of poetry dealing in different ways with aspects of the then new material of working-class life. But this should not detract from the completeness with which lyric poetry is taken over by participants in the war, and adapted and expanded as a vehicle to cope with experiences and situations that had never been written into literature before. Scouring the literary canon prior to 1915 may result in finding the occasional dead body, rat, rifle, or louse (Shakespeare, alongside the patriotic vision, places Falstaff's perception of soldiery, for example), but there is nothing like the outpouring of horrific experience which we encounter in anthologies of First World War poetry.

Again the homogeneity and size of this reaction needs to be stressed. The war may be (and usually is) approached through the work of a few poets chosen by critics as poetically skilful, or self-selected by their ambitious sense of themselves as 'poets' rather than soldiers who happened to write occasional verse. A standard critical strategy is to compare two soldier-poets (Owen and Sassoon, or Owen and Rosenberg) to the detriment of one. The history of twentieth-century criticism has been devoted chiefly to the examination of the work of individual poets, often in isolation from the poetic culture in which they wrote. But the 'major' war poets run the risk of being diminished if not seen in the context of the other work produced by the many writers now largely otherwise unknown. The anthology, with all the critical problems that its fissiparous, selective nature entails, has been a peculiarly appropriate medium for encountering and understanding this new departure in literary history.

The poems that grew out of this novel situation themselves often demonstrate a tension between the nature of the subject matter and its impropriety in relation to the perceived decorum of 'poetry'. Such texts exhibit self-contradictory qualities which anticipate deconstructive critical manoeuvres; as texts, they often offer explicit encounters with the break-down of literary language and meaning, dealing as they do with the disintegration of literary values and language itself in the face of experience. Some are texts about deconstruction, quizzical examinations of the ironic gulfs between content and form that stretch and map the limits of language and sensibility, and deny from the outset any simple, confident solidity of meaning.

A fragment from the opening of Owen's 'Insensibility' (1917) provides an example:

> The front line withers,
> But they are troops who fade, not flowers
> For poet's tearful fooling:
> Men, gaps for filling:
> Losses, who might have fought
> Longer; but no one bothers.

Owen initiates a metaphor, and then is overcome and angered by its trite associations, which he ascribes to the futile activity of the 'poet', no more than 'fooling', undercutting the purpose and meaning of the text itself. The poem's grammar collapses under the weight of the appalling irony of death into a pair of paratactic antitheses: Men/gaps for filling, and Losses/who might have fought longer. The final cynical assertion that 'no one bothers' is of course undermined by the fact that the poet is himself bothering. Each thought, as it occurs to the poet, seems to confute what went before: it is an extraordinary, ironic exercise in self-contradiction, nakedly at odds with the construction of any simple, direct meaning. Its ambiguities amount to self-cancellation. Literary language and responses are being explicitly tested to breaking point.

Not all the lyrics of war are exercises in the break-down of meaning like this. In general, lyrical forms and strategies remain peculiarly stable vehicles for war experience. They do not break under the strain. What is more, in the writing of a deliberate verse-craftsman such as Owen, there is a Keatsian play with the sounds of words, and decorative verse effects. This might be thought grossly inappropriate, applied to the grim subject matter of trench combat, as purveyed, for example, in 'Exposure' (1917):

Sudden successive flights of bullets streak the silence.
Less deadly than the air that shudders black with snow,
With sidelong flowing flakes that flock, pause, and renew,
We watch them wandering up and down the wind's nonchalance,
    But nothing happens.

The wrought complexity of the play of sounds, in the careful attention both to consonants and consonantal clusters as well as to the
modulation of vowels, the self-conscious enactment of the pause in
the third line, synaesthesia, the paradox of 'black with snow', the
dandled metaphorical combination of the 'wind's nonchalance', all
these rhetorical felicities, it might be argued, are at odds with the
poem's subjects – boredom, weariness, the 'merciless iced east winds'
(even these give rise to a neologism: 'knive'), the burying party,
and so on. Alliteration, assonance, and half-rhyme are the hallmarks
of Owen's verse style. It is ornate, metrical, traditional, highly pat-
terned, and as such refutes assumptions concerning the expressive
qualities of form: surely a fragmented, broken, free verse would
suit the fragmented, broken experiences that the war provided?[7]
    However, to set form against content in this way would be to
miss an essential point about the poetry of the First World War, and
not just about Owen's manifestly artificial writing. In the midst of
chaos the formal qualities of the lyric provide linguistic patterns
that momentarily give a sense of shape to experience. In the versi-
fication there is a constant and poignant ironic interplay between
the fragile verbal patterning and the overwhelming experiences that
it momentarily organises and keeps at bay. Edgell Rickword's
'Winter Warfare' (1919) invents a jaunty allegorical figure in appro-
priately childish metre, but a grim series of rhymes cancels the innocence of form:

        Colonel Cold strode up the Line
           (Tabs of rime and spurs of ice),
        Stiffened all where he did glare,
           Horses, men, and lice.

        Visited a forward post,
           Left them burning, ear to foot,
        Fingers stuck to biting steel,
           Toes to frozen boot.

Stalked on into No Man's Land,
   Turned the wire to fleecy wool,
Iron stakes to sugar sticks
   Snapping at a pull.

Those who watched with hoary eyes
   Saw two figures gleaming there;
Hauptmann Kalte, Colonel Cold,
   Gaunt, in the grey air.

Stiffly, tinkling spurs they moved
   Glassy eyed, with glinting heel
Stabbing those who lingered there
   Torn by screaming steel.

Wilfrid Gibson's equally simple lyric 'In the Ambulance' (1916)
juxtaposes the necessity of form with its ironic banality:

> *Two rows of cabbages,*
> *Two of curly-greens,*
> *Two rows of early peas,*
> *Two of kidney-beans.*
>
> That's what he keeps muttering,
> Making such a song,
> Keeping other chaps awake
> The whole night long.
>
> Both his legs are shot away,
> And his head is light,
> So he keeps on muttering
> All the blessed night:
>
> *Two rows of cabbages,*
> *Two of curly-greens,*
> *Two rows of early peas,*
> *Two of kidney-beans.*

The frame of the empty nonsense verse leads on to the irritation
of the 'other chaps' kept awake, and then the casual horror at the

centre of the verse: 'Both his legs are shot away'. Yet in 'making such a song', suggesting that empty form is an anodyne for pain, Gibson is offering a primitive theory of poetry.

In much war verse rhyme, rhythm, and the play of sounds are brought together to create an order that is neither rational nor logical – all reasoning may be in conflict with it – but which is none the less a moment of order, however temporary and arbitrary. This persistent lyric shaping offers the implicit possibility, or even proof, of human design and control, and therefore perhaps comfort in the midst of whatever desolation and confusion prevails. The lyric form is a charm to counter the evil of the war.

Yet however obvious, even strangely obtrusive, the lyric forms of poems like these are, it is the subject matter of war poetry that is still liable to possess the reader's imagination. The raw power of the information and the anger in a poem like Sassoon's 'Remorse' is liable to obscure the fact that it is a sonnet. Those poems that set out to describe the appalling conditions and events as vividly as possible overwhelm responses other than sympathy and horror. The poems come to be used as a window on history, as transparent fragments of a 'reality'. History also modifies our knowledge of the poems. The deaths of Owen, Rosenberg, Sorley, and other writers, or Gurney's war-induced mental instability, place their poetry in a special relationship with real events, with history and fact, that is sometimes used to validate the poetry unthinkingly. (The common use of war poetry in the classroom would seem to be based on this kind of premise: here is poetry about a special kind of intense experience, verifiable from historical sources, experience so 'real' as to have led to the death of some poets.) Foregrounding the factuality of war experience, while generating strong feelings in the reader, may lead to ignorance or circumvention of formal considerations. The poems cease to be poems, but just pegs on which to hang preconceptions about the nature of war, and the First World War in particular.

The poets themselves used the direct appeal to experience and history as a strategy to draw attention to their views of the war, and their poetry. Owen's much-quoted prefatorial notes offer a much cited instance of a poet seeking to divert attention from form to content. To repeat, he is 'above all ... not concerned with Poetry'. However, this comment has to be worked hard to sustain the view that Owen wished to 'subvert' literary tradition: it contradicts the whole texture of his poetry, as well as his pronouncements about poets and poetry in his letters. One example will have to suffice, from a letter of 31 December 1917 to his mother:

> I go out of this year a Poet, my dear mother, as which I did not enter it. I am held peer by the Georgians; I am a poet's poet.
> I am started. The tugs have left me; I feel the great swelling of the open sea taking my galleon.

There may be an element of self-parody in the reference to the Georgians, whom in other letters he does not value particularly highly, and in the mock-portentous language he deems suitable for conveying these feelings to his mother, but it is not sufficiently parodic to undermine his pleasure and excitement at the success of his poems.

But Owen's comment has been used to argue that his work is something harder and more 'real' than normal poetry, indeed that it is in some way antagonistic to poetry, something vividly 'real' and opposed to the usual falsities of 'poesy'.[8] From this perspective, war poetry is seen as subverting the poetic tradition, the Establishment, patriarchy, the masculine values of heroism in war (or it is chided for not subverting them enough). The element of truth in this approach needs careful discrimination. Of course the poets felt that they were participating directly and immediately in the drama of history. This fact, and their knowledge that the experiences they wished to convey through their writing were special, and in some respects 'unpoetic', shocking, or anti-authoritarian, forms part of the self-generated myth which sustained them in such adverse circumstances. The poets' perceived conflict with received ideologies has lead them to be reclaimed as part of a new 'subversive' canon. But the vogue for 'subversive' and 'radical' as validating and encompassing critical terms can be damagingly anachronistic and leads to obtuse and unjustifiable re-readings.

The obsession with the content and occasional didacticism of war poetry and the ignoring of its form, manifested in many different ways, is testament once more to the hegemony of realism in attitudes to literature. Approaches offered by feminist or new historicist perspectives often grow out of a crude political fundamentalism that seeks constantly to deny the fictionality, artificiality, and pluralism that is a *sine qua non* of all literary production and discourse, including criticism itself.

Though war poetry includes material which can be seen as offering a realism new in the history of English poetry, and though it exhibits shared subject matter and responses to historical events that allow it to be considered, unusually, as a homogeneous kind of poetry grouped by subject rather than genre, its common lyric form constantly works to contradict the ideologies of realism. Indeed, the lyric, in so far as it is non-narrative, is anti-ideological. Lyrics, by means of their intrinsic multifariousness, make a statement about the value and necessity of pluralism: each one is a new beginning, a new shaping of thoughts and feelings in language, a new and unique micro-ideology. And by their non-rational patterns of sounds and rhythms, organising momentarily the chaos of experience into new forms, they remind us of their constructed, artificial, and fictional aspects, and their status as creations of a specific kind within the wide realm of literary discourse.

Notes

1. *Georgian Poetry, 1911–12*, ed. Edward Marsh, was followed by further volumes in 1915, 1917, 1919 and 1922. *Des Imagistes*, edited anonymously by Pound, appeared in 1914. *Some Imagist Poets*, variously edited, also anonymously, appeared in 1915, 1916 and 1917. *Wheels*, ed. Edith Sitwell, came out annually in six 'cycles' between 1916 and 1921.
2. 'War Poetry', in *Poetry and Drama*, II, no. 8 (December 1914); this essay can be more conveniently found in D. Hibberd (ed.), *Poetry of the Great War: A Casebook* (Basingstoke: Macmillan, 1981) pp. 25–30).
3. Keith Robbins, in *The First World War* (1984) p. 16. The proliferation of verse in wartime in the twentieth century has long been wondered at, but never adequately explained.
4. As a category, 'war poet' is sometimes treated as problematic, most crucially in relation to a poet like Edward Thomas, who wrote much of his poetry between 1914 and his death in battle in 1917, but who only mentions war obliquely. 'War poetry', however, seems a clear enough category, as it refers to explicit subject matter. Thus a poet like Graves wrote some 'war poetry', and was for a while a 'war poet'. Those poets who died in the war are now designated 'war poets', frozen in this role, in spite of cross-classification as Georgians, Imagists, or whatever.
5. From a letter of 2 August 1924, in M. Newbolt (ed.), *The Later Life and Letters of Sir Henry Newbolt* (London, 1924); quoted by Paul Fussell in *The Great War and Modern Memory* (1975) p. 26, who cites as his source

Patrick Howarth, *Play Up and Play the Game* (1973). The relevant passage from the letter is also reprinted in J. Press, *A Map of Modern English Verse* (Oxford: Oxford University Press, 1969) p. 147, and in D. Hibberd (ed.), *Poetry of the Great War: A Casebook*, p. 65.

6. Graves gives his account of this in *Goodbye to All That* (London: Cape, 1929) chapter 24.

7. Notoriously, the poets of the First World War were omitted from Roberts's *The Faber Book of Modern Verse* because of their lack of formal experimentation. However, experiments were being made, if infrequently: for example, Robert Nichols's *The Assault*, published in *Ardours and Endurances* (1917) and also included in *Georgian Poetry 1916–1917* (1917), is in free verse of a crude kind, laced with obtrusive rhymes, a form devised in response to an attempt at narrative description.

8. For example, here is a comment from *Wilfred Owen: Selected Poetry and Prose*, edited by Jennifer Breen (London: Routledge, 1988): 'Owen's major poems, drawing upon his searing experiences of the Great War, comprise a sustained subversion of literary tradition.' And later in the same critical commentary Dr Breen remarks: 'readers of Owen's war poetry, if they throw off the restrictive practices of traditional 'lit. crit.', cannot but appreciate his radical exposure of a dehumanising patriarchy in church and state as well as in private lives'.

5

Recuperating and Revaluing: Edith Sitwell and Charlotte Mew

GARY DAY and GINA WISKER

The history of women's poetry in the early part of the twentieth century has been one of absence: absence from bookstores and library shelves and even from course lists. However, this situation is now changing and this chapter aims to contribute to that change by considering the work of Edith Sitwell and Charlotte Mew.

Edith Sitwell (1886–1964) has the reputation of being one of the bright young things of the twenties generation.[1] But it is more true to say that she was a critic rather than a celebrant of the frivolous worldliness which surrounded her. Similarly, the image of her as a right-wing versifier does not do justice to the huge and complex body of her work.[2]

The unwanted child of Sir George Sitwell and his seventeen-year-old wife, Ida, Edith was brought up by her grandparents and was a formidably precocious child who preferred the company of adults to that of children. By all accounts, her childhood was a harrowing affair, particularly as regards her mother, but it had its absurd moments as well, such as her falling in love with a peacock at the age of four and being singularly distressed when it wisely deserted her for one of its own kind.[3] In a house of ghosts, she identified with ghosts:

> I was always a little outside life –
> And so the things we touch could comfort me;
> I loved the shy dreams we could hear and see –
> For I was like one dead, like a small ghost,
> A little cold air, wandering and lost.[4]

In adult life, perhaps as a consequence of her childhood, Sitwell courted public recognition by dressing in a highly eccentric manner. Virginia Woolf described her as follows: 'Edith Sitwell is a very tall young woman, wearing a perpetually startled expression and . . . a high green silk head dress concealing her hair so that it is not known whether she has any.'[5] A description which was borne out by her appearance on the 1960s BBC 'Monitor' programme, her sharp, intelligent face offset by the slightly ludicrous turban balanced precariously on her head.

Her somewhat startling appearance made her seem rather formidable and, indeed, she was capable of lofty – and amusing – dismissals of her contemporaries, as when she wrote that the Georgians 'seem obsessed by the predilection for sheep'.[6] But she could also be very encouraging, championing, through her editorship of *Wheels* (1916–1924), the work of many young writers and artists, including Wilfred Owen.

As her ridiculing of the Georgians implies, Sitwell's sympathies lay mainly with modernism. But whereas critical commentary on male modernist poets is generally favourable, Sitwell's experiments have tended to be dismissed. Julian Symons refers to her as 'the arch-nurse of empty phrases'[7] while Aldous Huxley claims that though her poetry is 'exquisite', it is also for that very reason limited, confined to 'the immediacies of consciousness [rather than reaching] towards the universal'.[8] In today's post-structuralist climate, such a judgement is a reason for studying Sitwell rather than dismissing her. Her poetry is one of dazzling surfaces, full of artifice and fantasy, and its constant drawing attention to sounds, rhymes and rhythms alerts us to the primacy of the signifier in the constitution of meaning. This gives her work a radical edge, its brilliant coruscations are a refusal of the consolations of modernism's myths – such as Joyce's use of Ulysses – which seek to redeem the fragmentation on which they depend.

'When Sir Beelzebub', a fairly typical poem, is only superficially a comment on the hellish nature of cosmopolitanism. What is more striking is the layout and the repetition and variation on word sounds, producing an incantatory effect:

When
Sir
Beelzebub called for his syllabub in the hotel in Hell
Where Prosperpine first fell,

> Blue as the gendarmerie were the waves of the sea,
> (Rocking and shocking the bar-maid).
>
> (*CP*, p. 158)

Here the sounds, not the sense, of the words predominate. The overall impression is one of playfulness, the shaking loose of meaning instead of fixing it in some monolithic scheme. Sitwell's use of allusion is different from Eliot's, who uses it to revive or strengthen meanings in the European, Christian tradition. So instead of Eliotic resonance there is comic juxtaposition which distances both the Christian and classic reference, highlighting their protean as opposed to their 'essential' quality. In addition, the self-reflexive play with 'syllable' demystifies the poem, foregrounding its means of organisation and thus it contrasts with those other modernist works – again Eliot comes to mind – where the poem seems to be naturalised by the rhythms of consciousness; we seem to be in the presence of 'Prufrock' rather than of an artefact which gives us the illusion of such a presence.

Sitwell, however, never lets us forget the constructed nature of poetry and perhaps this has a bearing on her identity as a woman; her outlandish appearance a comment on the constructed nature of femininity in the same way that her verse is about the constructed nature of poetry. Certainly, the self-conscious aspects of Sitwell's poetry suggest that she had a more profound understanding of the implications of modernity than did some of her male contemporaries; she realised that it shattered all previous certainties and made it impossible to think in terms of new ones. Unlike them, she was prepared to embrace this freedom and her verse is a testament to the contingent nature of meaning rather than an expression of nostalgia for a lost essentialism. This would explain her debunking of Victorian culture, for example her mischievous references to Tennyson in 'Sir Beelzebub' (*CP*, p. 158), where the poet crosses the bar in 'classical metres' carrying workers' deputations all signed 'In Memoriam'. A critique of the Victorian age is also evident in 'The White Owl', where the period is characterised as the bustling Mother Bunch, who energetically parodies Matthew Arnold's 'Dover Beach':

> If once I begin to howl,
> I am sure that my sobs would drown the seas
> With my 'oh's' and my 'ah's' and my 'oh dear me's!'
>
> (*CP*, p. 38)

The rhyme scheme reinforces the satirical tone by mimicking the forced conformity of rhyme and metre in Victorian poetry.

Religion also comes under attack in 'Four in the Morning', which is reputed to be the time of Christ's betrayal. But this dramatic moment is robbed of its significance by being described in terms of 'the morning after the night before' of 'Mr. Belaker / the allegro Negro cocktail shaker' (*CP*, p. 123). His is a dream-like world of bars and seedy hotels where rootless and aimless people have faces 'flattened like the moon' (*CP*, p. 124). The senses are shaken together like drinks to make a cocktail producing a state of synaesthetic inebriation. The overall sense of delirium is compounded by vague and surrealist images and a rhyme scheme which disorganises any remaining lines of sense. In this aspect of her verse, Sitwell looks back to Victorian nonsense poetry and forward to the surrealism of David Gascoyne.

But this should not just be seen in aesthetic terms, for the refractions of sense also have to do with her position as a woman. The refusal of high modernist strategies for making sense of experience are perhaps akin to Virginia Woolf's attempts to escape what she considered to be the masculine structure of the sentence, with its emphasis on logic, clarity and orderly progression.[9] Such a language, Woolf felt, did not answer to the specific experience of being a woman. The trouble with this view is that it presupposes some essential female identity, which has the effect of reinforcing patriarchy since that is based on the binary opposition of male and female which constructs women as other.

A more fruitful approach might be to look at Julia Kristeva's notion of 'semanalysis'.[10] This focuses upon the tension between the symbolic and the semiotic orders in the construction of subjectivity. The symbolic order is the source of those rules and structures without which the subject could neither articulate nor be articulated. Its various grammars make signification possible. The semiotic, on the other hand, refers to all those aspects of language which are repressed by the operations of the symbolic and, as such, they remain a disruptive element within the signifying process. Kristeva's analysis is important because it underlines how the subject does not exist prior to language, as Woolf seems to imply, but is produced by it. Furthermore, the process of this production contains within it the possibility of resistance to the constraints of the symbolic order. Sitwell's seemingly nonsensical, sing-song verse seems to belong to Kristeva's semiotic order. It asserts possibilities of language other than those of control, fixity and appropriation.

However, this subversive and playful use of language did not survive the rigours of two world wars. Hence her poem 'Still Falls the Rain', which Geoffrey Thurley has described as being one of 'the finest and most serious statements about war in our time'.[11]

> The last faint spark
> In the self-murdered heart, the wounds of the sad
>   uncomprehending dark,
> The wounds of the baited bear, –
> The blind and weeping bear whom the keepers beat
> On his helpless flesh . . . the tears of the hunted hare.
>
> (CP, p. 273)

This poignant protest against the brutality of war belongs more to the symbolic than to the semiotic order, which suggests the latter's limitations when faced with the pressure of real events. Of course the word 'real' is highly contentious. There is no reality without language for it is through language that reality is organised and given meaning. Without it, everything that we know or think the world to be would disappear. Take away the specialist discourse of physics and the world which physics describes vanishes, and the same is true for any use of language, from the refinements of critical theory to conversations at bus stops.

At the same time it is important to remember that language is not a monolithic structure but the site of a constant struggle for meaning. For example, the history of feminism illustrates the struggle to change the meaning of the word 'woman' from something which signifies passivity, nurture and domesticity to one which signifies activity, decisiveness and independence.

When this struggle for meaning is intensified, as in war, the whole basis of a culture's ability to produce coherent interpretations of the world is fundamentally challenged. In such circumstances the normal strategies for making sense of the world are radically questioned, opening possibilities for new and more progressive meanings. Side by side with this positive effect, however, is the more conservative one of reaffirming those established perceptions which are, quite literally, under attack.

It is this dual condition of negation and affirmation which gives war poetry its resonance. It also helps to explain the sort of technical innovations which can be found in, for example, the work of Owen. Such innovations break with conventional structures of experience. However, this break does not represent an articulation of new possibilities since it functions to reaffirm, in true Derridian fashion, the perceptions which it apparently exceeds.[12] A true break is impossible, nonsense would be the result; any alternative has to be understood in relation to, and therefore include, the very system to which it is an alternative.

What can the semiotic transgress when the constraints of civilised life are destroyed by the machinery of war? But it is not just war which tempts Sitwell back into a more recognisable poetic discourse. For example, 'Myself in the Merry-Go-Round' expresses a desire for order in a world which 'shake[s] the body's equipose' (*CP*, p. 170) and where 'words [are] set all awry' (ibid.). The giddy procession of images is perhaps not just a rebuttal of Pound's demand that the image be hard, clear and precise,[13] it is also an enactment of the artifice, excess and riot of Sitwell's own social circle. Through her fantastical but largely forgettable images Sitwell evokes and indicts what she considers to be the superficial character of her age. Words such as 'giddy' and 'swirling' emphasise a world breaking apart under the force of its own momentum. And though Sitwell seems to speed up the process by piling rhymes on top of one another, 'Daisy and Lily / Lazy and silly' ('Waltz', *CP*, p. 144), so that meaning is lost in an acceleration of sound, there is nevertheless a desire for some sort of stability, to repair the '[f]rayed ends' ('Myself in the Merry-Go-Round', *CP*, p. 171) of sense which has been frayed precisely by the friction of movement. This desire to reach beyond the glittering cascade of the *bon vivants* finally becomes an appeal to traditional religious morality. In 'Gold Coast Customs' London is seen as 'Gomorrah' (*CP*, p. 251). It is also assimilated to Africa, which is portrayed as a swamp, 'mud and murk' from which 'arises everything' (*CP*, p. 240), and it is only through an act outside of history, 'God shall wash the mud' (*CP*, p. 252), that redemption can be imagined.

But the conservatism of Sitwell's verse needs to be set alongside the way in which it draws attention to the material aspects of poetry, thus preventing the reader from seeing it merely as a mode of self expression. Instead the emphasis on the constructed nature of poetry becomes a comment on the constructed nature of subjectivity.

Sitwell's sense of rhythm is particularly important here. Quite often, it approximates to what Antony Easthope calls 'four stress accentual metre',[14] which is usually to be found in nursery rhymes and football chants. These are heavily stressed, in contrast to the iambic pentameter – the dominant line in English verse since the Renaissance – and so can only be intoned in one way, compared with the different ways in which the iambic line can be expressed. Easthope's contention is that the iambic line is important in the formation of subjectivity. For instance, the self-contained nature of the iambic pentameter helps to present a picture of a unified and coherent subjectivity.

Sitwell's poetry relies not on the iambic but on the four stress accentual metre, 'Great Snoring and Norwich / A dish of pease porridge' ('One O'Clock', *CP*, p. 132), and so perhaps can be seen as a refusal of the subject position which the iambic gives. This analysis is fine as far as it goes but it fails to take into account the return of that traditional morality and religion which presupposes the kind of subject produced by the operations of the iambic.

The apparent radical implications of the four stress accentual metre are offset by Sitwell's conventional portrayals of women as vain and frivolous, 'Ladies, how vain, – hollow' ('Waltz', *CP*, p. 145). Such patriarchal perceptions perhaps account for why the technical experiments of the verse ultimately come to nothing. On the other hand, it is important not to forget those other poems which deal with historical or mythological incidents, where women's role has traditionally been relegated to that of an extra. 'Anne Boleyn's Song' (*CP*, p. 303) and 'Eurydice' (*CP*, p. 267) are attempts to give women a voice. But in doing so they implicitly posit an experience which is specifically female, suggesting an essential identity which other aspects of the poetry call into question. These and other tensions need further study before Sitwell's contribution to a feminist history of poetry can be properly assessed.

If Edith Sitwell was occasionally more modernist than the Modernists, Charlotte Mew (1869–1928) was more Georgian than the Georgians. This neglected group of poets are due for reassessment. In contrast to what they saw as the dream world of Victorian poetry, they wanted to write about 'life'. Poetry, they believed, should be confined to what had actually been experienced.[15] If this is accepted as the defining characteristic of Georgian poetry then very few of those who appeared in the five volumes of *Georgian Poetry*

(1912–1922) edited by Edward Marsh can be regarded as Georgians. Poetry such as the following speaks less of 'real experience' than of the desire to cut a poetic figure:

> I lingered at a gate and talked
> A little with a lonely lamb
> He told me of the great still night,
> Of calm starlight . . .[16]

It is not hard to see, given such excruciating sentimentality, why Edith Sitwell should have been so derisory about the Georgians.[17] Contrast this with Mew's description of a lamb, significantly a dead one, as '[t]he moon's dropped child'.[18] Significantly, because Charlotte Mew decided not to marry and have children in case she passed on the hereditary insanity which claimed her younger brother and sister and which was a factor in her own suicide at the age of fifty-nine. This decision cost her dear and the image of 'the child who went / or never came' ('Madeleine in Church', *CPP*, p. 25) haunts her poetry.

A number of points arise from this. The first is the precision of her images compared with the blurry impressionism of most of the Georgians. It is this vividness of conception which makes her poetry 'realistic' in a way that most Georgian poetry is not. Since poetic realism was the declared aesthetic of the movement, her non-inclusion in any of the volumes of Georgian poetry is highly surprising. In 1917 Edward Marsh asked Harold Monro, owner of the Poetry Bookshop, to suggest work by a woman poet for inclusion in *Georgian Poetry III*. Monro recommended Mew but to no avail. Marsh repeated his request, for *Georgian Poetry IV*, and Monro once more put forward Mew's name but again without success. This double rejection is even more bewildering given that John Masefield, whose work was generously represented in Marsh's anthologies, was so impressed by Mew's poetry that he, along with Thomas Hardy and Siegfried Sassoon, recommended Mew for a civil list pension in 1923.

It would be too glib to say that Mew was not represented because the sharply realised nature of her poetry exposed the pretentiousness of the Georgian claim to be realistic, though this was undoubtedly a factor. What is more likely is that she was not represented because certain features of her verse, notably her experiments with line length, allied her with modernism. Virginia Woolf referred to her as 'the greatest living poetess'; H. D. favourably reviewed her first collection *The Farmer's Bride* (1916); and Ezra Pound was sufficiently enthusiastic about her work to send it for publication to *Poetry* in Chicago.[19] Thus it would seem that Charlotte Mew's work was neither one thing nor the other; part Georgian, part modernist she resists classification and this perhaps explains why her poetry has been neglected over the years.

But again this is a too conventient explanation both for her exclusion from the Georgian anthologies and for the neglect of her verse. Charlotte Mew remains a problematic case and one of the reasons for this is because her work raises the thorny issue of the relation between art and autobiography.

Since 1968, when Barthes proclaimed the death of the author,[20] it has been unfashionable to see a writer's work as an expression of his or her life. But then, where in the history of criticism has the work ever been seen as an expression of the author's life? Such a view is a travesty of traditional criticism, which is far too diverse a phenomenon to be caricatured like this. The idea that the author's life explains his or her work is a myth circulated by some of the more extreme versions of critical theory in order to ground its claim that the author's life is irrelevant to an understanding of the work. If this is the case, then what are we to make of the efforts of feminist criticism to recuperate women's voices which have been repressed? To refuse to see women's writing as dealing with women's experience is to collude with patriarchy in its attempts to silence them. It is time to reconsider the complex relations between life and work. This is not to say that the work can be explained by the life, but that the life cannot be totally disregarded as an element of the work.

In the case of Charlotte Mew the life cannot be discounted as a factor in her poetry. Indeed, Val Warner argues that Mew's 'unresolved sexuality' was the basis of her work.[21] Perhaps the vividness of her verse, compared with the vague chirrupings about nature which characterised Georgian verse, can in part be explained by the problems of her life. However, these problems cannot be understood in a purely personal context. At the time of her writing, British cultural life was being reorganised along the lines of social Darwinism. The notion of the individual was giving place to that of the citizen. New discourses of social regulation emerged which addressed the subject less as a unique person than as an object for state concern. The subject was someone to be regulated and administered according to particular forms of knowledge which took no

account of the personal.[22] Indeed it is precisely at this moment that
the personal becomes pathological, for this is the period that gives
birth to psychoanalysis.

Mew's work can be read as a resistance to this redefinition of the
subject, which is more than can be said of either Georgianism or
Modernism. The traditional verse structure of the former merely
appeared as an archaism, while the much vaunted 'impersonality'
of the latter was nothing more than the poetic equivalent of the
regulative and administrative discourses which were increasingly
coming to dominate social life. Mew's work can be read as an attempt to preserve the personal by rendering Georgian concerns with
direct experience through modernist techniques.

Of particular importance here are her experiments with line length.
These are in direct contrast to the iambic pentameter which, as
remarked earlier, Easthope sees as constitutive of poetic subjectivity. 'Beside the Bed' opens with a thirteen-syllable line followed by
one of fifteen syllables, a third of seventeen syllables and a fourth
of three:

> Someone has shut the shining eyes, straightened and folded
> The wandering hands quietly covering the unquiet breast:
> So, smoothed and silenced you lie, like a child, not again
>   to be questioned
>   or scolded;   (*CPP*, p. 8)

It can be seen that such irregularity still manages to convey that
sense of the personal voice which Easthope maintains can only be
generated by the iambic. The only alternative he envisages to the
iambic is, as was noted earlier, the four stress accentual metre, but
Mew's verse moves beyond this simple binary opposition, showing
that subjectivity is not just the effect of a particular line structure
but can be the cause of one as well. Easthope's analysis fetishises a
coherent and unified subjectivity. Mew's varying line lengths, with
the inevitable use of *enjambement*, suggests a more fluid subjectivity, one which escapes the constraints of traditional verse while
preserving a sense of self from the encroachments of modernist
aesthetics. The open structure of her lines serves her well as she
explores different psychological states, and this is perhaps best
seen in 'Madeleine in Church', where she moves from one topic to
another more by association than by logical progression.

Of course it could be argued that Eliot achieves the same effect in 'Prufrock', in which case how can the reader tell the difference between the voice of a genuine consciousness and a dramatised one? The short answer is that he or she cannot. All consciousness and all writing and therefore all 'expressions' of consciousness are the effects of the play of *differance*.[23] Words do not deliver the person who speaks them; their meaning comes not from any correspondence with intentions or indeed objects but from the internal system of differences without which meaning would not exist. However, it is precisely because difference is the ground of meaning that our culture is articulated in terms of it, including that which pertains between what is genuine and what is false. We may never be able to tell the difference between them, and indeed that difference is a matter of convention and may therefore be changed, but we cannot operate without assuming that the difference exists. Accordingly we need to be attuned to those details which mark one text as more 'genuine' than another.

This is not something which can be examined in any depth here, but one way in which 'Prufrock' differs from 'Madeleine in Church' lies in the deployment of imagery. In 'Prufrock' it functions in an allusive manner, drawing attention to the European literary tradition. Furthermore, it exemplifies Eliot's doctrine of the 'objective correlative', which is 'a set of objects, a situation, a chain of events which shall be the formula of [a] particular emotion'.[24] The imagery of 'Madeleine in Church', by contrast, acquires its resonance not from a literary tradition but from its occurrence in other poems and from its connections with events in Mew's own life. An example of this would be the image of the child – that desideratum of her experience – which appears throughout her poetry.

The child appears in the title poem of the collection *The Farmer's Bride* (1916). The poem is written from the point of view of the farmer, who describes his bride as 'too young' (*CPP*, p. 1). Their wedding has the effect of making her 'afraid / of love and me and all things human' (ibid.). Thus in addition to the suggestion of the bride being more child than woman she is also linked to the world of animals. Indeed, she flies 'like a hare' (ibid.) and is 'like a mouse' (ibid.). In the farmer's own words' ''twasn't a woman' (ibid.). But it is important to remember that it is the farmer who is speaking here and so the bride is 'not a woman' only by his definition of the term. In this respect the poem can be read as resisting patriachy's definition of women.

The nature of this resistance is silence. The bride will talk only to animals. 'Happy enough to chat and play / With birds and rabbits and such as they' (ibid.).[25] The farmer himself has 'hardly heard her speak at all' (ibid.). The implication seems to be that language as it stands is of little use to women, whose only strategy is to withdraw from it altogether.

Or at least this appears to be their only strategy, for the poem also shows, since it is written by a woman, that women are able to occupy the position of a male speaker. This suggests that although language is organised in terms of gendered subject positions, these positions can be occupied irrespective of the gender of the speaker. This highlights their conventional nature. Furthermore, such a manoeuvre creates the possibility of changing the way in which men see women by parodying their usual view of them, though this possibility is not realised in the poem.

This broad analysis of the poem needs to be set alongside the little that is known of Charlotte Mew's life. Her possible lesbianism may be a factor in 'The Farmer's Bride', for the construction of the poem allows Mew, from the position of the farmer, to express desire for the female body:

> Oh! my God! the down,
> The soft young down of her, the brown,
> The brown of her – her eyes, her hair, her hair!
> (*CPP*, p. 2)

Hair is highly eroticised in Mew's verse: 'Only the hair / Of any woman can belong to God' (*CPP*, p. 7), while in 'The Forest Road' she describes 'the long sweetness of the hair that does not die' (*CPP*, p. 21). Thus it is by occupying a male subject position that subversive female desire can be expressed.

This desire can also be read in another way, that is for the speaker to be coincident with herself rather than marooned in a male subject position. This observation needs to be set in the context of remarks like the following: 'I think it is myself I go to meet' ('The Quiet House', *CPP*, p. 19) and 'I see my soul / I hear my soul, singing among the trees' ('The Forest Road', *CPP*, p. 22). The desire for self-unification helps to explain the frequent references to travel in Mew's work. There is a constant sense of journeying out which is evident even in the titles, for example, 'The Forest Road' (*CPP*, p. 20), 'On the Road to the Sea' (*CPP*, p. 29), and 'On the Asylum Road' (*CPP*, p. 19). In each case travel is partly understood as a movement towards the self.

But in order for the self to be unified it must have recognition from another, '[t]here must be someone. Christ! there must, / Tell me there *will* be someone' ('Madeleine in Church', *CPP*, p. 26). However, this recognition is not forthcoming. Marriage is one source of it but this is rejected in 'The Farmer's Bride'. Nor can this recognition be won from women, at least as far as the poetry is concerned because it is usually sought in the guise of a man, witness the farmer again. As a result, subjectivity in the poems remains deeply fissured, the desire to possess the self being counterpointed against the desire to avoid being possessed by the male, who wants '[t]he world that lies behind the strangeness of [the woman's] eyes', indeed the male speaker wants the woman's 'life' which she 'will not give' ('On the Road to the Sea', *CPP*, p. 29).

This self in pieces is related to the recurrent image of the child or children in Mew's poetry. As long as the self remains in this splintered condition the poetic persona remains a child, 'I shall . . . never grow up' says the speaker in 'The Changeling' (*CPP*, p. 14). The child in this poem is like the farmer's bride in that she (it?) too is associated with the animal kingdom, '[t]he word of a bird is a thing to follow' (ibid., p. 13).

But childhood should not just be seen as a negative state in the poetry – a sign of the failure to hold the self together – a more positive reading is possible. In the first place childhood, as it appears in these poems, is not gendered, and so it refuses the culturally imposed meanings of sexual difference. Secondly, the refusal of these meanings leads to the adoption of a language of nature which, in its refusal to differentiate, suggests Kristeva's definition of the semiotic, though this leads to various problems, as was seen in the discussion of Edith Sitwell.

More fruitful, perhaps, is the way in which childhood is linked to madness. In 'Ken', a poem about a village idiot, all the children are described as belonging to him, '. . . all the children and the deer / Whom every day he went to see / Out in the park, belonged to him' (*CPP*, p. 15). The most important thing about Ken is that he has the capacity to use language in a positive way, 'Nothing was dead: / He said 'a bird' if he picked up a broken wing' (*CPP*, p. 16). That is to say, he names the whole for the part and thus his use of language is healing and restorative. Moreover, in psychoanalytic terms, taking the whole for the part is a reversal of metonymy, in which, Lacan says, desire is forever doomed to move forward without encountering the object that can satisfy it. Ken's reversal of metonymy recalls desire from its banishment in the signifying chain and therefore holds out the possibility of its fulfilment.

So defined, Ken's madness is no longer something to be afraid of, but something to be desired. Perhaps we can detect here Mew's attempt to come to terms with her own fear of madness. This is not to say that her poetry can be regarded as a form of therapy, but rather that it offered resources implicit in the very density of poetic language which altered its meanings. This has to be distinguished from those elements of poetry which she could consciously manipulate, for example her fear of being possessed by madness is similar to the fear her female figures have of being possessed by the male ones. This analogy transforms madness from an hereditary and internal threat to an external one posed by predatory males. At this point, however, the rich texture of poetic language starts to make itself felt, for, as was seen in 'The Farmer's Bride', to flee the male is to find sanctuary in a language of childhood and nature which can only be heard as silence by the patriarchal ear. But this language speaks through its alliance with madness, which breaks with the language of reference and institutes a language of relation so that a broken wing becoming a bird opens up redemptive possibilities. Indeed, it is significant that 'Ken' deploys the image of a bird, since this too is another of Mew's recurrent image. It relates to the self, since the 'soul' of the poetic persona sings in the trees like a bird ('The Forest Road', *CPP*, p. 22), and the bird escaping from an upper window in 'The Sunlit House' is juxtaposed with the speaker going on her way (*CPP*, p. 31), suggesting a sense of release. Consequently the madness that she feared in life becomes in poetry the thing she desires, indeed it becomes the very language of desire.

Charlotte Mew's poetry presents women as childlike, avoiding men and speaking in a language which makes no sense from a patriarchal point of view. At the same time, it occupies male subject positions to voice desire understood either in lesbian terms or in terms of self-unification, and the use of the language of madness exemplified in 'Ken' shows how this may be achieved in respect of the latter. These features of Mew's verse need to be understood partly in relation to her anxieties about sexuality and madness and partly as a response to the emergence of the depersonalising discourses of administration which were increasingly coming to dominate cultural life. It is this latter aspect of her work which needs to be emphasised today, because it can still function as a source of resistance to the regulative bureaucracies which determine every aspect of life as we move towards the millennium. But this element of Mew's poetry can only be activated if we are prepared to reconsider the complex relations between a writer's life and his or her work.

Notes

1. See V. Glendinning, *Edith Sitwell: A Unicorn among Lions* (Oxford: Oxford University Press, 1981) p. 3.
2. Ibid., p. 5.
3. Ibid., p. 11.
4. E. Sitwell, 'Colonel Faxtock', in *Collected Poems* (London: Macmillan, 1965) p. 174; hereafter referred to as *CP* with poem titles and page references given in the text.
5. V. Woolf, quoted in V. Glendinning, *Edith Sitwell*, op. cit., p. 52.
6. E. Sitwell, quoted by R. H. Ross, *The Georgian Revolt: Rise and Fall of a Poetic Ideal* (London: Faber, 1965) p. 195.
7. J. Symons, quoted in V. Glendinning, *Edith Sitwell*, op. cit., p. 64.
8. A. Huxley, quoted in V. Glendinning, *Edith Sitwell*, op. cit., p. 89.
9. V. Woolf, *A Room of One's Own* (Harmondsworth: Penguin, 1967) p. 77.
10. See Julia Kristeva, 'The System and the Speaking Subject', *Times Literary Supplement*, 12 October 1973, pp. 1249–50.
11. Geoffrey Thurley, *The Ironic Harvest: English Poetry in the Twentieth Century* (London: Edward Arnold, 1974) p. 136.
12. 'we can pronounce not a single destructive proposition which has not already had to slip into the form, the logic and the implicit postulations of precisely what it seeks to contest' (J. Derrida, 'Structure, Sign and Play', in J. Derrida, *Writing and Difference*, trans. A. Bass (London: Routledge, 1978) pp. 278–93, at pp. 280–1).
13. E. Pound, 'A Few Don'ts By An Imagiste', in *Imagist Poetry*, ed. with an introduction by P. Jones (Harmondsworth: Penguin, 1976) pp. 130–4.
14. A. Easthope, *Poetry as Discourse* (London and New York: Methuen, 1983) p. 74.
15. See C. K. Stead, *The New Poetic: Yeats to Eliot* (London: Hutchinson, 1986) p. 82.
16. W. Kerr, 'Counting Sheep', in *Georgian Poetry V*, ed. E. Marsh (London: Poetry Bookshop, 1920–22).
17. See note 6.
18. C. Mew, 'Fame' in *Collected Poems and Prose*, ed. V. Warner (London: Virago, 1982) p. 3; hereafter referred to as *CPP* with poem titles and page references given in the text.

19. V. Woolf, quoted by V. Warner, introduction to C. Mew, *Collected Poems and Prose*, op. cit., p. xii.
20. R. Barthes, 'The Death of the Author', in *Modern Criticism and Theory: A Reader*, ed. D. Lodge (London and New York: Longman, 1988) pp. 167–72.
21. V. Warner, introduction to C. Mew, *Collected Poems and Prose*, op. cit., p. xvi.
22. For an excellent account of this process, see S. Hall and B. Schwartz, 'State and Society 1880–1930', in *Crises in the British State 1880–1930* (London: Hutchinson, 1983) pp. 7–33.
23. Difference is the process which enables language to signify. It is because words are different from one another, not because they correspond to objects in the world, that they have meaning. However, this meaning is never fully present in words because it always depends on other words which come before and after them. For this reason – given here in a brutally reductive form – Derrida argues that meaning is deferred. For a full account of this process, see J. Derrida, 'Difference', in J. Derrida, *Margins of Philosophy*, trans. A. Bass (New York and London: Harvester Wheatsheaf, 1982) pp. 3–27.
24. See T. S. Eliot, 'Hamlet', in T. S. Eliot, *Selected Essays* (London: Faber and Faber, 1976) pp. 141–6, at p. 145.
25. See J. Lacan, *Ecrits: A Selection*, trans. A. Sheridan (London: Tavistock, 1977) especially 'The Signification of the Phallus', pp. 281–91 and 'The Subversion of the Subject and the Dialectic of the Desire in the Freudian Unconscious', pp. 292–324.

6

Lawrence, Imagism and Beyond

NEIL ROBERTS

The importance of Lawrence's association with the Imagist movement – which meant for him, above all, the personality and poetic
example of H.D. – tends to be underestimated, probably because of
a stereotyped idea of the Imagist poem as something small, static
and precious. If, however, we think not of set-pieces like 'In the
Station of the Metro' but of what Imagism made possible, of what
the major Imagists went on to do, Lawrence's association with them
seems less incongruous.

What the most important of the Imagists – Pound and H.D. –
went on to do was, of course, to write long poems, or sequences.
Lawrence, too, habitually wrote in sequences, from *Look! We Have
Come Through!* on, and critics have of course noticed this fact, but
rarely is it given proper critical weight. His reputation is that of a
poet who wrote, or published, too much. It is assumed that he is
a very uneven poet, that his successes form a small proportion of
his total *oeuvre*, that reading through the whole of *Birds, Beasts and
Flowers*, still less, God forbid, *Pansies*, is a tedious and unrewarding
exercise. The fact that he wrote some poems, such as 'Snake' and
'Bavarian Gentians', that read very well in selections and anthologies, confirms the prejudice: these poems stand for Lawrence's
achievement.

'Snake' and 'Bavarian Gentians' are great poems, but appreciation of them in isolation misrepresents the nature of Lawrence's
poetry. Evaluation of poetry is still in the grip of New Critical criteria, despite all that has happened since. But Lawrence, in his famous Introduction to the American edition of *New Poems*, written
in 1919, entitled 'Poetry of the Present', wrote a proleptic challenge
to New Criticism. In the Introduction he rejects perfection, completeness and finality. 'In the immediate present there is no perfection, no consummation, nothing finished. The strands are all flying,

81

quivering, intermingling into the web, the waters are shaking the moon.'[1] There is some affinity between Lawrence's idea in this essay and Pound's 'intellectual and emotional complex in an instant of time',[2] but Lawrence's argument – or rather, perhaps, his characteristic idiom – makes the break with the well-made poem more inevitable. It can be argued that the instantaneousness of the image presupposes other instants, so that the Imagist poet could not rest in the small complete poem. But Lawrence's metaphor of the strands 'intermingling into the web' makes the consequence inevitable.

It is surprising that Lawrence does not refer to the importance of sequences in the essay; perhaps the campaign for free verse, which turns out to be the main theme, was more urgent. The relationship of the essay to the actual poetry is curious and complicated. The poems that it introduces, though called 'New', mostly antedate *Look! We Have Come Through!*, which had been published two years before. At the end of it he actually writes 'All this should have come as a preface to *Look! We Have Come Through!*'[3] However, I think Tom Marshall is right in saying (though he doesn't explain the comment) that the Introduction 'has most relevance not to *Look! We Have Come Through!* but to his achievement in *Birds, Beasts and Flowers*'[4] (and, I would add, in *Pansies*). In other words, the essay anticipates what Lawrence was to achieve in poetry in the next ten years, rather than describes what he had already done.

Sandra Gilbert suggestively remarks that 'the dialectic or repetitive essay-poems in *Birds, Beasts and Flowers* preserve the gestures of their composition in the way that action-painting retains the movements of the artist'.[5] This analogy is in the spirit of 'Poetry of the Present'. Lawrence employs a rhetoric of incompleteness and of process; the present is by definition incomplete, it cannot reflect upon and judge itself. The present of the poem is necessarily that of its own composition, so that the act of composition is partly its own theme. This does not mean that the poems are self-reflexive in a post-modernist sense (which would surely have been anathema to Lawrence) but that the poems are, in an important sense, unedited (by which I don't mean unrevised) or, in Gilbert's terms, 'preserve the gestures of their composition':

> Fig-trees, weird fig-trees
> Made of thick smooth silver,
> Made of sweet, untarnished silver in the sea-southern air –
> I say untarnished, but I mean opaque –
>
> ('Bare Fig Trees', *CP*, p. 298)

Of course, when Lawrence wrote 'untarnished' he *did* mean that; now, a line later, he means something else, and both moments of meaning are preserved. There is a limit of course to how much of this kind of thing a poet can do without it becoming a mannerism, and Lawrence does not make a habit of correcting himself.[6] But the subtle difference, here, between the connotations of 'untarnished' and 'opaque' is a microcosm of the much larger and more significant shifts of thought and feeling that occur, very often, *between* poems.

Sandra Gilbert, having proposed the interesting parallel with 'action-painting', is disappointingly conventional when she comes to criticise certain aspects of Lawrence's poetry that, understandably, she dislikes. Here, for example, she compares the notorious 'Figs' with 'Pomegranate':

> The terms in which Lawrence views the fate of the fig ... 'the secret is laid bare / And rottenness soon sets in. ... Ripe figs won't keep' – almost directly contradict the judgement with which he concludes 'Pomegranate': 'I prefer my heart to be broken. / It is so lovely, dawn-kaleidoscopic, within the crack.' In 'Pomegranate' the poet sees the process of nature as a positive good because he is writing of it for its own sake: the flowering, the fruiting, the ripening and the rupture are natural, inevitable. Lawrence knows, attending to the reality rather than intending morality, that it would be absurd to object on some human ground to so mysterious and uncontrollable a process ...
>
> In 'Figs' however, the rupture of the fig becomes an obscenity because the writer is not attending to his real subject, the fig as it is in nature, but rather imposing a puritanical, human horror on nature.[7]

There is some sloppy thinking about 'reality' here, as well as presumption in decreeing what is the poet's 'real subject', which would be unimportant if they had not been contradicted by Gilbert's intuition about the nature of Lawrence's poetry. Lawrence never writes about 'the process of nature ... for its own sake'. The present out of which the poem is written is always governed by a particular feeling or complex of feelings. Sometimes, as in 'Figs', some of these feelings may be ugly. But it is inconsistent to praise the poems for preserving the gestures of their composition, and then in specific instances to object to those gestures.

The problem is that to examine 'Figs' as a discrete poem, and compare it with another discrete poem, 'Pomegranate', is inappropriate to Lawrence's method. It is to consider 'Figs' as something whole, complete, final and would-be perfect: in other words to consider it according to, essentially, New Critical criteria. The presence of such criteria is evident in Gilbert's assertion that Lawrence's 'real subject' is 'the fig as it is in nature' rather than the 'puritanical, human horror'. What happens is that the subject shifts within the poem. To assert that the first subject is real and the second imposed is a strategy for translating an ideological objection into formalist terms.

The 'complete' poem is so by virtue of being closed to any possible objection the reader might make against it. Its implied author (or 'subject' in another sense) is completely in command of the relevant experience. This is the ideal poem of much twentieth-century criticism. In Lawrence's terms, it is the poetry of the past or the future. But if we step outside the charmed circle of literary criticism, it is evident that no such command of experience is possible. Lawrence's offence, in a poem such as 'Figs', is that the command is so blatantly absent. The second half of the poem is repetitive, assertive and linguistically thin. The mood has changed utterly from the amusing, slyly sexy opening. However, it is clearly not legitimate to condemn Lawrence for having these feelings: nor, if we take his poetics seriously, for expressing them so nakedly. What is objectionable is the arrogant complacency of embodying these feelings in a 'poem', with all the authority that has been invested in that word. 'Figs' so evidently fails to be a poem in this sense that the reader feels insulted.

All this is the consequence of reading 'Figs' in the traditional way. And, as long as it is read as a discrete poem, this will be the consequence. But it is not a discrete poem. Sandra Gilbert points out the contradiction of 'Figs' in 'Pomegranate': 'I prefer my heart to be broken. / It is so lovely, dawn-kaleidoscopic, within the crack.'[8] Her conclusion is that 'Pomegranate' is a good poem, and 'Figs' a bad one. But what we actually have here is a practical demonstration of Lawrence's poetic. 'Pomegranate', 'Peach', 'Figs', Medlars and Sorb-Apples' and 'Grapes' follow each other in sequence, the first five poems in the volume. With varying emphases and considerable contrasts of feeling these poems circle around a number of related themes: the body, sexuality, corruption, secrecy and 'candid revelation'. They are open to each other, though they do not subvert Lawrence's poetic by forming a 'poetic whole' together; one poem is not supplanted by another, and there is no teleological development. Rather, Lawrence's own metaphors apply: 'The strands are all flying, quivering, intermingling into the web, the waters are shaking the moon. There is no round, consummate moon on the face of running water, nor on the face of the unfinished tide. There are no gems of the living plasm.'[9] The strident anti-feminist sentiments in 'Figs' are flying strands, as are the lines from 'Pomegranate' or these from 'Peach':

> Why the ripple down the sphere?
> Why the suggestion of incision?
> (*CP*, p. 279)

Birds, Beasts and Flowers consists, substantially, of a series of 'sequences' such as this one: the 'Trees' 'Flowers', 'Evangelic Beasts', 'Creatures' and 'Reptiles' sections each consist mainly of a group of poems that form a thematic 'web'. Only the last three sections, 'Birds', 'Animals' and 'Ghosts' are collections of largely unrelated individual poems, though odd unrelated poems occur in the other sections as well – for example, the celebrated 'Snake' is tucked in with the sequence of tortoise poems, the most unified group in the volume. If, as I have said above, the act of composition is partly the theme of these sequences, but they are not self-reflexive in the post-modernist sense, it does not follow that they need to be completed by some kind of biographical reference to the circumstances in which they were written. This is how *Birds, Beasts and Flowers* (and *Pansies*) differ from *Look! We Have Come Through!* This collection is presented as a sequence; Lawrence prints a ponderous Foreword and Argument to instruct us to read the poems in this way.[10] But, despite, the quasi-narrative biographical foundation, the connections are not made in the poems themselves. There is no 'web' of discourse in which the flyings 'strands' of the poems meet. This is, perhaps, reflected in the notorious fact that despite their subsequent classification as 'Unrhyming Poems', most of them are in rhyme and metre, and so make gestures towards the 'static perfection' that Lawrence associates with these devices. Even the famous 'Song of a Man who has Come Through', one of the most successful poems in the volume, which is in free verse, claims in its idiom and its title a finality that few of the later poems claim. The more naked, often courageously confessional poems, such as 'First Morning', 'Mutilation' and 'Humiliation' are remarkable in their way, but they connect up through Lawrence's biography, not through the poetics of the sequence.

The two essays that Lawrence wrote to introduce the two editions of *Pansies* in 1929 are more self-deprecating than the introduction to *New Poems*, but they offer similar guidance to the reader:

> It suits the modern temper better to have its state of mind made up of apparently irrelevant thoughts that scurry in different directions yet belong to the same nest: each thought trotting down the page like an independent creature, each with its own small head and tail, trotting its own little way, then curling up to sleep. We prefer it, at least the young seem to prefer it to those solid blocks of mental pabulum packed like bales in the pages of a proper heavy book. Even we prefer it to those slightly didactic opinions and slices of wisdom which are laid horizontally across the pages of Pascal's *Pensées* or La Bruyère's *Caractères*, separated only by *pattes de mouches*, like faint sprigs of parsley.[11]

The delightfully apt and satirical touch of the *pattes de mouches* alerts us to the great importance of presentation, and comes to mind when I consider the comparison of at least one extreme of the *Pansies* with Imagist poetry. David Ellis has recently published a good essay contributing to the rescue of *Pansies* from the contemptuous or at best apologetic manner in which they are commonly treated – and makes, though he does not develop, an important point about sequences within the volume – but seems to me to betray prejudice when, in discussing 'Sea-Weed', he refers to 'the mistaken belief that [Lawrence] was an Imagist'.[12] Here is the poem in question.

> Sea-weed sways and sways and swirls
> as if swaying were its form of stillness;
> and if it flushes against fierce rock
> it slips over it as shadows do, without hurting itself.
>
> (*CP*, p. 467)

And here is an extract from a representative early poem by H.D., one of the ones on which Lawrence based his high opinion of her.

> They say you are twisted by the sea,
> you are cut apart

> by wave-break upon wave-break,
> that you are misshapen by the sharp rocks,
> broken by the rasp and after-rasp.[13]

There are evident differences, which it is tempting to call differences of temperament. Lawrence's longer line suggests a more relaxed voice, and in 'without hurting itself' he permits himself a looser, more colloquial diction. And yet the similarities, against the general background of the kinds of poetry being written in the second and third decades of the twentieth century, are very striking. Would either of them be very obviously out of place in a volume that included the other? Among the reasons why we might think so is the difference in the ways we have become conventionally accustomed to read H.D.'s *Sea-Garden* and Lawrence's *Pansies*. I don't know whether H.D.'s poems have ever been printed with *pattes de mouches*, but it would be no surprise to find that they had. They have accrued an aura of preciosity. Yet there is nothing precious about 'Sea-Rose', even if it is a little more self-consciously poised and considered than Lawrence's poem. Reading it with the more brisk attention that we give to *Pansies* might bring out an energy that is stifled by the *pattes de mouches* – actual or metaphorical – that surround it. Lawrence's admiration of H.D. was real and based on a sense of affinity if not indebtedness that is still evident more than ten years after he broke his friendship with her.

However, even if we were to read *Sea-Garden* in the way we read (or should read) *Pansies*, we should undoubtedly miss one of the characteristics that David Ellis rightly considers 'a crucial feature' of Lawrence's volume: variety.[14] With or without *pattes de mouches*, the reader of *Sea-Garden* is bound to feel that a particular way of writing is being privileged, even if the moment of the individual poem is not. Ellis has demonstrated the variety of the kinds of poem that might be defined as 'pansies', drawing on poems from *More Pansies*, *Last Poems* and even *Birds, Beasts and Flowers*. I want to show that the experience of this variety, of contrasting but related themes and modes, is built into the structure of the volume, at least its first two thirds: the later part of the book is more monotonous, consisting predominantly of the kind of didactic poems often wrongly thought to be typical of the book as a whole. My argument is not that Lawrence's poems cannot be criticised, but that criticism should attend to the sequence, not just to the isolated poem.

Pansies is, as much as *Birds, Beasts and Flowers*, a structured volume – more systematically so than Ellis implies – though its structure is not signalled like that of the earlier book. Most of it consists of a series of mini-sequences of poems 'clustered together in coherent groups',[15] as Sandra Gilbert says. Gilbert itemises several of these groups, but I prefer not to do so formally because I think this would misrepresent their character. They are like pulses, or series of pulses, of thought, feeling, and sometimes form, that often merge into each other, so that while all readers would recognise their existence, they might place the divisions differently. 'Sea-Weed', for example, belongs to a small sequence of short poems about the natural world. It is immediately preceded by two other 'imagistic' poems, 'Spray' and 'New Moon', though neither of these has the H.D.-like intensity of 'Sea-Weed', and 'New Moon' is, unfortunately, more reminiscent of T. E. Hulme. More interesting is the relation of 'Sea-Weed' to the other four poems of the group, which, though equally short, are not predominantly imagistic. For example, 'Little Fish':

> The tiny fish enjoy themselves
> in the sea.
> Quick little splinters of life,
> their little lives are fun to them
> in the sea.
>
> (CP, p. 466)

This is as slight, or slight-seeming, as *Pansies* gets. The language of four of its five lines is almost provocatively casual and childish – perhaps the language in which adults address(ed) children rather than that of children themselves. One might go so far as to suggest that it is an early twentieth-century equivalent of a 'Song of Innocence', in which this kind of language functions as the language of conventional children's poetry functioned for Blake. At the same time, the poem is hinged on a middle line that *is* imagistic, or (perhaps the same thing) comes from a particularly attentive and imaginative adult addressing a child. It is the quality of this line that justifies foregrounding the style of the other lines as I have done: it would be naive to call it the only poetic line in the poem, but perhaps it makes the others poetic. This poem's thematic relation to 'Sea-Weed' is obvious, but what is interesting is the stylistic relationship. The Imagist poem encapsulates what Hopkins might have called the instress of the sea-weed through a (for Lawrence) unusually intense sound patterning and something between a Yeatsian resolved paradox and a Blakean clash of contraries, of violence and stillness. This piling up of poets' names is deliberate. 'Little Fish' looks at the self-delight of the creatures in a language that is almost innocent of poetic precedent, as if its sub-text were that this is, or ought to be, all that need be said, it ought to be as simple as this. But it doesn't, of course, supplant the other poem; the support of the context is needed to be able to read it like this. 'Fun', for example, is a word commonly associated with cocktails, jazz and triviality, in Lawrence. Here it is redeemed by the proximity of 'Sea-Weed', and perhaps even more by the immediately preceding poem, 'The Gazelle Calf':

> The gazelle calf, O my children,
> goes behind its mother across the desert,
> goes behind its mother on blithe bare foot
> requiring no shoes, O my children!
>
> (CP, p. 466)

(This obviously also influences my reading of a very different way of addressing children into 'Little Fish'.)

Two poems after 'Little Fish', we have Lawrence in more didactic mood, in 'Self-Pity':

> I never saw a wild thing
> sorry for itself.
> A small bird will drop frozen dead from a bough
> without ever having felt sorry for itself.
>
> (CP, p. 467)

This works on its own as something between a proverb and a short homily, but it works better for picking up the 'blithe bare foot' of the gazelle calf, the 'fun' of the fish and the stillness-in-motion of the sea-weed. Finally, 'The Mosquito Knows – is the most aphoristic of the group:

> The mosquito knows full well, small as he is
> he's a beast of prey.
> But after all
> he only takes his bellyful,
> he doesn't put my blood in the bank.
>
> (CP, p. 466)

This also works perfectly well on its own but, like all the poems, it interacts with the sequence. This gives us, within a broad thematic consistency, a sharp and rapid alteration of mode – imagism, satire, homily, innocent-eye, mock-oratory – corresponding to shifts of focus within the thematic field.

Most importantly, this thematic field does not produce a tight sequence isolated from the rest of the volume. 'Self-Pity' encapsulates the message of the series of longer homilies, a few pages earlier, about 'fighting'; and 'The Mosquito Knows –' obviously relates to the sequence of poems about money. A reader might with some justice point out that I have made this little sequence artificially tight, and point out that 'The Gazelle Calf' is preceded by 'Sex and Trust':

> If you want to have sex, you've got to trust
> at the core of your heart, the other creature.
> The other creature, the other creature
> not merely the personal upstart;
> but the creature there, that has come to meet you
> trust it you must, you must
> or the experience amounts to nothing,
> mere evacuation-lust.
>
> (CP, p. 466)

This is probably more typical of *Pansies* than any of the other poems I have quoted, all of which could hold their own in an anthology (in the case of 'Little Fish', perhaps a children's anthology). 'Sex and Trust' is decidedly not anthologisable. The repeated words 'trust' and 'creature' insist on a significance that the poem does not supply. Even more obviously than 'Figs' it is, considered as a discrete poem, unsuccessful. But the various evocations of creatureliness in the following poems *do* supply a context of significance for that word, while the blitheness, self-delight, sufficiency, lack of self-pity, and stillness of the various creatures supply a penumbra of connotations for 'trust'. At the same time 'Sex and Trust' provides a framework of human meaning for the nature-poems, both by itself and by linking this sequence with the one that precedes it, which includes 'The Risen Lord', 'Beware, O My Dear Young Men –' and 'Sex Isn't Sin –'. These are all longer didactic poems, Lawrence's most notorious kind: these poems particularly gain from being read not as complacently self-sufficient monuments but as strands 'flying' to connect with other very different poems in a web that is itself not complete.

It would be inconsistent with the way of reading *Pansies* I am describing to suggest that there is a pattern or a central controlling idea. There are, however, repeated expressions of a particular feeling that I want to privilege here because it has an important bearing on so much else in the book, and so much else in Lawrence. This is the feeling expressed in what I imagine all readers would agree to be the beautiful short poem, 'Desire is Dead':

> Desire may be dead
> and still a man can be
> a meeting place for sun and rain,
> wonder outwaiting pain
> as in a wintry tree.
>
> (CP, p. 504)

This poem needs no context or sequence. It is not 'poetry of the present': it returns upon itself and completes itself with the best of them.[16] But many poems of various kinds, and on various ostensible themes, are touched by this exquisite expression of acceptance – meet momentarily at this still point. 'Self-Pity' takes on a different shade of meaning, the poems about old age assume a more personal note, the didactic poems about sex in the head seem less like obsessional ranting, the references to the phallus seem more impersonal, and any accusation of wish-fulfilment in them has to test itself against this and other confessions of the death of desire. In the larger and troubled arena of Lawrence and sexuality, this group of poems, and their pervasive echoes throughout *Pansies*, may contribute to an argument that Lawrence explores a large range of sexual perspectives, among which his fantasies about virility and male dominance are not definitive.

The history of modernism has always found Lawrence an awkward figure to deal with. His poems look out of place in a movement defined by the work of Eliot and Pound, just as his novels look out of place in a movement defined by the work of Joyce, Woolf and Faulkner. So he looks increasingly marginal and, as a poet, amateurish. But any concept of modernism worthy of the name has to embrace all the innovative work that was being done during the relevant period. To call Lawrence a modernist is not to measure his work by standards derived from other writers, but to assert that it is part of the defining body of modernist texts. At least as early as 1916, when he was working on the main draft of *Women in Love*, he was incorporating Imagist techniques into the novel,[17] and he consistently praised the work of H.D.,[18] with which, as I have briefly shown, certain of his poems have affinities, not only during the period of their friendship but many years later. Most importantly, for the purpose of this chapter, Lawrence made a significant and, though not unnoticed, as yet critically unassimilated contribution to the most distinctive genre of modern poetry: the long poem/sequence. That this may have come about almost by accident, a by-product of Lawrence's habits of writing and even (in the case of *Pansies*) state of health, with only the most casual theoretical foundation, does not detract from its importance.

I have tried to show that *Birds, Beasts and Flowers* and *Pansies* are more similar than they are usually considered to be: that the appreciation of a few 'perfected' poems in the one, and the dismissal of the other for its comparative lack of such poems, alike miss the point. Both volumes are open and informal sequences, with numerous interconnections of 'strands', in which poems in a large variety of modes, often individually incomplete, representing various thoughts, moods and feelings, form a 'web' whose pattern, always provisional, will be different for every reader, and every reading. As such they are eminently *scriptible* texts, but with their predominantly conversational tone, their concern with the present moment of experience, the absence of provocatively deliberate fragmentation, they are also, in the older but I hope not entirely discredited sense, eminently readable. They should be read whole, and more rapidly than one normally reads a volume of poetry. Only when a number of readers have reported on the results of such readings will a proper debate on their importance be possible.

Notes

1. D. H. Lawrence, 'Poetry of the Present', in V. de Sola Pinto and W. Roberts (eds), *The Complete Poems of D. H. Lawrence*, vol. 1 (London: Heinemann, 1964) p. 182; hereafter referred to as *CP* with page numbers given in the text.
2. E. Pound, 'A Retrospect', in T. S. Eliot (ed.), *Literary Essays of Ezra Pound* (London: Faber, 1954) p. 4.

3. D. H. Lawrence, 'Poetry of the Present', *Complete Poems*, p. 186.

4. T. Marshall, *The Psychic Mariner, A Reading of the Poems of D. H. Lawrence* (London: Heinemann, 1970) p. 5. See also, D. Ellis, 'The place of "pansies" in Lawrence's poetry', in D. Ellis and H. Mills, *D. H. Lawrence's Non-fiction* (Cambridge: Cambridge University Press, 1988) p. 147. Ellis refers to the greater use of free verse in *Birds, Beasts and Flowers*.

5. S. Gilbert, *Acts of Attention, The Poems of D. H. Lawrence* (New York: Cornell University Press, 1972) p. 141.

6. Another pertinent example is when the 'He is dumb' of 'Lui et Elle', in the Tortoise sequence (*Complete Poems*, vol. 1, p. 362), is corrected by 'I thought he was dumb / I said he was dumb, / Yet I've heard him cry', in 'Tortoise Shout' (ibid., p. 363).

7. S. Gilbert, op. cit., pp. 144–5.

8. D. H. Lawrence, 'Pomegranate', *Complete Poems*, vol. 1, p. 279; cited by Gilbert, op. cit., p. 144.

9. D. H. Lawrence, 'Poetry of the Present', *Complete Poems*, vol. 1, p. 182.

10. D. H. Lawrence, *Complete Poems*, vol. 1, p. 191.

11. D. H. Lawrence, 'Introduction to *Pansies*', *Complete Poems*, vol. 1, p. 417.

12. D. Ellis, op. cit., p. 159.

13. H.D., 'Sea Gods', in *Collected Poems 1912–1944*, ed. L. L. Martz (Manchester: Carcanet, 1984) pp. 29–30.

14. D. Ellis, op. cit., p. 164.

15. S. Gilbert, op. cit., p. 256.

16. There are numerous poems in *Pansies* (though not as high a proportion as in *Look! We Have Come Through!*) in rhyme and metre. However, most of these – such as 'Red Herring' and 'The Little Wowser' – are in a rough metre deriving from street-ballads that Lawrence uses, mainly, to find a voice for the working-class environment in which he grew up. They evoke a completely different tradition, popular, oral and improvisatory, from that conjured by the beautiful cadences of 'Desire is Dead'. Such poems neither achieve nor aspire to the 'perfected' state; their rhyme and metre are as open and 'present' as free verse.

17. I have discussed the importance of Imagism for Lawrence's development as a novelist in a paper, 'Lawrence and Imagism', to be published in W. Pratt and R. Richardson (eds), *Homage to Imagism* (New York: AMS Press) forthcoming.

18. See letters to A. W. Macleod and Edward Marsh, in *The Letters of D. H. Lawrence*, vol. 3 (Cambridge: Cambridge University Press, 1984) pp. 61, and 84.

7

Deconstructing the High Modernist Lyric

ALISTAIR DAVIES

I

'One of the anomalies of criticism in the late twentieth century', the American critic Marjorie Perloff has recently stated, 'is that the lyric poem, the great genre of the Romantics, as of the High Modernists, no longer seems central to its discourse.'[1] Whether we agree with Perloff's implicit judgement of the importance of the lyric form or not, her comment reminds us that the radical transposition of the lyric – particularly of the High Modernist lyric – from centre to margin is one of the most notable events in the recent history of literary criticism. For forty years, from the early 1920s to the late 1960s, the lyrics of Yeats and Eliot enjoyed an almost unimaginable prestige in Anglo-American letters. They provided the models which younger poets, from Auden to Plath, sought to emulate; they inspired in Practical and New Criticism institutionally powerful and influential doctrines of criticism; and they constituted for many critics the poles within which poetic writing itself was deemed possible. So overpowering was their prestige that few thought odd the view that the significant history of English literature was to be found in the development of the lyric.

There are, of course, may reasons for the change to which Perloff refers, and we need look no further than her own work if we wish to understand one of the more important reasons for this. In *The Poetics of Indeterminacy* she distinguishes between two traditions of post-Romantic lyric poetry, the Symbolist tradition originating with Baudelaire and running through the work of Yeats, Eliot and Stevens, and the anti-Symbolist tradition originating with Rimbaud and running through the work of Pound, Carlos Williams and Ashbery. It is the first tradition – the tradition of High Modernism – which has been, she suggests, predominant in twentieth-century criticism, and she is at pains to reveal its shortcomings in order to champion in criticism as well as poetry the alternative anti-Symbolist one. Like a number of her fellow American critics, she finds this other, subordinate tradition, in which the relation of lyric to narrative is fully explored, more adequate to contemporary, post-modernist experiences and concepts.

Perloff's study assumes (and it is an assumption which derives from the impact of Derrida on Romantic and post-Romantic studies) that the lyrics of High Modernism depend upon an unquestioned and hierarchical set of dualisms inherited from the Romantic lyric; the 'I' and the other, the self and the world, inner and outer, spirit and sense, the supernatural and the natural, the transcendent and the real. As in the Romantic lyric, these dualisms are resolved (and to the advantage of the first term) within coherent, symbolic structures. This is possible because the lyrics of High Modernism leave 'essentially intact' the conventional relationship between the word and its referents, drawing upon 'multiple relational meanings' within the system of the poem, within the intertextual system of which the poem is a part, and within the world conceived as systematic totality. 'What makes *The Waste Land* such a thickly textured poem', she writes, 'is that the symbolic threads are woven and designed so intricately that the whole becomes a reverberating echo chamber of meanings.'[2] Even though the poem is one of great complexity, she has no doubt that the poem is intended finally to be decoded.

At the same time, the High Modernist lyric is 'about' a particular mental or spiritual state and, while it might represent the anguish or anomie or sense of fragmentation of modern life, it invariably provides glimpses of the transcendent: Yeats's 'Miracle, bird or golden handiwork' ('Byzantium') or Eliot's 'hyacinth girl', or fishermen lounging at noon, or images of 'Ionian white and gold' (*The Waste Land*). Perloff is, however, less concerned with the compensatory function of such lyrics, which she takes to be the most explicit debt of the modernist lyric to its Romantic predecessors, than with their conservative signifying practice. Within such poetry, the points of view of the speaker, the poet and the reader, she suggests, are both determinate and determined.

By contrast, in inaugurating the anti-Symbolist tradition, Rimbaud undermined such dualisms: 'It is wrong to say: I think. One ought to say: I am being thought. I is Another.' 'If the "I" becomes "another,"' Perloff continues, 'the Romantic dualism of subject and object is resolved; the self no longer contemplates nature but becomes part of its operational processes.' Nor is the poet a visionary judging others or the world: he or she stands back and judges his or her self as if it belonged to someone else. 'The poet is no more able than is his reader to explain the content of his visions.'[3] Nor is the poem a determinate symbolic structure but an indeterminate verbal field in which the word and its referents have been sundered and in which the identities of the speaker, of the poet and of the reader have been dissolved.

What gives particular weight to Perloff's argument is the awareness that her criticism of the Symbolist tradition is not simply a matter for literary historians but belongs to the very line of epistemic rupture along which the most important theoretical work of the post-structuralist tradition, from Barthes to Derrida, has been taking place. This is by now a familiar story. The dualisms which the High Modernist lyric ('a regressive semiological system', in Barthes's dismissive phrase[4]) inherited from Romanticism not only sustained the ideology of the transcendent subject, but also made inevitable the reactionary differentiations which followed when it posited itself against those it identified as non-transcendent, and inevitably degraded others: women, members of the the lower middle and working classes, non-Europeans and Jews.[5] (Eliot's 'Burbank with a Baedeker: Bleistein with a Cigar' may cause as many difficulties for his admirers as do Yeats's 'A Prayer for My Daughter' or 'The Statues' for his.) By working beyond these dualisms, the anti-Symbolist tradition called their dangerous and reactionary differentiations into question. The recovery of this tradition would release, as Julia Kristeva has argued, the revolutionary potential of the literary avant-garde. Its energies had been repressed by the institutional hegemony of the Symbolist tradition (of which New Criticism was an early and structuralism a late epiphenomenon) but would be renewed within the theoretical practice of post-structuralism itself.

There is a powerful and convincing rhetoric at work here. What is regressive necessarily needs to be left behind, while that which gives birth to the new necessarily needs to be applauded. It is hardly surprising that those who have employed it have been remarkably successful in challenging the canonical status of the High Modernist lyric. But matters are perhaps not quite so straightforward. Perloff's insights, in keeping with deconstructive practice, have been gained by unsettling dualisms, and I want for a moment to unsettle the new ones which she herself has established by exploring further the implications of her view that 'Modernism was itself a time of tension between rival strains.'[6] Is it not possible that the poetry of Yeats and Eliot, even if it was a successor to the Symbolist tradition, also bore within itself the anti-Symbolist tradition as well? The seemingly irresolvable differences between grammatical and rhetorical modes of understanding which Paul de Man, for instance, explores in his famous analysis of the final stanza of Yeats's 'Among School Children'[7] not only establishes the disciplinary differences between philosophy and literature but also undermines the kinds of easy congruence between mind and nature, literature and reality upon which a certain reading of Romantic and post-Romantic poetry has defended. Do we not have in Yeats and Eliot a double practice of writing, at once closed and open, determinate and indeterminate, symbolic and allegorical? Have some critics in fact missed the true source of productivity in the lyric poetry of High Modernism?

The footnotes to *The Waste Land* are perhaps the most obvious sign of this double practice, inviting us on the one hand to fix the poem in one framework of interpretation while mocking us on the other for our very desire to do so. Perhaps less obvious is the Dantean epigraph at the head of 'The Love Song of J. Alfred Prufrock'. Is this an indication of the poet's mind? Or of Prufrock's? Or does it by its very status as a quotation remind us that the poem as a whole is an intertext, a verbal field of references and allusions within an almost unbounded larger one, in which we find less a speaking subject than a ventriloquial point? What are we to make of the fact that the quotation which forms the epigraph itself remains untranslated from its original language? Do the processes of translation not provide the best analogy for the process of reading itself?

We can agree with Perloff that the poem's 'carefully chosen images – the empty evening sky, the "patient etherised upon a table," the streets that lead nowhere, the "sawdust restaurants with oyster-shells" – create a symbolic complex that defines the anaesthetized consciousness, the life-in-death of the man who speaks these words'.[8] His erotic fantasies will not be realised, nor will the mermaids sing for him. But no sooner have we conceded this than the overwhelmingly derivative and mediated forms of most of the images in the poem, and the late Victorian or Decadent sentiments they convey, make their impact upon us. What is important about these images is not so much that they are visually striking or unconventional – products of that process of defamiliarisation of which the Russian

Formalists speak. It is that they are, on the whole, the stock images of the literature of the period. Prufrock's conscious and unconscious worlds have always already been occupied.

By this, I wish to suggest more than the obvious point that Eliot dramatises in Prufrock the second-hand responses of a turn-of-the-century American aesthete, although the degree to which Eliot makes specific the material conditions of his speaking subjects, including those of social idiom and cultural code, has not received adequate attention. In reading the poem, I am struck by two antithetical processes at work: one, a process of extraordinarily rapid shifts from one identification to another, as if the subjectivity at its centre is still undefined, both a void and a vortex; and the other, a process of painfully heightened self-consciousness (and Perloff is wrong to speak of Prufrock's "anaesthetized consciousness') which is made possible because the individual has been able to stabilise himself, through a particular cultural code, by means of ascetic imitation:

> But though I have wept and fasted, wept and prayed,
> Though I have seen my head (grown slightly bald)
>   brought in upon a platter,
> I am no prophet – and here's no great matter;
> I have seen the moment of my greatness flicker,
> And I have seen the eternal Footman hold my coat, and
>   snicker,
> And in short, I was afraid.

The two processes interweave: as if the spiritual man – the martyr, the man of torment – is reproduced, in demonic parody, by his aesthetic double, the martyr to his sensibility.[9]

Eliot's poem, far from reproducing the ideology of the subject, actually interrogates the means by which the subject is constructed. Prufrock's 'life-in-death' comes not from some particular and remediable failure of perceptiveness but from acknowledging that ascetic imitation denies all notions of originality, for it is only made possible through entry into language, into discourse. Prufrock's I is Another. It is an understanding which might usefully be read in the light of Foucault's analysis of the subjection of language or (as Maud Ellmann has recently done[10]) in the light of Lacan's exploration of the links between narcissism and aggressivity, and it calls into question not only the distinctions made by Perloff but also the conclusions which follow from them.

II

It is the recognition of such self-conscious textuality – in the theory of impersonality, in the doctrine of the mask, in the idea of an intertextual tradition – which has caused others to find in the High Modernist lyric an anticipation of the critique of the subject and the foregrounding of language associated with deconstruction. The High Modernist lyric, in which words are quotations, utterances of other texts and discourses, not only puts under question notions of presence and of voice, but also grows out of a larger intellectual challenge to the notion of origin. Can we not, for instance, find in Yeats's image of history as a 'widening gyre' a view of history as a creative process of repetition and difference? Or, even more so, can we not find in Eliot's poetry of fragments and shreds the very manifestation of a Derridian art of writing? Is *The Waste Land*, in Ruth Nevo's phrase, an 'ur-text of deconstruction?'[11]

What is surprising, however, is that the three major scholars of Romantic and post-Romantic poetry, Harold Bloom, Paul de Man and Geoffrey Hartman, who have responded most fully to deconstruction, albeit in a complex revisionary process of assimilation and antithesis, have found Yeats rather than Eliot to have explored more creatively and more resolutely the poetic and philosophical implications of textuality. The issues at stake are complex and, of course, their original determination in the criticism of Bloom, de Man and Hartman not only pre-dates the arrival of deconstruction but also conditions their response to it.

We may find an indication of what is involved by examining briefly Geoffrey Hartman's most recent work. In *Criticism in the Wilderness* and *Saving the Text*, he undertakes an increasingly allusive meditation, at once vigil and celebration, on the appropriate style of commentary in the wake of 'the seeming impotence of traditional humanistic philosophies, together with the obvious success science has had in turning its provisional mastery of the world into a real imposition'.[12] His principal concern, however, intermittently in the first study and constantly in the second, is the challenge to traditional concepts of the text and of commentary posed by the writings of Jacques Derrida. How could Hartman sustain his belief in literary study as an engagement with the monumental texts and the monumental figures of the tradition after Derrida's aleatory style of exegesis in *Glas*, with its cutting up or rather cutting down of the great texts and great figures of the past? 'How can mind accept rather than subvert or overlook (by sophisticated scanning techniques, which are the opposites of close reading) the language of great writers, both in philosophy and literature?'[13]

Derrida estranges, but in a way which allows Hartman to re-define and practise a new style of commentary which is open to the situation of debris and ruin which Derrida evokes – 'there is no single, unifying logos: there is, at most, a divine parapraxis imitated alike by medieval jongleur and modern grammatologist'[14] – but which is resistant to his negating rigour: 'Even if we do not seek to monumentalize our nothingness in the form of some perman-ent double,' Hartman writes, 'even if we understand the need for sacrifice and dissemination, must we spend our intellectual lives decomposing the vanity of the monumentalists: the writers, artists, philosophers, and theologians among us?'[15] The grounds for a hu-manism restored after Derrida's 'timely' provocations (one which knows precisely the degree to which anti-humanist propositions must underlie it), seem to lie in the understanding of such vanity, in a certain patience (a favourite mood or mode in Hartman's work) in the face of the monumentalising stratagems by which writers, artists, philosophers and theologians respond to the fact that we live in the void, in an 'economy of death'. The question is ulti-mately, as Hartman suggests, as it always has been in his criticism, a matter of time.

Like Derrida, he accepts the loss of origin and the condition of exile, but unlike Derrida (whom he links on this point with the Eliot of *The Waste Land*), he does not engage in a 'fashionable meditation in the graveyard of Western culture'.[16] Even Derrida's song of de-composition – his Hegelian rag (like Eliot's *Shakespeherian Rag*) at the ending of history and of art – was, he suggested, dependent upon the great figures and texts of the past. The laughter of Derrida involved the elation rather than the sublation of the monuments of the past. It was a form of Dada: Derridadaism. What was required, if we were to cure rather than prolong the wound of our condition, was patience in the 'work of mourning', in the personal reading and incorporation in their otherness of the great texts of the past.

For some, Hartman's 'criticism in the wilderness', (like that of Bloom and de Man), is a throwback to the aestheticism of the 1890s and reflects the alienation and the redundancy of a humanist view of the function of criticism and of the humanities at the present time.[17] It can easily be seen as an elitist turning away, in the spirit of the the High Modernist lyric, from the levelling wind of modern culture. Certainly, it is not difficult to find warrant for it in Yeats.[18] In 'Sailing to Byzantium', for instance, the need for seeking a monumental double and for engaging with monumental and monumentalising texts (to produce and reproduce history itself) is fully understood, just as the indifference of the larger political society (in the figure of 'the drowsy Emperor') to the fate of letters is also accepted:

> An aged man is but a paltry thing,
> A tattered coat upon a stick, unless
> Soul clap its hands and sing, and louder sing
> For every tatter in its mortal dress,
> Nor is there singing school but studying
> Monuments of its own magnificence;
> And therefore I have sailed the seas and come
> To the holy city of Byzantium.

Yet Hartman arrives at this position – in relation to Yeats and to Derrida – as the result of an attempt over three decades (and it is paralleled in the careers of Bloom and of de Man) to analyse a contradiction within Modernism itself, a contradiction which has had important implications both for their understanding of the High Modernist lyric and for their understanding of the relationship between commentary and text. It is a contradiction which needs to be examined because, they suggest, we continue to read in the wake of the High Modernist lyric, under the shadow of the achievement of Modernism and within its unresolved problematic.

This arises from the recognition, expressed most fully and decisively by de Man in his essay 'Literary History and Literary Modernity' (1969), that the will to renewal at the heart of Modernism cannot be reconciled with the inevitable duration (and the inevitable anteriority) of the act by which this is attempted. When writers 'assert their own modernity, they are bound to discover their dependence on similar assertions made by their literary predecessors; their claim to being a new beginning turns out to be the repetition of a claim that has always already been made'.[19] Nevertheless, Modernism is motivated – and this is its most powerful and distinctive desire – by the desire to annul time. (For Bloom, de Man and Hartman this desire takes many different forms, from the parricidal desire of the literary son to kill his stronger literary father, to the quest for organic forms and theories of being; from the yearning for 'life', significance or action beyond the text, to the very decomposition of the inner duration of a text and of the larger duration within which texts have their being.) Yet why does the analysis of this desire become so important? Is it because this desire is the temptation to which all writing is subject and which it needs to resist in order to be literature? 'Or is it because this desire – however necessary it is to give existence to both literature and history – has and has had dangerous consequences not only for literature but for history as well?

Let us look, for a moment, at the example of Eliot. From its first to its last section, *The Waste Land* depicts scenes of contemporary life through parodies and echoes of numerous discourses, ranging from those of high literature to those of popular journalism, and it does so in order to make clear that the lives of those represented within those scenes are parodic and repetitious. Nevertheless, what is most striking is the way in which Eliot presents them, with his lofty and sorrowful awareness of their anteriority (what Tiresias sees, we are told, is the substance of the poem), yet repossesses them, in the instantaneousness of denunciation, as signs of worthlessness, depravity, emptiness, and absence 'a heap of broken images' (*The Waste Land*, I, 22). The will to renewal coincides with – or is perhaps the condition for – an even stronger yearning to bring time, as duration and as repetition, to a final end.

What the poem expresses most consistently are feelings of derision and disgust, authorised at one and the same time by St Augustine and the Buddha, for all forms of material embodiment, from the physical flesh to words themselves. These are sentiments which focus on literature itself – because, on the one hand, its mediated or embodied meanings derive from mankind's fallen condition and because, on the other, it holds out the illusion of meaningfulness in a world in which individuals find themselves bereft of meaning – like the disinherited Prince d'Aquitaine evoked at the end of the poem, 'à la tour abolie' (*The Waste Land*, V, 429). Indeed, in a poem which finds affirmation only in the voiced reverberations of thunder, there remains a striking ambiguity about the function and value of the textual fragments which the speaker, at its conclusion, shores against his ruins. Do these not support the pretences that ought to be swept away? Is the spiritual state about which the poet writes, not the absence of meaning but its terrifying and uncontrollable excess? Is the poem not moved by a desire for an immediacy which its very mode negates, and does it not thereby experience the unbearable condition of literature?

We might wonder if Eliot's explicit acceptance of the doctrines, practices and institutions of Anglo-Catholicism in mid-career did not bring such desires to an end. The rhetorical uses of language, no less than traditional literary forms of self-exploration, were self-consciously presented in *Four Quartets* as age-old and supra-individual vehicles for seeking and making available the revealed truth of God. God's Word had been translated, as if through a linguistic act of incarnation, into the specific vernacular in which Eliot's English and American predecessors had written and in which he too was writing. His poetry was in this sense a concrete enactment of tradition, an act – within time – of receiving and of handing on, by which history itself was constituted and the past linked with the present and the future.

Yet, for Eliot, this living but historic language was not only threatened with decay, but subject to a disturbing, uncontrollable multiplicity:

> Words strain,
> Crack and sometimes break, under the burden,
> Under the tension, slip, slide, perish,
> Decay with imprecision, will not stay in place,
> Will not stay still.
>   ('Burnt Norton', IV, 149–53)

It may well be that Eliot again draws here upon St Augustine, in the hope that the multiplicity of language caused by the Fall will be redeemed by the fullness of language promised by the Incarnation. Yet how are we to judge Eliot's desire, here and elsewhere in the poem, to go beyond the states of mediation (whether of language, or culture or national institution) by which the historical world was sustained, to a fusion in which the impossible union of spheres of existence was made actual, of the temporal with the eternal? Let us look for a moment at the following lines from the fourth section of the fourth culminating quartet, 'Little Gidding'. The lyric reflects upon the significance of a German fighter-bomber dropping its incendiary load on London during the Second World War:

> The dove descending breaks the air
> With flame of incandescent terror

Of which the tongues declare
The one discharge from sin and error.
The only hope, or else despair
Lies in the choice of pyre or pyre –
To be redeemed from fire by fire.
('Little Gidding', IV, 200–6)

It might seem that Eliot is here playing off literal and metaphorical realms of reference, somewhat as an exercise in modern metaphysical poetry. The descent of the fighter-bomber (in the First World War, the German war plane, the Dove, was much talked of in England) is akin to the descent of the Holy Spirit, 'descending from heaven like a dove' (St John, 1, 32).[20] But in the passage, it is difficult to decide quite where literal and metaphorical realms begin and end. The metaphorical realm not only lays claim to unveiling the hidden truth of the literal – that this is not only a moment of destruction but of apocalypse[21] – but to do so in terms of a willed annihilation of the temporal world within which the differentiation between the two realms is possible and meaningful. What the dive-bomber threatens to destroy are the grounds of poetry as well as of history, because both depend upon duration.

Yet what compels this understanding? There is, it seems, a yearning for punishment from the angry, mocking Father mankind has spurned. 'Water and fire deride / The sacrifice that we denied.' ('Little Gidding', II, 72–3). In the next stanza of the fourth section of 'Little Gidding' quoted above, Eliot poses and answers his own perplexing question: 'Who then devised the torment? Love.' ('Little Gidding', IV, 207). We are saved by being destroyed.[22] We should embrace the terrifying destruction of God's Love, which promises us eternal life, rather than the flames of lust, which can only promise us eternal death. Eliot's mode of questioning, no less than the capitalised noun by which his question is answered, point to the linguistic means by which such propositions are expressed and necessarily called into doubt, but what perhaps needs to be answered is not the mocking mysteriousness but the sadism (or sadomasochism) of Eliot's apocalyptic sublime.

I have taken this detour through Eliot in order to detail examples of elements in his writing against which, I believe, Bloom, Hartman and de Man have defined themselves. (A detour through Yeats would have shown how the poet, reflecting upon time, continuity and inheritance, not only celebrates the ancient tower in which he lived as a monument, a family home and the site of literary and symbolic power but also resigns himself – on account of his belief in the persistence of emblem or text – to the disappearance of the cultural world and the magnanimous values he most cherished.) It is a commonplace that the writings of these critics advocate a post-modern practice of interpretation which acknowledges the indeterminacy of meaning inherent in language and which resists all attempts to contain the infinite deferral of signification within the authoritarian assurance of one single meaning (or Word). What is less of a commonplace is that their resistance to this follows from their resistance to Eliot's understanding of Modernism as a stylistic and cultural transformation, or break-through or rupture, by which the present is put under annihilating judgement, a new meaning is given to things, language is purified, literature is superseded, and a new time is inaugurated. Their resistance to this drive is absolute, even if it is marked by the awareness that such a drive is both necessary and necessarily contained by the mediatedness of all things and by the burden of echo, or repetition, or intertext. 'We are born with the dead: / See, they return, and bring us with them' ('Little Gidding', IV, 230–1). The text of Modernism, like the modernist text, undoes itself.

We might construe all this as a claim for the primacy of literature (albeit a highly self-reflective and self-resistant literature) against the claims of speculative reason: Hegel's judgement on the end of art may be right, but not yet. But there were, I believe, more immediate political and moral commitments in making such an analysis. For a generation writing in the wake of the Second World War, it was necessary to understand the urge to 'make it new' on the grounds that this drive, either in its revolutionary and millennarian forms or in its organic and nostalgic ones, turns (and in this century has turned) too readily to catastrophe. Impatience in the face of temporality and the impetuous will to shape it, or end it, or transform its content, can lead to terrifying and destructive effects.[23]

The poet, it seems, needs the strength, both moral and epistemological, to accept, on the one hand, that he or she lives in an ungrounded world and to resist, on the other, the temptation which might follow from that situation for immediacy or for permanence. It is a strength which Yeats possessed and Eliot did not, for while Yeats made of his writing 'befitting emblems of adversity', Eliot as a young man failed to create a monumental self out of the fragments of the waste land, and as a mature man sought self-annihilation.[24]

Our position as readers requires a similar heroism, in the face both of groundlessness and of the monumental texts from which an identity and a tradition have to be formed. It may well be that the true provocation of Derrida's challenge lies in his resistance to the male and other presuppositions upon which such views are based, and upon his refusal to reassemble himself without question in the mirror of texts which, in his view, work and have worked for his dispossession. Yet this critique may not be final. Is the post-modern reader of the High Modernist lyric, even an unsympathetic one, not fated to participate in the desire and the resistance at the heart of Modernism itself?

Notes

1. Marjorie Perloff, 'New Nouns for Old: "Language" Poetry, Language Game, and the Pleasure of the Text', in Matei Calinescu and Douwe Fokkema (eds), *Exploring Postmodernism: Selected Papers presented at a Workshop on Postmodernism at the XIth International Comparative Literature Congress, Paris, 20–24 August 1985* (Amsterdam/Philadelphia: John Benjamins Publishing Co., 1987) p. 95.
2. Marjorie Perloff, *The Poetics of Indeterminacy: Rimbaud to Cage* (Princeton, N.J.: Princeton University Press, 1981) p. 16.
3. Ibid., p. 61.
4. Roland Barthes, *Mythologies*, selected and translated from the French by Annette Lavers (London: Jonathan Cape, 1972) p. 133.
5. For a recent discussion, see Patrick Williams, 'Cultural Coherence and Contradiction in Yeats', and Mick Burton, 'The Imperfect Librarian: Text and Discourse in *The Waste Land* and *Four Quartets*', in David Murray (ed.), *Literary Theory and Poetry: Extending the Canon* (London: Batsford, 1989). Burton's essay is particularly useful for its analysis of the ways in which the 'woman reader' of Eliot is 'hailed as inferior'.
6. Perloff, *The Poetics of Indeterminacy*, p. 33.
7. Paul de Man, 'Semiology and Rhetoric', *Allegories of Reading: Figural Language in Rousseau, Nietzsche, Rilke, and Proust* (New Haven: Yale University Press, 1979) pp. 3–19.
8. Perloff, 'New Nouns for Old', p. 117.
9. See Geoffrey Galt Harpham, *The Ascetic Imperative in Culture and Criticism* (Chicago: Chicago University Press, 1987) pp. 3–66.
10. Maud Ellmann, *The Poetics of Impersonality: T. S. Eliot and Ezra Pound* (Brighton: Harvester Press, 1987) pp. 62–90.
11. Ruth Nevo, '*The Waste Land*: Ur-Text of Deconstruction', *New Literary History*, 13:3 (Spring 1982) pp. 453–61.

12. Geoffrey H. Hartman, *Saving the Text: Literature/Derrida/Philosophy* (Baltimore: Johns Hopkins University Press, 1981) p. 2.

13. Ibid., p. xv.

14. Ibid., p. 7.

15. Ibid., p. 6.

16. Ibid., p. 9.

17. See, for a brief account of responses to deconstruction, Howard Felperin, 'The Anxiety of American Deconstruction', in Rajnath (ed.), *Deconstruction: A Critique* (London: Macmillan, 1989) pp. 180–96.

18. See, for a discussion of the centrality of Yeats to Bloom and de Man, Daniel O'Hara, 'Yeats in Theory', in Richard Machin and Christopher Norris (eds), *Post-structuralist Readings of English Poetry* (Cambridge: Cambridge University Press, 1987) pp. 349–68. For a discussion of the centrality of Yeats to Hartman, see Daniel O'Hara, *The Romance of Interpretation: Visionary Criticism from Pater to de Man* (New York: Columbia University Press, 1985) pp. 98–146.

19. Paul de Man, 'Literary History and Literary Modernity', *Blindness and Insight: Essays in the Rhetoric of Contemporary Criticism* (London: Methuen, 2nd rev. edn, 1983) pp. 161–2.

20. Harry Blamires, *Word Unheard: A Guide Through T. S. Eliot's Four Quartets* (London: Methuen, 1969) p. 143.

21. See Genesius Jones, *Approach to the Purpose: A Study of the Poetry of T. S. Eliot* (London: Hodder and Stoughton, 1964) p. 265: 'The Kingdom finally comes, and the Earthly Paradise is realised in a transcendent form as the Kingdom of the Son, when the Holy Spirit invades the earth. And it is this invasion which Mr. Eliot celebrates in *Little Gidding*. The figure of the invasion is the *Luftwaffe*. But it is precisely the Stuka bomber – "The dark dove with the flickering tongue" – which is the agent of the Holy Spirit.'

22. A. D. Moody speaks of a 'rhetorical ultimatum' in *T. S. Eliot: Poet* (Cambridge: Cambridge University Press, 1980) p. 256.

23. They perform an aestheticist reading, of the kind analysed by Allan Megill, *Prophets of Extremity: Nietzsche, Heidegger, Foucault, Derrida* (Berkeley and Los Angeles: California University Press, 1985). A Derridian reading would pose questions about the cultural effects, not least of inclusion and exclusion, following from the 'onto-theology' of *Four Quartets*. Purification through fire has different connotations for those identifying with the purifying force and for those identifying with its victims.

24. See the conclusion to de Man's early 'Image and Emblem in Yeats', *The Rhetoric of Romanticism* (New York: Columbia University Press, 1984) pp. 145–238. 'Those who look to Yeats for reassurance from the anxieties of our own post-romantic predicament, or for relief from the paralysis of nihilism, will not find it in his conception of the emblem. He cautions instead against the danger of unwarranted hopeful solutions, and thus accomplishes all that the highest forms of language can for the moment accomplish.' See also, Hartman's discussion of 'Leda and the Swan' and of Yeats's interrogative mode in *Criticism in the Wilderness: The Study of Literature Today* (New

Haven: Yale University Press, 1980) pp. 21–5 and pp. 272–5. See also, de Man's comments on Eliot and on salvational criticism in 'The Dead-End of Formalist Criticism', *Blindness and Insight*, pp. 229–45. 'Instead of saying that Wheelwright's thought, or, for that matter, T. S. Eliot's to whom it is so close, sacrifices consciousness to faith, it is better to say that it alternates moments of faith without consciousness with moments of consciousness without faith. This is possible only if negation and affirmation are both wielded carelessly' (p. 244).

8

Ruined Boys: W. H. Auden in the 1930s

STAN SMITH

RUINED BOYS

Ruin was fashionable in the 1930s. Cyril Connolly's 'Theory of Permanent Adolescence', set out in *Enemies of Promise* in 1938, gave it a rationale which has become part of the mythology of the 'Auden generation':

> It is the theory that the experiences undergone by boys at the great public schools, their glories and disappointments, are so intense as to dominate their lives and to arrest their development. From these it results that the greater part of the ruling class remains adolescent, school-minded, self-conscious, cowardly, sentimental, and in the last analysis, homosexual. Early laurels weigh like lead and of many of the boys whom I knew at Eton, I can say that their lives are over . . . now, in their early thirties, they are haunted ruins.[1]

The fiction of Evelyn Waugh, Aldous Huxley and Christopher Isherwood, the criticism of Christopher Caudwell (*Studies in a Dying Culture*) and Stephen Spender (*The Destructive Element*), all subscribe to the theme. As a literary topos, it has its sources in that founding father of Modernism, T. S. Eliot, whose 'broken Coriolanus', in 1922, ended in fragments and ruins, and whose lectures on *The Use of Poetry and the Use of Criticism*, in 1933, spoke of Coleridge as 'a haunted man . . . a ruined man'. Eliot added, with characteristic double-take, 'Sometimes, however, to be a "ruined man" is itself a vocation.'[2]

In 1934, C. Day Lewis's polemic study of what he called 'post-war poetry', *A Hope for Poetry*, had drawn a link between Eliot's disenchantment and the disillusion of the war poets as dual influences on his own generation:

Wilfrid [sic] Owen, killed on the Sambre canal, spoke above the
barrage and the gas-cloud, saying to us, 'The poetry is in the
pity.' When it was all over, it was left to an American, T. S. Eliot,
to pick up some of the fragments of civilization, place them end
to end, and on that crazy pavement walk precariously through
the waste land.

Post-war poetry was born amongst the ruins.[3]

Connolly's diagnosis has regularly been applied to his friend W. H.
Auden, usually with the suggestion that ruin was a vocation intimately related to homosexuality. But Day Lewis's formula, merging the waste lands of Modernism and the Great War, provides the
interpretative context within which such vocation can be understood. The *locus classicus* for such a reading is 'Consider this and in
our time', in *Poems* (1930):

> It is later than you think; nearer that day
> Far other than that distant afternoon . . .
> They gave the prizes to the ruined boys.[4]

The phrase 'ruined boys' is usually read as a flippant reference to
public-school homosexuality: the prize-winning pupils, heroes to
their families, already corrupted by a sinister and secret precocity.
But the image is much more central and more serious in Auden's
writing than this would imply.

The list of symptoms with which the poem ends suggests why.
From fugues, through irregular breathing and alternate ascendancies,
to the explosion of mania and classic fatigue, they are all, like the
neurotic dread of the previous paragraph, the symptoms of neurasthenia, that 'shell shock' diagnosed in survivors of the Great War
by the psychologist W. H. R. Rivers, who treated several of the war
poets, including Owen, Sassoon, and Graves. For Auden's generation memoirs such as Graves's *Goodbye to All That*, published in
1929, rapidly became a *cause célèbre*. Linking the sham and sexual
hypocrisy of a public-school upbringing with the greater hypocri-
sies of the War, the book posited a continuity between the world of
manipulated schoolboy heroism and the mass murder at the Front.
These young men had volunteered to be victims because school
had constructed them into an ideology which closed off any alternative vision. The trauma of the War had then, for many, exposed
the futility of the very self they inhabited.

In the poem later called 'A Free One' the nonchalant pauses of one such ruling-class hero are exposed as imposture. In the year *Goodbye to All That* was published and Byrd flew over the South Pole, this figure is emphatically neither a returning conqueror nor polar circumnavigator, but, like the shell-shocked veteran, his 'balancing subterfuge' can counterfeit the hero's striking profile and erect bearing. Like Graves in his Majorcan exile, he has to make the longest journey to an intrinsic peace – a peace more difficult than that external, extrinsic one effected at Versailles, for he still carries the scars of war within him. 'Will you turn a deaf ear' likewise deploys the effects and after-effects of the War (concrete air-raid shelter and the gas mask's porcelain filter against germ warfare, death wheeled around in the veteran's invalid chair, saluting the flag along with soldiers' wives), before contrasting the broken promises of 'A Land Fit For Heroes' with the treatment actually meted out to the returning 'heroes', as observed by the next generation ('later other'), who learn there is neither income, bounty, nor 'promised country', but only a 'neutralising peace'.

Representatively, 'Sentries against inner and outer' deploys the imagery of war to describe a hysteric, uncommunicating self; while 'Again in conversations' seems to explore the talking cure of Rivers's psychotherapy, encouraging the shell-shocked to speak their fear, and thereby shed their sickness. Here, the process does not seem to work, for though the voice comes closer, it remains as confused as memories of first love or (in a peculiar conjunction) 'peacetime occupations'.

This closing phrase in the 1930 text was altered in the second edition of *Poems*, in 1933, to 'boys' imaginations'. Together, the two phrases forge an unassailable link between prewar peace and prepubescence, in the cadence and idiom of Wilfred Owen. Sex and war alike in this poem are thrust prematurely on boys whose precocious knowledge exceeds their capacity. While the poem's cryptic phrases pastiche the idiom of Graves's mentor Laura Riding, whose *Love as Love, Death as Death* Auden was reading in December 1928, 'Saying goodbye but coming back' gestures ironically towards the title of Graves's autobiography, shortly to be published.

Auden developed Graves's thesis about the continuity between the psychological manipulations of the educational and military–imperial apparatuses in an essay in Graham Greene's collection, *The Old School*, in 1934, published as 'Honour' but originally called 'The Liberal Fascist'.[5] His own, he says, was 'a modern school', 'liberal',

with 'vague ideals of service', yet it too manipulated the schoolboy mélange of emotional immaturity and sexual precocity for
ultimately sinister ends. Just as most the teachers were 'silted-up
old maids' or 'earnest young scoutmasters', 'afraid of the mature
world', 'the would-be children', so they conspired, largely unconsciously, to produce a similar retardation in their pupils:

> the only emotion that is fully developed in a boy of fourteen
> is the emotion of loyalty and honour. For that very reason it is
> dangerous. By appealing to it, you can do almost anything you
> choose, you can suppress the expression of all those emotions,
> particularly the sexual, which are still undeveloped; like a mod-
> ern dictator you can defeat almost any opposition from other
> parts of the psyche, but if you do, if you deny these other emo-
> tions their expression and development . . . they will not only never
> grow up, but they will go backward, for human nature cannot
> stay still; they will, like all things that are shut up, go bad on you.

Thus a new generation of 'ruined boys' is produced, with a 'moral
life . . . based on fear, on fear of the community', as the fertile soil
in which Fascism may flourish; and, as Auden comments with
characteristic panache, 'fear is not a healthy basis. It makes one
furtive and dishonest and unadventurous. The best reason I have
for opposing Fascism is that at school I lived in a Fascist state.'
These boys are doomed to repeat the catastrophe of their predecessors, because, as 'To ask the hard question' suggests, they cannot
be sure of what they learn simply from the repeated re-enactment
of old deeds. Trapped in the strangely exciting lie, these ghostly
inheritors are driven to re-enact that which cause their pain. Thus
they become the new recruits of Fascism, their cowardice crying to
be chastised and their will to obey seeking a master.
    In *Lions and Shadows*, in 1938, Christopher Isherwood recorded
that in the late 1920s the experience of the generation of 1914 had
'shaken my faith in the invulnerability of my generation':

> Yes, they had all had to go through it; and one day, perhaps, it
> would be our turn. . . . Our little world which seemed so precious
> would burst like the tiniest soap bubble, unnoticed, uncared for
> – just as [their] world had exploded, thirteen years ago.

Isherwood detected in a representative war-veteran a 'puzzled air
of arrested boyishness', as if he 'belonged forever, like an unhappy

Peter Pan, to the nightmare Never-Never-Land of the War. He had no business to be here, alive, in post-war England. His place was elsewhere, was with the dead.'[6] The image of the veteran as 'a ghost – the ghost of the War' elucidates that imagery of posthumous youths haunting a ghostly world so frequent in Auden's early verse. Learning is an alienating process, as in 'Paid on Both Sides',[7] recruiting the child as a new ghost to a superannuated order where it learns about death from the 'old termers', posthumous before it sets out. To imitate the father is to become the mere reprint of the older generation, a simulacrum, assuming faces not one's own. At the heart of such learning is betrayal, an emigration from weakness which simply reinstates weakness in the postures of heroism. If the fathers taught their sons ostensibly to find themselves in the false sureties of war and conquest, they omitted the crucial lesson, which only failure could reveal.

Again and again, the shadow of the father falls across volition. In 'Get there if you can', copying 'perfect pater' and 'marvellous mater' will never lead to authentic selfhood. But renouncing their models, doing the reverse of all that they would do, equally results in catching their disease. In 'Under boughs between our tentative endearments', the speaker responds with furtive pleasure to the distant sound of drums, harking back to the last war and forward to the inevitable next one. For the new generation's features each day resemble more closely those in the family albums. Fathers who fought in the old war can hear their own tricks of speech and pronunciation reproduced in their sons' voices. Just as assuredly, the ancestral curse, restrained for years, will one day finally erupt in a new and violent conflagration.

Many of Auden's early poems fall into place as obsessive reprises of the experience of the Great War, which is then predicted as a doom for the next generation. In 'Between attention and attention' there is the same uneasy transition between winning at a school Sports Day and the 'crucial test' of war. Isherwood records in *Lions and Shadows* that, 'Like most of my generation, I was obsessed by a complex of terrors and longing connected with the idea "War." "War", in this purely neurotic sense, meant The Test', which was then translated into 'a cult of the public-school system . . . the daydream of an heroic school career'.[8] In the poem later called 'Missing', the training of leaders likewise moves from the prize competitors of a school Sports Day to the battlefield where skyline operations present a perfect target, bringing death to heroes who thought themselves immortal. The title, which Auden added later, remains obscure until we recall the conventional phrase for soldiers lost in action: 'Missing, believed dead'.

In *The Orators*, in 1932, classroom and battlefield are overlaid in a sinister homology of practices at once ludicrous and distressing, and the opening 'Address for a Prize Day' turns, by the end, into a drilling for war. As late as 'Oxford', in 1937, the correlation persists, speaking of a college ethos which promises the glittering prizes to the sharpest sword, silences outrage with a testament, and discloses to the eager child a more serious revelation: 'That Knowledge is conceived in the hot womb of Violence'.[9]

DRUNKEN PROPHETS

Fused, however, with this modern conjunction in Auden's poems, as that ambiguous word 'testament' in 'Oxford' suggests, is a more archaic element: an eschatological vision that looks down the generations of men with the clairvoyant ferocity of a Biblical prophet. The leader looking down upon the happy valley in 'Missing' echoes typologically Moses on Pisgah, looking upon the promised land he cannot enter, dying the other side of the border, a leader who, in the Exodus, had once himself to migrate. An earlier version of these and other lines, in *Poems* (1928), joins school, war and Biblical prophecy in a single bathetic image, speaking of death, like a schoolmaster as much as Moses, leading his chosen people to a 'mildewed dormitory'.[10] This fusion of prophetic and pedagogic discourses points to a key convergence in Auden's poetry.

In a letter to Stephen Spender in 1930 Auden wrote gnomically that 'All poetry in our time is comic. These are two modes (1) The drunken prophetic (2) The legal disclaimer.'[11] Auden attempts to come to terms with what he sees as the doubly absurd vocation of his ruined generation by combining both postures. His poems sonorously proclaim a prophetic rhetoric which fuses revelationary and revolutionary modes as, left-handedly, they disclaim the heroic pretensions of phrases which reinstate the patriarchal voice as they denounce it. Seeing as a child is one way of drunkenly disclaiming the fathers.

The generation which came to maturity in the late 1920s had experienced the Great War with the distorted clarity of children.

Born in 1907, Auden almost automatically associates the War with his schooldays, not simply because they were contemporaneous, but because the simplicities of infancy and prepubescence seem intimately related to the infantilism of war. 'Letter to Lord Byron'[12] reduces the Great War to schoolboy banality, confused by the new recruits at prep school with thumpings from older boys or a beating from the headmaster. But if the boys' perspectives are askew, so is that of the teachers. Failing at lessons becomes hyperbolically a form of fifth-column activity: when half the class mistake the gender of the Latin word for 'war', writing masculine *Bellus* for neutral *Bellum*, the Latin master accuses them of working for a German victory. To master Latin, the imperial language, is to qualify for entry to the patriarchy, another kind of 'test'. To the child, the War exhibits all the immature emotions of a schoolboy stone-throwing squabble, just as his view of his father's homecoming diminishes it in a bathetic conjunction, 'Butter and Father' returning simultaneously to the family table. Similarly, the three Auden boys' singing of the hymn 'Eternal Father' on the seafront conflates the absent earthly patriarch with his heavenly analogue. The father's return was sure to bring disappointment, a disillusion like that which, the poem suggests, induced postwar nihilists to convert that 'Eternal Father' into the baby-talk of 'Visions of Dada'.

The conflation of playground and battlefield in *The Orators: An English Study*[13] draws its inspiration from the drunkenly prophetic spirit of Dadaism. Usually seen as proleptic of Fascism and the next war, *The Orators* also derives much of its urgency from the war that has just passed. It self-consciously occupies an interbellum period, a between-time indicated by the 'Prologue' and 'Epilogue' which bracket the text. In the former, a soldier who is little more than a boy returns home to an 'odd welcome' from the country he fought for, greeted not as a conquering hero but as a coward and deceiver. The poem calls up the Babylonian exile of the Old Testament (straying among green pastures and still waters) and of the foolish virgins ('unwise daughters') unprepared for the Second Coming in the New. Like one of the apostles, he carries the good news to a world ignorant of its danger (cf. Proverbs 25: xxv, 'As cold waters to a thirsty soul, so is good news from a far country'). If 'this prophet' returns in the 'Prologue' to a home where he is rejected, the 'Epilogue' shows him riding away from a doomed house, taking the Gravesian path of renunciation and exile which is the prophet's ancient prerogative.

Most of the Odes in *The Orators* take up the Psalmic impulses of 'Prologue', while Ode VI parodies the linguistic convolutions of the Scottish Metrical Psalm appropriate to the school prize day with which the book opens, mimicking the unnatural contortions demanded by a vengeful Father God. Ode V, a poem full of echoes and pastiches of Old Testament prophecy addressed 'To My Pupils', casts the latter as already ruined boys. Its imagery evokes the last war only to prefigure the next one, the youngest drummer as versed in peacetime stories of war as the oldest soldier. Brought up to pray for their Daddy fighting far away, these boys inherit war as a patrimony which cannot be renounced. The quarrel began before their time, the aggressor is no-one they know; nevertheless, they must live up to the names of the famous dead and fight without questioning. The only permitted question begs them all: whether they can be sure of passing the 'endurance test'.

Though the ode recalls that fraternisation in No-Man's-Land on the first Christmas Eve of the War, walking about on the skyline, exchanging cigarettes, exchanging phrases, it dismisses any prospect of a more than momentary truce as naivety. A 'scarecrow prophet' out of the Old Testament offers an unremitting vision of perennial misery, stretching before and after, in which the rhetorical question of the bitter psalm, 'How long shall they flourish?', answers itself. The Enemy will flourish perpetually, like the green bay tree. The boys will fight till they lie down beside the lord they have loved, and the last stanza presages the punctual restoration of hostilities, all leave cancelled. With remarkable prescience, Auden dons here the mantle of true prophet even as he warns us of its threadbare ('scarecrow') quality: the pupils addressed here, ten to twelve years old in 1930–32, came to manhood just in time to become, in 1939, conscripts to the next war.[14]

Like *The Orators'* Airman with his obsessive kleptomania, the traumatised figures of Auden's poetry are locked in compulsion repetitions which reproduce ontogenetically a phylogenetic fate. For history itself is a series of recurrences, in which each generation relives the same crisis of destruction and dispersal from which a remnant survives whose children will repeat it all again. In 'Consider this', the initially unclear antithesis between 'that distant afternoon' and 'that day / Far other' relates a quotidian history to the larger, prophetic pattern. 'That day' is far from being a casual locution: it calls up the *dies irae*, the 'days of wrath' of the Apocalypse, prefigured as 'that day' in numerous texts of Old and New

Testaments, of which Zephaniah, 1: xv, is an apposite instance: 'That day is a day of wrath, a day of trouble and distress, a day of wasteness and desolation.' D. H. Lawrence's last book, *Apocalypse*, published in 1931, was a commentary on the contemporary significance of the book of Revelation, and his *Pansies*, published in 1929, which Day Lewis claimed would elucidate 'much that is difficult in post-war poetry',[15] contains poems called 'Dies Irae' and 'Dies Illa' ('that day'), and provides, in 'To Let Go or to Hold On – ?', the image which was to haunt a generation, speaking of 'the dark flood of our day's annihilation'. For Auden, the perspectives offered by his Christian upbringing provided a narrative paradigm which underlies all these poems, facilitating an easy transition from Revelation to Revolution and back again. Already 'handsome and diseased youngsters' on that distant prize-giving afternoon before the War, the moral ruin of these boys prefigures and prepares the way for the physical devastation of 'that day' when the powerful forces latent in brutalising soils emerge into the open.

'Consider this' is a compendium of Biblical prophetic semes, from Psalm 50's vision of 'the day of trouble' (xv), with its admonition 'consider this . . . lest . . . there be none to deliver' (xxii), to II Timothy, which urges 'Consider what I say' (2: vii) and three times refers to the expected end as 'that day'. The densest cluster of allusions, however, points to the modern poet who mediates its prophetic postures. Ezekiel, whose voice Eliot mimics to admonish the 'son of man' in the opening section of *The Waste Land*, foresees that 'rumour shall be upon rumour' (7: xxvi) in the unfolding of a divine vengeance which 'will scatter toward every wind all that are about him . . . scatter them among the nations. . . . But will leave a few men of them' (12: xiv–xvi). So, in the poem, it is a rumour which, 'spreading magnified', will become a 'peril, a prodigious alarm', scattering the people in a sudden gust, from which the supreme Antagonist will summon the survivors as his chosen people. The 'haunted migratory years' of the last lines then call up an eschatology of perpetually renewed exile encompassing Old and New Testaments, in which 'That day / Far other' translates quotidian prize-giving into a cosmic event of final rewards and retributions.

Everywhere in these poems, the 'son of man' stands rebuked under the shadow of the father. The topos is established in one of the earliest of Auden's published poems, where, in spite of the 'new heroism' of adolescence, the callow young still stand in real awe of the doddering Jehovah they pretend to mock.[16] The stern patriarch is reinstated as the addressee in the last poem of *Poems*, 'Sir, no man's enemy', even as he is called on to be prodigal – a word which in its ambivalence recalls not only the generous forgiving father but also the defeated prodigal son of the New Testament parable, returning home in abjection. Ingrown virginity, a weaning which brings exhaustion not freedom, the liar's quinsy with its barely suppressed hint of Oedipal self-castration, all focus the paradoxes of a poem in which *turning* cannot be dissociated from *returning*. Though the poem attempts to move from inversion to conversion, closing the volume on the rising note of a change of heart, what it reinscribes everywhere is the patriarch's power to prohibit and correct, whose blessing is needed for that very change, and whose searchlight must be beamed on that great retreat before it can be turned round. Such salvation seems to reinstate rather than transgress the name of the father.

From the 1928 *Poems*, privately published for Auden by Stephen Spender, through the 1930 and 1933 volumes, the same impasse recurs: an urgent need to move on, go beyond, is thwarted by a neurotic arrest, flight halted even before the frontier is reached, which is intimately linked to the father/son relation. In 'Since you are going to begin today', the superannuated subject cannot abdicate (which is to say, hand over to a son–successor). This dilemma is projected onto the Enemy, the father's generation, in poem after poem. But in reality it is the deepest anxiety of the son, who can neither flee from nor finish the job he has inherited. He too will be abandoned in his turn, as his father was and as his son shall be, even though he now rejects the father's world to join the 'opposing team' (class war cast as school sports).

Within this almost gloating joy in supersession lies its contrary, a sense of being frozen, immobile, at a moment of crisis which demands action. None of these holders of one position can escape what they don't so much *hold* as are *held by*, as if in a kind of hysterical paralysis. In 'Under boughs . . .' the very rhymes and syntactical inversions of the poem enact this introverted paralysis: 'Escaping cannot try; / Must wait though it destroy'. In 'Who stands, the crux left of the watershed' the frustrate subject is turned back by a cut-off land which refuses communication. Sap rises unbaffled at the end of the poem, and the hare poises before decision; but the subject, a mere empty, indeterminate pronoun, stands baffled at the crux, unable to effect a psychological watershed. The social and the physiological parallel each other, for both are traumatised. In

another 1927 poem[17] mind reproaches body that, though often eager
to start, it equally often refused to go further. As if in ironic confir-
mation, the last line speaks of a body frozen into impotence, the jaw
unable even to reply.

The intercepted restlessness of the poem later called '1929' derives from the subject's unsureness as to whether he is one of the
chosen who will carry forward 'seed in time to display / Luxuri-
antly in a wonderful fructification', or merely part of 'a degenerate
remnant / Of something immense in the past' which now survives
only as an infectious disease. The poem speaks of a process in which
living is thinking and thinking changes living; but this positive
feedback is constantly shortcircuited in practice. Only a complete
rupture, the revolutionary 'destruction of error', offers a way forward. Once more, it is the children who are under threat. Now,
however, they, unlike their parents, have progressed to foreknow-
ledge of their fate, know even at play that 'This is the dragon's day,
the devourer's.'

The dragon of the last days (Revelation 12: iii–iv) 'stood before
the woman . . . for to devour her child as soon as it was born'; seeking to interrupt the apostolic succession of the generations, 'the
dragon . . . went to make war with the remnant of her seed' (12:
xvii). These ancient discursive lineages in '1929' are mediated by
the profane immediacies of a more recent history, in a poem whose
very title adds ten years' incremental doom to that immediately
post-bellum text, Yeats's 'Nineteen Hundred and Nineteen', where
'Now days are dragon-ridden, and the nightmare / Rides upon
sleep'. Likewise, reiterating the verb 'know' in its prophetic sense
of revealed knowledge, the poem calls up not only Eliot's ancient
Ezekiel ('for you know only / A heap of broken images') but also
his up-to-date neurotic woman ('Do you know nothing?').

Throughout the 1930s, Auden was obsessed with the idea that
knowing and doing were no longer synchronised. In the immediately preceding poem, 'Control of the passes', knowledge is value-
less without the ability to act on it. The trained spy is always-already
too late, his training unable to save him from betrayal by the old
tricks. He can't get his message through because 'They' ignore his
wires. Knowledge of what could and should be done only intensifies panic. In '1929', it may well be time for the destruction of error;
but things no longer arrive at their appointed time. Apocalypse has
long been predicted by those who, like Cassandra, can expect to be
ignored, their keener vision dismissed as sickness or insanity by the

indifferent and supercilious. '1929' struggles to find a knowledge uncorrupted by the conditions of its acquisition. In the prophetic vision, time is compacted, offering a 'forethought of death' so that, dying, we may not find ourselves 'hopelessly strange to the new conditions'. 'Finding ourselves' means also, in Pauline terms, losing ourselves.

A deep ambiguity infects the early poetry, in which the renouncing subject angrily realises his complicity with that which he rejects, and fears that even in rejection he is perpetuating it. In *The Orators*, the Enemy triumphs by infecting the Airman with his deathliness. But if the Enemy is within, then the death of the old gang means quite literally 'our death'. It is ruin itself that, following the paradox adumbrated by St Paul, Auden finds the opportunity of salvation.

Look, Stranger!,[18] that volume which dominates the middle years of the decade, constitutes in Auden's work a move from Old to New Testaments, from angry denunciation that sometimes revels in destruction to a gospel of redemption which offers a way out, looking towards the lolling bridegroom waiting, at the end of '1929', the other side of destruction, acknowledging that poem's final access of knowledge, that love 'Needs death, death of the grain, our death'. This politicised, collective 'love', which communists might call solidarity and St Paul 'charity', evokes not only contemporary revolutionary slogans but also the Pauline chiliasm of I Corinthians (15: xxxvi–xliii) in the Anglican Burial Service: 'Thou fool, that which thou sowest is not quickened, except it die . . . thou sowest not that body that shall be, but bare grain. . . . So also is the resurrection of the dead. It is sown in corruption; it is raised in incorruption. . . . It is sown in weakness; it is raised in power.' That last antithesis is central to Auden's thought.

ARDENT APOSTLES

In *Illusion and Reality*, in 1937, Christopher Caudwell cited C. G. Jung's account of a mechanism, *enantiodromia*, by which the psychological 'ruin' induced for Auden by formal schooling might be reversed in the psyche. By this mechanism, 'the development of one function at the expense of the other . . . [which] sinks into the unconscious and becomes correspondingly barbaric and crude', when carried to extremity, brings about 'a kind of conversion or complete reversal of personality, as when the cold, Christian-hating Saul becomes the ardent apostle Paul'.[19] St Paul's conversion, a frequent reference point for Jung, whose work Auden read at an early age, provides a model for a generation of revolutionary converts. Jung's *enantiodromia* is the pattern of conversion for Auden too, explaining how the subject constructed by ideology can transcend false consciousness, breadking through to a clearer perception of the real.

'Who will endure', a new poem in the 1933 edition *Poems*, is ostensibly about the impossibility of conversion. It proclaims, absolutely, that (in the words of its subsequent title) there is 'no change of place'. Significantly, however, the line's antecedents reach back to a famous convert, St Augustine ('Place is there none; we go backward and forward, and there is no place') via the state of despair of Milton's Satan in *Paradise Lost*, Book IV, lines 21–3: 'nor from Hell / One step no more than from Himself can fly / By change of place'. In the poem the son remains under the interdict of the father and his surrogate, that gamekeeper whose command to turn back dominates the poem's last verbal frontier, a secular equivalent of the angel with the flaming sword before the gates of Paradise. Unlike Augustine, saved from a life of debauch in the 'brilliant capital' of Carthage, the modern subject will never even know what (spiritual or economic?) conversion that capital awaits.

Yet the poem does imaginatively transgress these frontiers. The half-acknowledged destiny waits over the border as, in *On the Frontier* (1938), the young lovers from either side of the Ostnia–Westland frontier intuit a future which unites them even as they struggle against the hatred and narrowness of their own families and states. Even negatively, a new note is struck in that intuitive aspiration towards a 'brilliant capital' where the provincialism of the ruined boy could be transcended, if only he knew. In the sonnet sequence 'In Time of War' (later renamed 'Sonnets from China') in 1939, expulsion from Eden and the fall from animal innocence into knowledge which occasioned it are the preconditions of human evolution.[20] Coming into knowledge as if it were both birthright and curse is the motif of the poetry that follows 'Who will endure', and conversion is its figure. A 1930 review which refers to the work of W. H. R. Rivers speaks of 'the inhibition rather than the development of desires . . . their underground survival in immature forms' as 'the cause of disease, crime, and permanent fatigue', but speaks also of conversion, in terms heavily charged with Christian resonance:

The only duality is that between the whole self at different stages of development – e.g. a man before and after a religious conversion. The old life must die in giving birth to the new. That which desires life to itself . . . casts itself, like Lucifer, out of heaven.[21]

In its exploration of 'the history of knowing', '1929' had tried to work out how such a rebirth into knowledge was possible, if consciousness was totally usurped by the parental discourses. Central to the poem is the idea of a faltering. The child, weaned from its mother, leaves home, but falters, vexed, in its first steps, unable to go further. A similar thing happens in 'Taller to-day', where the peace of a prewar childhood and the present transitory 'peace' are interrupted by that War in which Captain Ferguson disappeared, one instance in a litany of ruin characterised by a faltering at the moment of breaking through to triumph.

At the centre of Auden's idea of the 'ruined boys' is a conviction that such falterings can be *educative*. Just as, in the testimony of Graves and Sassoon, shell-shock broke through the clouds of ideological unknowing to reveal the real contours of the world they had miscognised before the War, so, for Auden, trauma becomes the very ground of knowledge. This is how, in '1929', the 'finer perception' of illness and neurosis can bring insight. For madness and illness are not only symptoms but also signs (in a prophetic sense) of 'what is to be done'. In 'Psychology and Art To-day', in 1935, Auden argued that 'all illness is purposive. It is an attempt at cure. All change, either progressive or regressive, is caused by frustration or tension.'[22] In the poetry, this frustration, what '1929' calls the 'restlessness of intercepted growth', reaches such a pitch that Jung's *enantiodromia* supervenes. For Auden, psychology and art decipher 'what the impersonal unconscious is trying to tell them, and by increasing their knowledge of good and evil, to render them better able to choose, to become increasingly morally responsible for their destiny'. In that great elegy 'In Memory of Sigmund Freud',[23] in 1939, Freud's talking cure teaches the hapless subject to recite its past like a school poetry lesson until it falters at those words which point to the primal accusations, the internalised accuser and judge.

Auden's 1935 essay in *Christianity and the Social Revolution* deploys the Pauline idea of 'charity' or *caritas* as analogous to Freud's talking cure, combining teaching and loving in a carnal and material union where the 'going bad on you' of education can be transformed into grace:

What we call evil is something that was once good but has been outgrown. Ignorance begets the moralistic censor as the only means of control. Impulses which are denied expression remain undeveloped in the personal unconscious. . . . What can be loved can be cured. The two chief barriers are ignorance and fear. Ignorance must be overcome by confession – i.e. drawing attention to unnoticed parts of the field of experience; fear by the exercise of *caritas* or *eros paidogogos*.[24]

'Letter to Lord Byron' actually casts what seems to be an early homosexual encounter with a teacher as an educative experience.[25] Unlike headmasters, he says, 'little children bless your kind that knocks / Away the edifying stumbling blocks' (the phrase recalls 'the stumbling-block of their iniquity' of Ezekiel 7: xix), for disabusing rather than edification is the true path of learning: what a prep school actually teaches is 'knowledge of the world we'll soon be lost in', offering, like the Fall, an insight snatched from loss. A child, he argues elsewhere, seeks traumatic experience 'in order to find a necessity and direction for its existence, in order that its life may become a serious matter', for 'a neurosis is a guardian angel; to become ill is to take vows'.[26] Ruin is a vocation, as the poem makes clear, in a theological sense. The 'modern trick' of straightening out the psychological kinks of the young is actually harmful, creating conformity and spiritual deadness. Each child should actually be encouraged to acquire 'As much neurosis as the child can bear'. Byron, he says later, stumbled into genius because of his lame foot, and because his mother in a temper cursed him as a 'Lame Brat', for which she is to be thanked. Heaven is full of dull, perfect souls who never suffered a childish trauma: 'For no one thinks unless a complex makes him, / Or till financial ruin overtakes him.' The falterings and stumblings of ruin issue in rupture, displacement, and a new knowledge. According to a much later poem, 'A Thanksgiving', 1929 was the year when 'financial ruin', overtaking so many, found in Auden a ready pupil and convert, for, as the whole western economy crumbled, ready in waiting to instruct the liberal poet Auden was the Marxist poet Brecht.[27]

The War still haunts the poems of *Look, Stranger!*, but now they speak of it as the opportunity for knowledge, offering a way forward in the exploration of neurosis. Poem XVII condemns previous prophets who muffled their warnings in 'the common language of collective lying'. It sees the modern crisis focused in the death-wish revealed in 1914–18, society's customs hardening into the habits of death. Now, however, the war dead admit their complicity. Self-hatred, another form of the death-wish, they say, lay at the heart of their defeat, even as they played at fathers and assumed the soldier's insouciance or the heroic sexual pose for the benefit of 'the little ladies'. Their deaths were more farcical than tragic, their bravery really the insanity of those who will their own suffering. The chiming of the Priory Clock (shades of Brooke) calls the poet to return alive to his situation, his will effective and his nerves in order. 'Nerves' recalls Graves's account, in *Goodbye to All That*, of steeling himself to return to the Front. But the poem also invokes another of the illustrious dead, and a rather different emphasis, by quoting Wilfred Owen's famous phrase about his war poetry, 'The poetry is in the pity', familiarly and appropriatively referring to his homosexual predecessor only by his forename. The poem ends by refusing idleness with the Marxist axiom that men are changed by what they do. It is doing, not thinking, which brings the epistemological break. Conversion may come about through loss and anger, in which the unlucky learn to love one another in practice.

Love, that wooziest item in Auden's gospel in the 30s, is everywhere in *Look, Stranger!*, invoked in the opening line of the 'Prologue', explored in its private and collective forms in 'Out on the lawn', given a communist twist in 'Brothers, who when the sirens roar', transformed into the 'wooing poses' of dictator and demagogue in the poem later called 'A Bride in the 30s', absorbed into the combinedly Laurentian and Dantescan flood of love in 'Love had him fast'. 'May with its light behaving' explores love's relation to the death-wish in terms which transform the Miltonic expulsion from paradise (the 'dangerous apple', the real world lying before them) into Wordsworthian delight in the 'animal motions' of youth recalling 'Tintern Abbey'. Though it brings the death-wish into the world, and all our woe, love also urges a Laurentian blood-knowledge, a carnal, material doing which transcends the abstractions of look and endearment.

Learning involves unlearning too, which can come only from the moment of fall and faltering – ruin as an education. The 'Epilogue' to *Look, Stranger!* speaks of those who, unlearning hatred, have turned towards a better (implicitly socialist) world. It brings together, in this collective turning, or conversion, Groddeck, Freud and Lenin, and writers such as Lawrence, Kafka, Proust, who refused to comfort with lies, but exposed instead the shame, guilt and self-regard at the heart of bourgeois culture. Lenin, in 'Our hunting fathers', is the apostle of a love different from that which, in the patriarchs' fine tradition, rages for personal glory: a love suited instead to the intricacies of guilt, prepared for anonymity, illegality and hunger. Nevertheless, at the end of *Look, Stranger!* the cause of virtue and true knowing seems to be in shock, hearing 'the glittering / Brass of the great retreat'.

This retreat is identified in a review[28] of Liddell Hart's biography of T. E. Lawrence in the spring of 1934 as

> blind action without consideration of meaning or ends... an escape from reason and consciousness; that is indeed to become the Truly Weak Man, to enlist in the great Fascist retreat which will land us finally in the ditch of despair, to cry like Elijah: 'Lord take away my life for I am not better than my fathers.'

T. E. Lawrence, he says, has 'demonstrated the truth that action and reason are inseparable; it is only in action that reason can realise itself, and only through reason that action can become free. Consciousness necessitates more action not less, and *vice versa*.' That other Lawrence, D. H., is also invoked, to dismiss 'the Western-romantic conception of personal love [as] a neurotic symptom only inflaming our loneliness, a bad answer to our real wish to be united and rooted in life', in which 'sexual relations [only] postpone a cure'. So too, is Lenin, offering 'the way back to real intimacy ... through a kind of asceticism' in the phrases deployed in 'Our hunting fathers': 'The self must first learn to be indifferent; as Lenin said, "To go hungry, work illegally and be anonymous".' T. E. Lawrence's life is 'an allegory of the transformation of the Truly Weak Man into the Truly Strong Man, an answer to the question "How shall the self-conscious man be saved?"' He and Lenin together are 'the two whose lives exemplify most completely what is best and significant in our time, our nearest approach to a synthesis of feeling and reason, act and thought, the most potent agents of freedom and to us, egotistical underlings, the most relevant accusation and hope'.

If the doctrine of 'The Truly Strong Man' is '"absolutely modern"', it relies not only on Lenin but also on Elijah, and indeed, the allegory of conversion deploys the archetypal Christian topos of strength through weakness figured in II Corinthians 12: ix–x:

> my strength is made perfect in weakness.... Thesefore I take pleasure in my infirmities, in reproaches, in necessities, in

persecutions, in distresses for Christ's sake: for when I am weak,
then am I strong.

This brief review articulates most of the key motifs of *Look, Stranger!*.
The 'great retreat' of the 'Epilogue' involves a desire to revel in
one's sickness, as in *The Orators'* 'Letter to a Wound'. The alternative is to apply to it that surgeon's idea of pain spoken of in the
'Prologue', a surgery that is necessary and curative, wielding a
Leninist scalpel. This alternative 'fine tradition' unfolds a 'possible
dream' of salvation at odds with the dream of the fathers, who
looked down a different future. But the dream of linking the dead
in the splendid empire of Tradition now retreats into England's
'maternal shadow'. The 'great retreat' of Fascism is the last illusion
of a bourgeoisie whose demise is figured in the economic collapse
of Lancashire, Glamorgan, Dumbarton's gasping furnaces.

The 'Epilogue' speaks of this world as a place of the dead, bound
tight in hatred, where 'the wish to wound has the power'. The new
tomorrow of opening and closing poems may burst upon 'actual
History' somewhere beyond the bounds of the volume. What we
are left with, though, for all the verbal élan of *Look, Stranger!*, is the
sense that love lies bleeding from an unstaunchable wound, as in
an uncollected poem in *New Verse* in 1933, 'Deepening daily, discharging all the time / Power from love'.[29] Personal loves, lives,
hopes are here quack remedies that do more harm than good. The
wound has to deepen, the suffering intensify, before it can get better, as the ambiguity of 'discharging' suggests, for in losing power
it is also putting power into the world.

The analogy is between the new gospel of communism, a kind
of Joachite Third Testament, and the Christian gospel proclaimed
throughout Acts and Epistles. Indeed, in the *New Country* version
of another poem in *Look, Stranger!*, 'The chimneys are smoking', it
is the *communist* orator who lands at the pier, bringing a message
which strikingly recalls St Paul's mission to the unconverted. This
poem also spells out how the love of 'Our hunting fathers' can suit
itself, in this alternative patristic tradition, to the intricate ways of
guilt:

And since our desire cannot take that route which is straightest
Let us choose the crooked, so implicating these acres
These millions in whom already the wish to be one
    Like a burglar is stealthily moving.

Auden deploys here a cluster of tropes from the Epistles and Revelation. 1 Thessalonians 5: ii–iv in particular brings together many of the motifs of apocalypse ('that day') in Auden's early verse:

> For yourselves know perfectly that the day of the Lord so cometh as a thief in the night. For when they shall say, Peace and safety, then sudden destruction cometh upon them . . . and they shall not escape. But ye, brethren, are not in darkness, that that day should overtake you as a thief.

The reference to 'crooked' ways is more complex, heretically redefining Christian themes. It recurs throughout Auden's thirties writing, always in the context of a love which has to find devious routes to fulfilment. Thus, for example, in 'A Bride in the '30's', love may choose to be as 'Crooked to move as a moneybug or a cancer / Or straight as a dove'.

In 1939 a poem about Pascal spells out its theological implications. Pascal's inteligence shares the insight of the 'spoilt' and deserted child whose adolescent 'day / Of diagnosis' exposes its ruin, its talent cutting like a knife into 'the closed life the stupid never leave'. What the enlightened, disabused Pascal discovers is the intimate relation between ruin and revelation, where, in a troping of conversion as *turning*, 'The crooked custom takes its final turning / Into the truth it always meant to reach'. Sin brings forth good – a Pauline paradox Milton set out to construe in *Paradise Lost*. The last stanza of 'The chimneys are smoking' likewise resorts to Christian heresy in rationalising subterfuge as the key to survival: 'For our joy abounding is, though it hide underground', out of fear of death playing dead. This recalls the 'charity of every one of you all toward each other aboundeth' of 2 Thessalonians 1: iii (where 'charity' translates Auden's 'love' as communist solidarity). But more obviously it challenges the narrative of Romans 5: xx–6: vi, which moves from the empirical observation that 'where sin abounded, grace did more abound', to rebuke the antinomian conclusions drawn from it, 'Shall we continue in sin, that grace may abound? God forbid.'

Auden's 'communist' gospel of love in the 1930s, then, repeatedly finds its imagery and idiom in that earlier gospel, which, in an essay such as 'The Good Life', is explicitly recruited as the authentic tradition of revolt. Within this tradition, with Milton as precedent, Auden could find an eschatology in which good could come forth from the intensification of evil, salvation from ruin. For it is in the faltering of the self constructed in sin (that is, in the falsehood of bourgeois ideology) that knowledge can be found. The ruined boys of 'Consider this' lurch forward to 'that day / Far other' in which all shall be revealed and set right.

In 'September 1, 1939',[30] contemplating the final coming home to roost of a low dishonest decade, Auden discerned a continuity between the quotidian consciousness of an average day and the euphoric dream of Fascism. Both comprise an ideological stupor in which we imagine ourselves to be adults, masters, and thereby refuse to recognise that we are in reality lost children, fearing the night in a haunted wood, who have never really been good or happy. Precise scholarship, he says, may uncover the intimate relation between the larger repressions of German history since Luther and the personal defeats of what *F6* called 'the stilted schoolboy lives'; may establish what 'huge imago' gave birth to Hitler's 'psychopathic god'. But such scholarship will only tell us what we know already, what we all learn in school, that the victims of evil in time become its agents. The poem's enjambement on 'done / Do' transforms ruined boy into avenging angel, in an endless handing-on of misery. Like the naughty children lost in the wood, we are not disinterested surveyors of the human condition but simultaneously its victims and agents, perpetually renewing ruin.

In 'Now from my window-sill', in *Look, Stranger!*, Auden had looked out on New Year's Eve 1931 on the grounds of the school where he taught, hoping to journey beyond the father's long shadow, imagining, ambivalently, desire unfastened like a police dog amidst the uncertain futures of the boys in his care. Addressing the Lords of Limit, he foresees like some starving visionary the carnival of anarchy unleashed, the bodies of such father-figures kicked about the streets, only to conclude that, in our sickness, we still need the power represented by these 'Oldest of masters, whom the schoolboy fears'. History in this poem becomes some kind of final examination set by the Lords of Limit, which we all have to sit. In 1944, contemplating a second war to end all wars in which the clever hopes of another generation of ruined boys had expired, Auden retitled the poem, with a sad schoolmasterly irony, 'Not All the Candidates Pass'.

For Auden, throughout the thirties, then, to be a 'ruined boy' was a vocation, but a vocation in which, as both drunken prophet and ardent apostle, he felt obliged to understand the nature of his calling. In a 1939 poem, he was to reject the dream prototype of Napoleon, ruined boy turned patriarchal dictator, in favour of another, anonymous 'son of man', at once more knowing and more innocent, who carries in his ruin the burden but also finally the inheritance of history: that terrified imaginative child who must assume responsibility for the future he will become, whose 'weeping climbs towards your life like a vocation'.[31]

Notes

1. Cyril Connolly, *Enemies of Promise* (London: Routledge & Kegan Paul, 1938; revised edition, London: Deutsch, 1988) p. 271.
2. T. S. Eliot, *The Use of Poetry and the Use of Criticism* (London: Faber and Faber, 1933; this edition 1970) p. 69.
3. C. Day Lewis, *A Hope for Poetry* (Oxford: Blackwell, 1934) p. 4.
4. W. H. Auden, *Poems* (London: Faber and Faber, 1930; second edition 1933). Auden's prefatory note to the second edition records that he has omitted some poems from the first edition and substituted others. All poems not subsequently tagged in the present essay can be found in these volumes.
5. W. H. Auden, 'Honour', in Graham Greene (ed.), *The Old School: Essays by Divers Hands* (London: Jonathan Cape, 1934) pp. 9–20.
6. Christopher Isherwood, *Lions and Shadows* (London: The Hogarth Press, 1938; this edition, London: Methuen, 1979) pp. 157–8.
7. W. H. Auden, 'Paid on Both Sides: A Charade', in *Poems* (1930); originally published in T. S. Eliot's journal, *Criterion*, vol. IX, no. 35 (January 1930) pp. 268–90.
8. Christopher Isherwood, op. cit., pp. 46–8.
9. W. H. Auden, 'Oxford', *Another Time* (London: Faber and Faber, 1940); originally published in *The Listener* (9 February 1938).
10. W. H. Auden, *Poems* (1928), privately printed by Stephen Spender (n.p.: S. H. S., 1928) poem II.
11. Katherine Bucknell and Nicholas Jenkins (eds), *W. H. Auden: 'The Map of All My Youth', Auden Studies I* (Oxford: The Clarendon Press, 1990) p. 60.
12. W. H. Auden, 'Letter to Lord Byron', in W. H. Auden and Louis MacNeice, *Letters from Iceland* (London: Faber and Faber, 1937). The passages referred to can be found on pp. 205–8.
13. W. H. Auden, *The Orators: An English Study* (London: Faber and Faber, 1932; 2nd edition, 1934; 3rd edition, 1966); 1934 text, pp. 7, 112, 110, 103–9 passim. All Biblical references in the present essay are to *The Holy Bible, containing the Old and New Testaments . . . appointed to be read in Churches: Authorised King James Version* (London: Collins, 1953).

14. On Auden and the Larchfield School, Helensburgh, with some recollections by former pupils, see Stan Smith, 'Loyalty and Interest: Auden, Modernism, and the Politics of Pedagogy', in *Textual Practice*, vol. 4, no. 1 (Spring 1990) pp. 54–72.

15. C. Day Lewis, op. cit., p. 43.

16. W. H. Auden, *Poems* (1928), privately printed by Stephen Spender (n.p.: S. H. S., 1928) poem IV; reprinted in *Poems* (1930).

17. Ibid., poem X; reprinted in *Poems* (1930).

18. W. H. Auden, *Look, Stranger!* (London: Faber and Faber, 1936).

19. Christopher Caudwell, *Illusion and Reality* (London: Macmillan, 1937; new edn, London: Lawrence and Wishart, 1946) p. 257 ff. For a further discussion of this issue, see Stan Smith, *W. H. Auden* (Oxford: Blackwell, 1985) pp. 49–50. As I suggest there, the words 'conversion' and 'capital' in the poem 'Who will endure' are both polyvalent. I have developed this argument in Stan Smith, 'The Dating of Auden's "Who will endure" and the Politics of 1931', in *Review of English Studies*, vol. XLI, no. 163 (August 1990).

20. W. H. Auden, 'In Time of War', in W. H. Auden and Christopher Isherwood, *Journey to a War* (London: Faber and Faber, 1939) pp. 259–301.

21. W. H. Auden, review of G. B. Dibblee, *Instinct and Intuition: A Study in Mental Duality, Criterion*, vol. IX, no. 36 (April 1930) pp. 567–9.

22. W. H. Auden, 'Psychology and Art To-day', in Geoffrey Grigson (ed.), *The Arts To-day* (London: Bodley Head, 1935) pp. 1–21.

23. W. H. Auden, 'In Memory of Sigmund Freud', *Another Time* (London: Faber and Faber, 1940).

24. W. H. Auden, 'The Good Life', in John Lewis (ed.), *Christianity and the Social Revolution* (London: Victor Gollancz, 1935) pp. 31–50.

25. W. H. Auden, 'Letter to Lord Byron', in W. H. Auden and Louis MacNeice, *Letters from Iceland* (London: Faber and Faber, 1937). The passages referred to can be found on pp. 206 and 234.

26. See W. H. Auden, 'The Wandering Jew', *New Republic*, vol. CIV, no. 1367 (10 February 1941) p. 186; 'Democracy is Hard', *The Nation*, vol. CXLIX, no. 15 (7 October 1939) pp. 386 and 388.

27. W. H. Auden, 'A Thanksgiving', *Thank You, Fog* (London: Faber and Faber, 1974).

28. W. H. Auden, review of B. H. L. Hart, *T. E. Lawrence*, in *Now and Then*, vol. 47 (Spring 1934) pp. 30 and 33; reprinted in *Then and Now: A Selection . . .* (London: Jonathan Cape, 1935).

29. W. H. Auden, Five Poems, *New Verse*, no. 5 (October 1933) pp. 14–71.

30. W. H. Auden, *Another Time* (London: Faber and Faber, 1940).

31. W. H. Auden, 'Not as that dream Napoleon', ibid.; subsequently entitled 'Like a Vocation', in *Collected Shorter Poems 1930–1944* (London: Faber and Faber, 1950).

9

Alternative 'Modernists': Robert Graves and Laura Riding

JEFFREY WALSH

With the exception of a few perceptive studies, such as those by Douglas Day, Michael Kirkham and Daniel Hoffman, academics surveying twentieth-century poetry have tended to classify Robert Graves as a poet of secondary importance whose main achievement is the writing of a handful of elegant love poems.[1] The hegemony of Eliot and Pound in critical orthodoxy is, of course, principally responsible for the academy's downgrading of Graves's reputation since he is a poet of a very different kind, as also is the resistance his work throws up to fashionable belletristic categories: it is impossible, for example, to encompass his massive corpus of work within such narrow definitions as 'Georgianism' or 'anti-Modernism'. Graves, for a large part of his writing life, challenged the dominant views of the literary establishment, and is too independent a poet to be reductively pigeonholed by it.

Graves's diversity and copiousness renders his poetry impervious to facile classification, and his poetic output rivals that of Hardy and Yeats as among the most prolific of modern poets. All his professional life Graves wrote uninterruptedly to support a large family, and he continued doing so up to and throughout his seventies. One result of this fertile creativity is that any researcher of his sixty years of published poems will come up against his editorial severity; Graves frequently discarded poems that failed to satisfy him, and many poems, often admired by readers, are now out of print. Indeed, a corollary of this is that the poet's selection of his own canon is problematical, for example, his 1975 *Collected Poems*. Although Graves himself valued the poems he wrote during his last twenty-five years as equal to those of his middle period, say, from

131

1925 to 1950, an impartial reader may very well disagree with such an assessment.

In responding to Graves's substantial output, then, a thorough and wide sifting is necessary in order that a central core of representative work becomes identified. As an example of such a method of analysis, this essay seeks to study Graves's middle years by focusing on his collaboration with the American poet, Laura Riding. Inevitably any discussion of this period will involve a consideration of the intellectual relationship of the two poets to the discourse of poetic modernism because Graves is often excluded from the Modernist movement: in fact, he was well aware of the theory of poetic avant-gardism and chose consciously to depart from it.

Two recent biographies, the magisterial one by Martin Seymour-Smith, *Robert Graves: His Life and Work* (1983), and two companion volumes by Richard Perceval Graves, including *Robert Graves: The Years With Laura, 1926–40* (1990), contribute centrally to a revaluation of the poet's work, especially by reminding us of the breadth and intellectual energy of Graves.[2] It is understandable that both of these books, as they are primarily concerned with Graves, tend to present the British poet as the senior partner in the relationship, and neither considers in much depth the poetry or theory of Laura Riding, although Seymour-Smith and Perceval Graves acknowledge the range and vigour of her intellectual concerns. It is important, therefore, to recognise the influence of Riding on Robert Graves, and to understand properly why he admired her poetry and was interested in her ideas. Their collaboration in co-authoring *A Survey of Modernist Poetry* (1926) was highly effective, and this combative and well-informed book emerges, in retrospect, as a significant modernist document on a par with other key texts such as T. S. Eliot's *The Sacred Wood* or Virginia Woolf's *The Common Reader*. Through their poetic practice and by their theoretical enquiry Graves and Riding situated themselves at the centre of modernist debate about such paradoxical issues as the merits of free verse as against established metre, the roles of personality or impersonality in poetic composition, and the importance of taking into account tradition while searching for relevant and progressive verse forms.

Graves's biographers testify to the force of Riding's personality and suggest that her commitment to poetry matched his own: more importantly she complemented the British poet's growing interest in some of the younger American poets, such as John Crowe Ransom and e. e. cummings. Riding had for a short time been a contributing

member of the southern group of US poets known as the Fugi-
tives, whose number included Allen Tate, Donald Davidson, John
Crowe Ransom, Hart Crane and Harriet Monroe. In a critical account of Riding's life and work, Joyce Piell Wexler, in *Laura Riding's
Pursuit of Truth* (1979), describes Riding's association with the Fu-
gitives, and her belief that a new kind of poetry, taking account of
the breakdown of established communal values, should symbolise
'peace and reconciliation between the inner nature of a man and the
external world without him'.[3] Riding's own poems of this period,
which she later came to feel were over-personal, were brought together in her first collection when she was twenty-five, *The Close
Chaplet of Thought* (1926). In the Carcanet revised edition of her 1938
collection, *The Poems of Laura Riding* (1980), many of these poems
are more accessibly gathered together in the section entitled 'Poems
of Mythical Occasion'.[4] They are an impressive achievement, and
such poems as 'Because I Sit Here So', 'The Mask', 'The Signature',
'Chrysalis', 'So Slight', 'The Tillaquills', 'Take Hands', 'Lucrece and
Nara', 'Mortal', 'The Quids', 'As Well As Any Other' and the two
Helen poems, 'Helen's Burning' and 'Helen's Faces', have a lyrical
harmony, grace and idealism that she rarely attained in her suc-
ceeding work. Her later poetry demonstrated a more abstract set of
interests and was infused with the passionate intellection that so
often intimidated visitors to Deya.

It is easy to see how Graves, who was in 1926 an established
poet with several collections of poetry behind him, could admire
a poem with the exquisite tact and delicacy of 'As Well As Any
Other', which includes the lines,

> As well as any other, Erato,
> I can dwell separately on what we know
> In common secrecy,
> And celebrate the old, adoréd rose,
> Retell – oh why – how similarly grows
> The last leaf of the tree.
>
> (p. 54)

Riding's poems in *The Close Chaplet* are the equivalent of her own
songs of innocence; they signify the virginal, chrysalis world of true
and constant love, a region illuminated by pastoral myth and with
the potential for transcendent joy. Although there are poems that
hint at lovelessness and lack of faith, her poems of this period lack

overall the angst, cynicism and sense of betrayal that her later work shows, after her suicide attempt and what she considered to be her abandonment by Geoffrey Phibbs, her lover and Graves's friend. Typical of the unified world view evident in *The Close Chaplet of Thought* is 'Lucrece and Nara', which suggests that earthly lovers can partake mysteriously of the timeless devotion of the mythical pair who remain,

> True to their fading,
> (p. 36)

Like other poems in the volume, 'Lucrece and Nara' treads a line between romantic naivety and eloquent stylisation of direct feeling. At her best, Riding enunciates a control of emotional expression rarely surpassed in twentieth-century love poetry, as in the soulful lyric of past love, 'So Slight'. By means of assonance, vowel colouring and an expressive rhythm of falling cadences, a mixed mood of regret and acceptance is hauntingly communicated which wistfully celebrates the vanished affair,

> Such faint rebellion
> Was lately love in me.
> (p. 33)

Such verbal felicities and restrained evocation of the beauty of natural phenomena are explicitly rejected in Riding's later work, which is far tougher, less romanticist in tone and more philosophically probing and precise.

In one of her finest short poems, 'There is Much at Work' from a later volume, she explicitly dismisses her earlier representation of multiple beauties in such acerbic lines as,

> There is much at work to make the world
> Surer by being more beautiful.
> But too many beauties overwhelm the proof.
> Too much beauty is Lethe
>
> (p. 79)

After writing the poems which appeared in *The Close Chaplet of Thought*, Laura Riding experimented widely in poetic forms and styles until she renounced poetry in 1940. More so than Robert

Graves she followed the twin modernist creeds of 'make it new' and 'make it difficult'.

If there is a common concern which is found throughout all of her mature work it is the disciplined task she undertook to find her own voice and to define her own complex vision as a woman poet. A large proportion of her poems are written in an interrogative form, and often utilise a literal question and answer format. She is especially concerned to understand her own core of selfhood, as in, for example, 'I Am', 'As many Questions as Answers' or 'And I'. Continually searching for her experiential identity, she associates it with three areas of her life: her destiny as a poet, her self-statement as a woman, and her renunciation of sex and the old smiling accoutrements of romantic love.

A series of poems address the problematical issue of using words poetically to refine meaning, for example, 'Hospitality to Words', 'The Troubles of a Book', 'The Courtesies of Authorship', and perhaps the most interesting of all, 'As To A Frontispiece'. The latter poem is part of an imaginary dialogue between the poet and a reader or patron who wishes to commission a text which will illustrate verbally the features shown in a portrait. The poet rejects such limitations, and instead offers an autonomous poem that transcends any frontispiece: the poem, as in all of Riding's statements about poetry, is an ideal construct, a visionary offering demanding literacy and close reading. To read poetry, the reader is obliged to give all of his attention entirely without preconceptions.

After the poem has been read intensely, then a shared process of constructing identity is possible because its words are subsequently alive and will continue to live in language.

A case could be made out that Laura Riding espouses in her work feminist causes. Her early humorous poem 'The Tiger' asserts women's independence, and acknowledges the 'inner animal', the tiger that every woman cages 'inside her lofty head'. In this poem the menacing tiger woman, proud, cognizant of 'abolished pleasures', is appropriated by pursuing men, mischievous rapists, and she formally chooses to conform socially to 'sanctioned' feminine roles as shepherdess or ladylike Queen. 'The Tiger' concludes with images of woman lamenting the concealment of her tigerly self. In less overt form the psychological conflict between men and women as expressed from the woman's point of view is also found throughout other poems of a less mythical and popular kind. 'The Biography

of a Myth' is a particularly interesting, although difficult, example
of such an exploration. In common with 'The Tiger' it represents
woman's role-playing in order to accommodate men's voyeuristic
desires. A similar poem, less sophisticated but slightly more polem-
ical in its investigation of male dominant specularity, is 'Auspice of
Jewels',

In its penultimate passage 'Auspice of Jewels' envisions a trium-
phant womankind which has passed 'into total rareness' and is
'otherwise luminous'. Riding's witty elaboration of the jewel metaphor finds space at the end to include, with diminutive irony, men
who are trying to put the clock back. The women are ultimately
attended by 'restless knights' who urge 'the adventure past return'.
Women, the poem implies, can do without the adornment of trin-
kets, and can recapture a striking otherness of beauty, one free from
the taint of maleness.

Laura Riding developed through her poetry and prose an ethical
system that rejected conventional romantic love, affirmed celibacy
and eschewed sexual stereotyping of women. Her philosophical
starting point is the pain she suffered after her suicide attempt,
when she begins to record her subsequent efforts at reordering her
life. Through such representations she frequently transcends the
stigma of victimisation, gaining in the process moral poise. In such
a category fit a series of poems like 'An Ageless Brow', 'Then
Wherefore Death', 'Death as Death', 'After So Much Loss', the long
allegorical poem, 'Then Follows', and the short, haunting lyric,
'Celebration of Failure', which includes the recuperative lines,

> Through pain the land of pain
> Through tender exiguity
> Through cruel self-suspicion:
> Thus came I to this inch of wholeness.
>
> (p. 132)

As here indicated, Riding wore the poetic mask of survivor proudly
in much of her work, a position which contributed experientially to
the development of her vocabulary and sources of imagery. This
linguistically hard edge was complemented by her fondness for
joking, for riddles, word play and surreal comedy as demonstrated
in *Poems: A Joking Word* (1930).

Towards her own earlier idealisation of romantic love, and especially those amorous relationships which involved womanly sub-

mission, she maintained an adverse critical posture. At least four poems, for example, express a tough-minded dismissal of unreal sentimentality and her former indulgence in the traditional niceties of sexual love; these are 'Rhythms of Love', originally entitled 'Love as Love' (1928), 'When Love Becomes Words', 'In Due Form', and the ideologically confident, 'After Smiling'. In these poems, and in others that are closely related in substance and mode, such as 'The Definition of Love' or 'Memory of Mortalities', the clichés of love poetry are deconstructed. For example, 'In Due Form' playfully prefers a tangible manifestation of love to fanciful notions; 'Rhythms of Love' explores through ironic counterpointing the banal, often foolish behaviour that inevitably characterises a relationship; and 'When Love Becomes Words' theorises about the nature and consequences of sexual abstinence.

Critics have frequently found Riding's work conceptually opaque and abstract, yet her intelligent and ebullient manner can often explore psychological truths in an unremittingly honest way. One of her most interesting and complex poems, 'After Smiling', functions in this way. Ostensibly the poem illustrates, as do many of her others, how Riding and Robert Graves adjusted to each other personally and creatively over a period of years. Essentially it dramatises the proposition that men and women (using the model of herself and Graves) are fighters who must necessarily engage in psychological conflict, but who are equally as capable of a glorious compatiblility once rivalry is acknowledged. The opening lines of 'After Smiling' convey well the poem's querulous, pugnacious tone; the speaker argues, in effect, for a reversal of 'complaisance' and its replacement by a more hard-headed acceptance of woman's continuing quarrels that must rage with man,

> Now not to smile again.
> Those years of softening
> To this one and to that one
> Because the body has a meaning
> Of defeat and dread unless
> It advertises cheerfulness –
> Those years of life-feigning are done.
>
> (p. 185)

Interweaving a pattern of metaphor derived from warfare, conquest and mutual detente, 'After Smiling' innovates linguistically in grammar, syntax and vocabulary: its rhythms are flexible and alternating, creating a witty mobility of tone which irreverently undermines staidness and social orthodoxy.

'After Smiling', through its robustness, attests to the force of Riding's personality, a quality that appealed to Graves, who enjoyed being dominated by women. Her restless energy also fascinated him: Riding, as her fiction *Progress of Stories* (1935) and *Lives of Wives* (1939) demonstrates, was exceedingly inventive and interested in formal experiment. She did not flinch from extraordinarily ambitious projects such as *Epilogue*, the review journal she edited which addressed issues of major historical and philosophical significance. Clearly her avant-gardism exposed Graves to what we should today, with hindsight, describe as high modernism: it challenged him to clarify his own artistic procedures in relation to the new practice.

Graves, though, has some claims to be part of modernist culture himself. Before he met Riding he had shown an interest in psychology and the processes of the unconscious mind, and his early books, *On English Poetry* (1992) and *Poetic Unreason* (1925) theorise about the interrelations between the production of and responses towards poetry and underlying neurotic and hypnotic states. Graves was interested in the work of W. H. R. Rivers, who had treated cases of neurasthenia, and he explores how poetry often derives from pressing emotional problems. He argues that poetic images defy logical explanation, share common features with dreams, and are related culturally to older anthropological memories. Although both of these treatises, *On English Poetry* and *Poetic Unreason*, are unsystematic (they do not, for example, exemplify a coherent knowledge of Freud's theories), they are nevertheless pioneering investigations into the latent rhythmical and structural effects of language.

Neither of the two earlier hypotheses possess the excellence or sophistication of *A Survey of Modernist Poetry* (1926), a classic that greatly influenced the growth of both Empsonian analysis and New Criticism.[5] *A Survey of Modernist Poetry*, as its title suggests, examines the work of a wide range of contemporary poets, including T. S. Eliot, Yeats, Pound, e. e. cummings, John Crowe Ransom, Allen Tate, Hart Crane, the Sitwells, William Carlos Williams, Wallace Stevens, Richard Aldington, Carl Sandburg, John Drinkwater and Gertrude Stein. The quality of these contemporaries is measured against the integrity, or lack of it, shown by such earlier poets as Milton, Wordsworth, Shelley, Browning, Bridges or Gerard Manley Hopkins.

The quirky connecting hypothesis that identifies a 'genuine modernism' within the dross of the 'false variety' is supported by ingenious and highly original linguistic analysis, sometimes dazzling in its inventiveness. e. e. cummings is frequently adduced in order to serve as a model of a fresh and innovative poet who breaks with conventional metre and regularity of form. Perhaps the most acclaimed section of *A Survey* is the seminal analysis of Shakespeare's sonnet, 'The expense of Spirit in a waste of shame', which defends the primary text over later versions as being true to Shakespeare's punctuation and syntax. The witty and erudite discussion of this sonnet, together with cogent and subtle analyses of other poems such as T. S. Eliot's 'Burbank with a Baedeker: Bleistein with a Cigar', influenced William Empson, who put it to famous use in his *'Seven Types of Ambiguity'* (1930). Graves and Riding can legitimately be regarded as the pioneers of New Criticism as practised by Wimsatt, Frye and Brooks and their followers, and also the progenitors of 'prac. crit'. Certainly the spirit of *A Survey* emphasises the autonomy of the poem as verbal artefact. Graves and Riding argue for self-referentiality and autotelic poems. The genuine modernist poem is not dependent upon how successfully it reflects or translates external particulars; on the contrary it is free-standing, capable of generating its own meanings, which do not need to be validated by context or contingent circumstances,

> The ideal modernist poem is its own clearest, fullest and most accurate meaning. Therefore the modernist poet does not have to talk about the use of images 'to render particulars exactly', since the poem does not give a rendering of a poetical picture or idea existing outside the poem, but presents the literal substance of poetry, a newly created thought-activity: the poem has the character of a creature by itself.   (p. 118)

This passage is at the heart of Graves's and Riding's argument, and illuminates well their own imperatives. It distinguishes between a factitious poem that is full of topical reference and simply mirrors what is 'historically new', and a more profound work of 'a new and original kind' where the poet is not merely a 'servant and interpreter of civilisation'. Their own work aspired to transcend the immediate occasion and thereby relate to wider time scales. This stance, consciously held by Graves and Riding, in their own opinion differentiated them from the thirties poets, Auden, Spender, Day Lewis who were content merely to record events of the present.

Quite often *A Survey* displays attitudes that are recognisably modernist. In the matter of the independence of the poem as text from the personality of the poet who created it, Graves and Riding are not far removed from T. S. Eliot's celebrated doctrine of 'impersonality': they dismiss the 'dead movements' of Anglo-Irish Romanticism, Imagism and Georgianism which fostered the cult of the poet. The modernist poet should be invisible:

> He does not have to describe or docket himself for the reader, because the important part of poetry is not the personality of the poet as embodied in a poem, which is its style, but the personality of the poem itself, that is, its quality of independence from both the reader and the poet, once the poet has separated it from his personality by making it complete – a new and self-explanatory creature.
>
> Perhaps more than anything else characteristic modernist poetry is a declaration of the independence of the poem. This means first of all a change in the poet's attitude toward the poem: a new sense has arisen of the poem's rights comparable with the new sense in modern times of the independence of the child, and a new respect for the originality of the poem as for the originality of the child.   (p. 124)

Towards tradition, the living presence of past poetry, *A Survey* discriminates between fresh poetry such as the intelligent work of Shakespeare and 'dead poetry' such as the pontifications of Tennyson during his most sage-like posturings. If older poetry fulfils the criteria of displaying integrity, having an 'intellectual slant', and showing 'simplicity and naturalness' even in difficult references, then it possesses modernist credentials; 'Most of all, such poetry would be characterised by a lack of strain, by an intelligent ease.'

During the years 1929 to 1940, when he worked closely with Laura Riding, Robert Graves was at the height of his powers, and wrote the majority of his finest poems, all of which he submitted to her for critical approval. It is likely that her subtle intelligence and technical craft as a practising poet contributed to the intellectual coherence and sophistication of his work published during this period. In general, his work at this time displayed a robustness and urbane control that it frequently lacked later when he wrote his White Goddess sequences or his idealised celebrations of women as Muses.

For convenient analysis, the seventy or so poems included in his 1975 *Collected Poems*, dating from 1929 to 1940, may be thematically grouped into those treating six recurrent concerns: the body's needs and desires; the vagaries of love; poetic truth and falsehood; the significance of cultural tradition; fulfilment in love; and the moral state of England. A discussion of these six problematical issues, exemplified by close textual analysis of key poems, will be undertaken during the remainder of this chapter, as will Graves's ambiguous relationship to modernist practice and theory.

The pressures of male sexuality, whether expressed as lust or as manifestations of unconscious instincts and desires, are explored in such poems as 'Trudge Body', 'Down, Wanton, Down!', 'The Succubus', 'Leda', 'A Jealous Man' and the much-praised 'Ulysses'. In representing disparity between the physical nature of the sex act and the sought after perfection of love Graves wrote some of the most effective anti-phallic, 'Freudian' poems of the century. 'The Succubus', for example, illustrates the contradictions of physical love: carnal desire brings the reality of a woman, 'gulping away your soul, she lies so close', instead of 'longed for' 'beauty' of male fantasy. Graves, so fastidious of temperament, offers in this poem more than a hint of distaste. Sexual fantasy is represented as animalistic, the poet's 'ecstasy of nightmare' conjures forth a 'devil woman'. A similar theme is treated more elegantly in the Rochester-like 'Down, Wanton, Down!', the poet's eloquent priapic conceit.

In classic quatrains, underscored by a loose patterning of iambic metre and regular, formal rhyme, 'Down, Wanton, Down!' commingles apostrophe and questioning in almost equal measure. Its tone, a mixture of pride at his virility yet interspersed with mock-shame, creates a poised detachment. 'Down, Wanton, Down!' shows Graves at his best, controlled and witty, offsetting the vocabulary of courtly love against such clichés as 'rule of thumb' or 'love may be blind', as in the concluding lines,

> Will many-gifted Beauty come
> Bowing to your bald rule of thumb,
> Or Love swear loyalty to your crown?
> Be gone, have done! Down, wanton, Down!
>
> (p. 78)

Wryness, cynicism, and hauteur inform the aristocratic mode of this playful reproach which displays a mock-heroic edge of characteristic audacity. 'Down, Wanton, Down!' is effective because of its urbane treatment of a taboo subject, a description that might equally be applied to 'Ulysses'.

In this poem Graves transforms the Ulysses myth into a fable of sexual compulsion. The mythical imagination found throughout the poet's work accords the poem an assurance in narrating the hero's fruitless search for an equilibrium between love and sexual satisfaction. Ulysses's quest is doomed to failure because it is a self-destructive one: the danger he faces compounds his inner restlessness: he is not merely storm-tossed but 'love-tossed', tormented by the raging currents of the flesh, as in the fourth stanza,

> One, two and many: flesh had made him blind,
>   Flesh had one pleasure only in the act,
> Flesh set one purpose only in the mind –
> Triumph of flesh and afterwards to find
>   Still those same terrors wherewith flesh was racked.
>
>   (p. 56)

The rhythmical and lexical repetitions here apparent suggest the frenetic state of his mind. Ulysses, the poem implies, is a man fatally attracted to women and yet one for whom sexual contact is unfulfilling because 'he loathed the fraud, yet would not bed alone'. By formal management of mobile syntax and a regular rhyme scheme, 'Ulysses', in the manner of Graves's historical novels, skilfully punctures an established myth, deconstructing earlier stereotypes such as the Tennysonian one. Its imagery of disillusionment and its metrical compactness, especially appropriate in a poem concerned with a combative hero, extends to related poems that explore the inconstancy of love and sexual betrayal.

Notable among this category of poems are 'Sick Love', 'The Foreboding', 'Never Such Love', 'At First Sight', 'With her Lips Only' and 'A Former Attachment'. All of these poems display a scepticism towards conventional romantic or marital love, a recognition of faithlessness, deceit and the inevitability of passion's end. Perhaps the most cogent poetic expression of such attitudes occurs in the widely anthologised poems, 'Never Such Love' and 'With Her Lips Only'. 'Never Such Love' is one of the great poems about love in the English language, affirming silence and restraint against verbal protestations of enduring commitment, which are represented as illusory given the heart's inconstancy.

The fatalism of 'Never Such Love' (expressed through the rhythmic conduits of assonance or internal rhyme) is paralleled in 'With Her Lips Only', which portrays a wife who desires her lover for the sake of her children and remains trapped in a loveless marriage bed. The themes of repression, sexual despair and the corruption of love are also treated in 'Sick Love' and 'The Foreboding'.

The latter, a visionary poem, describes how the poet prophetically sees himself in a distraught condition, death-like and abandoned by his beloved. He has written her name, and awaits in his 'unkempt' and 'abstracted' state her inexorable betrayal with its accompanying pain. 'The Foreboding' lacks the impersonal power of 'Sick Love' because of its masochistic and self-pitying resonances. 'Sick love' registers an altogether more widely symbolic premonition by elaborating ironically upon the traditional *Carpe Diem* motif. Gathering rosebuds is envisioned here not as a youthful diversion, but as a temporary state before the destructiveness of the unconscious is unleashed. The 'smiling innocent' exists only in 'listening horror for the cry / That soars in outer blackness dismally'. The regality of spiritual love, it is implied, will lead, through 'tainted blood', to death of the spirit; the lovers, therefore, inhabit, '. . . a shining space / With the grave's narrowness, though not its peace' (p. 49). This concluding image, reminiscent of Marvell, is wholly typical of the contrasting phraseology deployed in 'Sick Love' whereby such rhetorically elevated phases as 'royal array' or 'heavenly causeway' are undercut linguistically by the vocabulary of madness, 'the dumb blind beast, the paranoiac fury'. In 'Sick Love' duality goes beyond the usual mind–body separation to prevision degeneration and insanity. The body's gross domination of the higher aspirations of love is signified through the poem's air of menace. Other poems of this period, though, explore more hopeful themes, none more so than when Graves addresses the role of the poet and the social function of poetry.

Writerly independence and poetry's ability to reveal unique truths preoccupied him throughout the late twenties and all of the thirties, as, indeed, they did for the whole of his life. In a series of poems, he treated the falsehoods of the impure poet, critic or dilettante, who all shamed genuine creativity. In 'Any Honest Housewife', for example, a case is made out for empirical discrimination between 'the workers' and their opposite, 'the lazy, the liars and the petty thieves'. Behind this poem stands Graves's conviction that meretricious and fake poets are easy to detect,

Is it any mystery who are the sound,
And who the rotten? . . .

(p. 89)

We may legitimately surmise (from the tone of parts of *A Survey* where he dismisses, for example, Wallace Stevens, William Carlos Williams and some of the Georgians) exactly what he had in mind. He expresses contempt for misuse of language in 'Hell'; for cocksure rationalists, 'In Broken Images'; and attacks in 'The Laureate' a burned out poet who stays a nuisance. 'The Laureate' also draws upon the symbolism of a lizard to suggest the arid nature of the sterile ex-poet. In contradistinction to such negative renderings are those poems which espouse the cause of inspirational poetry, such poems as 'Ogres and Pygmies', 'Flying-Crooked', 'The Reader Over My Shoulder', 'The Devil's Advice to Story-Tellers', and 'Gardener'. In all of these the autonomy of the poet and the poem is affirmed. In 'Flying-Crooked' and 'Gardener' the poet is likened to an intuitive creator and nurturer; in 'The Devil's Advice' art is associated with the humanly erratic and contradictory.

'Ogres and Pygmies' and, to a lesser degree, 'The Reader Over My Shoulder' somewhat romantically discriminate between the reader and the critic and, on the other hand, the wild, creative spirit of the artist. (Graves's lifelong infatuation with the conception of the poetic muse as inspiration situates him broadly within the Romantic legacy.) A vigorous exposition of the doctrine is expounded in 'Ogres and Pygmies', which exalts the redblooded poets (the Ogres), together with their gargantuan behaviour, and concludes by scorning the literary critic (the Pygmy). The 'thunderous' power of the text dwarfs the 'snivelling commentary'. In 'Ogres and Pygmies' fairy-tale connotations suggest a cultural traditionalism that is replicated throughout Graves's work, and is a relevant factor in evaluating his attunement or otherwise to the prevailing poetic orthodoxies of twentieth-century British poetry.

Valuing clarity, intelligent ease, lack of strain and pretence, Graves looked to a sturdy pragmatism in responding to social and cultural matters. Experience was called upon to legitimate ethical conduct, and to supply a straightforward test and guide for action. In particular he celebrates the concepts of moral independence, intellectual autonomy, affectionate rebellion against family and ancestors, and the emotional power of trusted friendship. Such attitudes draw heavily upon the imperatives of common sense and personal judgement; as a set of ideas they lack the consistency of, say, T. S. Eliot's high-church anglicanism or the socialism of certain thirties poets. Graves is open to the criticism of quirkiness or prejudice, but such a stance was poetically necessary to him albeit smacking of random empiricism. Generally speaking, he fostered his own separateness from grand theories, and preferred to rely upon his individual opinions of persons or social issues. Such judgements, although occasionally extreme, were underpinned by a life of intellectual enquiry.

In such poems as 'Front Door Soliloquy', 'William Brazier', 'To Evoke Posterity', 'The Advocates' and 'The Great-Grandmother' the humanising values of tradition and cultural connectedness are evaluated. Most powerful of these is 'The Great-Grandmother', a poem which communicates in sophisticated and trenchant fashion a deconstruction of patriarchal values and symbolic systems. The 'aged woman' who was 'honest with herself' lived a conformist life, in accord with gender stereotypes of good wife and mother, yet nurtured a core of feminist selfhood, a 'hard heart', secretly resentful of female role-playing. The great-grandmother conceals a 'wrathful irony' which can now at last be exorcised through disclosure to her great-grandchildren. The poem, said by Martin Seymour-Smith to be a barbed but respectful tribute to Laura Riding,[6] is one of Graves's best, tinctured with unsentimental irony and subversive, warning cadences particularly evident in the resonant conclusion.

The acute free-verse form of 'The Great-Grandmother' contributes effectively to its presentation of the oracular woman, confident at last in the open pleasure of her womanly desire.

It is, in an arcane way, an oblique love poem, and Graves did write love poems to Riding. There is justice in the view that Robert Graves is perhaps the finest English love poet of the century, whose love poems are ingenious, resourceful and often audaciously modulated. Poems written to Laura Riding have a claim to be considered among his most subtly disciplined and tactful, especially 'On Portents', 'The Terraced Valley', 'The Chink' and 'No More Ghosts'. All of these works resist verbal excess through their quality of intellectualism: structural tension and linguistic restraint also assist in the articulation of passionate feeling. 'On Portents', often said to be a prototype White Goddess poem, typifies the group of love poems, including also 'Lovers in Winter', 'New Legends' and 'Like Snow', which communicate Graves's love for his fellow poet. It is a poem that sets Riding at a distance, its tone seeming to include a frisson of awe and psychic bondage,

If strange things happen where she is,
(p. 107)

In such poems as 'The Chink' and the more complex, 'The Terraced Valley', Graves practised several of the ideas formulated in *A
Survey of Modernist Poetry*. Poems should be civilised, urbane and
well-proportioned, free from narrow prescriptiveness. On the whole
Graves preferred 'clearness and restraint and proportion' to con-
temporaneity or obscurity flaunted for their own sake.[7] He argued
that even traditional-sounding poetry could be 'progressive' in its
own way, providing that it demonstrated integrity and genuine
creativity. Such a premise underlies 'The Chink', a sophisticated
love poem that recalls the resourceful stretching of intellectual
conceits often found in Metaphysical verse.

'The Chink' is based upon the analogy between a sunbeam pen-
etrating a darkened hall and the speaker's wish that his love will
break through into his lover's 'grief-occluded' mind. The suggestion is that, nature triumphs over culture; once through the chink
it floods the darkness with light. The images of transformation,
perfectibility and active natural joy in 'swims' are gracefully subsumed in the linking metaphors of fertility and power. The chink is
penetrated; the sunbeam is both fertilised by the 'well waxed oak'
and disseminates its power, becoming an agent of reproduction,
'The sun's plenipotentiary'. It is an astonishingly poised poem combining sexual desire and need, in verse one, with intellectual need,
in verse two. The lover seeks entry into his beloved's mind, not her
body, but the parenthetical 'rising' implies his physical urgency in
the concluding line,

But, rising, open to me for truth's sake.
(p. 108)

The speculative power of mind is thus allied in 'The Chink' to an
underlying repressed passion. The poem's high degree of formal-
ity and purity of diction, its overall elegance, permits aspects of
the unconscious to surface: imagery of entered houses, swimming
sunbeams and 'ragged chinks' circumvent the possibilities of vul-
gar naming (of wombs, vaginas and seminal fluid, for example)
because of rhythmic dignity and balanced language use.

Although it lacks the stylisation and concealed artifice of 'The
Chink', Graves's other great poem of this period, 'The Terraced

Valley', originally published in *Poems 1926–30*, exhibits an identical speculative power. In his study of Graves's work Michael Kirkham has reported Charles Tomlinson's admiration for the older poet and also Tomlinson's criticism that Graves usually refrains from exploring the full implications of the experiences he treats.[8] 'The Terraced Valley' surely transcends any tendency to oversimplify experience: it is a poem that amply repays dense verbal analysis of the Empsonian kind.

'The Terraced Valley' relates what has come to be termed in modernist discourse, an epiphany, whereby processes of mental discovery find significant outlet. The poem focalises how the lover temporarily finds himself cut off from his beloved in a way that reminds us of the primal experience of losing one's mother for a short period of time and then joyfully finding her again. The poet reports his almost visionary experience of being caught in a 'counter earth' of contraries and paradoxes where mystical things happen: the sky and horizon disappear, the left-hand glove slides easily onto the right hand, and out of doors is heard the domestic 'singing of kettles'. The sophisticated manoeuvring of the poet's voice registers the dance of opposites and vocalises the beloved's absence,

> Neat outside-inside, neat below-above,
> Hermaphrodizing love.
> Neat this-way-that-way and without mistake:
>   (p. 107)

It is interesting to compare these lines, which convey in dialectical fashion the collision of antitheses, with, say, a passage from Eliot's *The Waste Land* or *Prufrock*. Graves is here successful in communicating a sense of emotional confusion through his enunciation of contradiction; his imagery, though, lacks the auditory or visual precision of Eliot's. A phrase such as 'hermaphrodizing love' essentially appeals to the reader's intellect, as does the image of the shell delivering the young snake. Whereas the passage from *The Waste Land* describing the loveless encounter between the house agent's clerk and the secretary gains its impact from allusion, explicitness and ironic juxtaposition of the seedily tactile present and the glorious literary past, Graves's language is less innovative. 'Hermaphrodizing love' is an inventive usage, suggesting castration and androgyny, yet does not have the topicality or ironising potential of Eliot's somewhat voyeuristic passage. 'The Terraced

Valley', commingling clarity and nebulousness, hints at sexual potency in tactful images of snake's eggs, kettles and the drawing on of gloves. It ends with a reversal or peripeteia when the lover's voice resolves his little-boy-lost situation, when he 'cried disconsolately', and 'broke' the 'trick' that time had played upon him. As Michael Kirkham has noted, 'The Terraced Valley' manifests a particularly felicitous verse form, intricate yet relaxed, expressive of the modernist ideal sought for in *A Survey*.[9] Graves, commenting on a passage from the Bible, might have been describing the effect of his own poem, 'The effect of regularity is here again achieved by the recurrence of ideas in varying alternations to show the movement of the poem'.[10] Graves's method, in central ways, differs from Eliot's perhaps in some deeply cultural sense hinting at a British reserve which contrasted with Eliot's characteristically American willingness to experiment. Although Graves has Irish and German strains in his family tree, he thought of himself as a British poet and wrote broadly within such cultural traditions.

In the 1980s, when conceptions of Britishness have been ideologically foregrounded (for example during and after the Falkland's war) Graves's poetic encoding of what it is to be culturally 'British' is especially interesting. Like Graham Greene or Evelyn Waugh or W. H. Auden's visions of Britishness, Graves's is necessarily a personal and class-defined one. He was frequently attacked for seeming in his work to be isolated from many of the important political and historical events of his time, yet had close experience of war and of such evils as Fascism.[11] It is perhaps understandable to think of such poets as Auden, Spender or Day Lewis when considering the poetic representation of social and cultural issues during the interwar years. However, as Martin Seymour-Smith has shown, Graves, in such poems as 'The Fallen Tower of Siloam', effectively treats the historical dilemmas of his time in obliquely coded and mythical fashion.[12] Paralleling the Modernists' visions of apocalypse, Graves articulates a sense that materialism and corruption lie at the heart of the British Empire. 'The Cuirassiers of the Frontier', for example, contrasts the integrity of the honest soldiers at the perimeter with the decadence of organised religion and spurious patriotism.

It is possible to read 'The Cuirassiers of the Frontier', therefore, as a critique of imperialism, especially shaped by its opening lines,

Goths, Vandals, Huns, Isaurian mountaineers,
Made Roman by our Roman sacrament,

We can know little (as we care little)
Of the Metropolis ...

(p. 91)

Graves's position, as evident here, is to celebrate the pride of the
exile (as in 'The Cloak'), to refrain from meaningless poetic gestures
(which is the sub-theme of 'The Fallen Tower of Siloam') and to
confront proudly the values of cultural inheritance, which forms
the theme of 'A Country Mansion'.

In 'A Country Mansion' Graves's favourite country-house symbolism suggests the ties and family customs of the British tradition.
In expansive unrhymed quatrains the poem's speaker ranges over
the house's history in a tone that is at times affectionate and celeb-
ratory, as in the pivotal stanzas,

A smell of mould from loft to cellar,
Yet sap still brisk in the oak
Of the great beams: if ever they use a saw
It will stain, as cutting a branch from a green tree.

(p. 102)

These lines can be justly praised for their resonance of hope, and
for their affirmation of living communal values. Not a bad model
for these divided times.

Notes

1. Douglas Day, *Swifter Than Reason: The Poetry and Criticism of Robert Graves* (Chapel Hill: University of North Carolina Press, 1963). Michael Kirkham, *The Poetry of Robert Graves* (London: University of London, Athlone Press, 1969). David G. Hoffman, *Barbarous Knowledge: Myth in the Poetry of Yeats, Graves and Muir* (London: Oxford University Press, 1967).

2. Martin Seymour-Smith, *Robert Graves: His Life and Work* (London: Abacus, Sphere Books Limited, 1983). Richard Perceval Graves, *Robert Graves: The Years with Laura, 1926–40* (London: Weidenfeld and Nicolson, 1990).

3. Quoted in Joyce Piell Wexler, *Laura Riding's Pursuit of Truth* (Athens, Ohio: Ohio University Press, 1979) p. 12.

4. Laura (Riding) Jackson, *The Poems of Laura Riding; A New Edition of*

the 1938 Collection (Manchester: Carcanet New Press, 1980). All quotations from Laura Riding's poems are taken from this edition, and page numbers are indicated in parentheses.

5.   Laura Riding and Robert Graves, *A Survey of Modernist Poetry* (New York: Haskell House Publishers Limited, 1969). [The original publication was 1927, London: Heinemann.] Quotations are from the 1969 edition, with page numbers indicated in parentheses.

6.   Seymour-Smith, op. cit., p. 305.

7.   Graves and Riding, op. cit., p. 47.

8.   Kirkham, op. cit., p. 129.

9.   Graves and Riding, op. cit., see, in particular, chapter II.

10. Ibid., p. 48.

11. Seymour-Smith, op. cit., p. 283.

12. Ibid., pp. 285–6.

10

Hugh MacDiarmid: Lenin and the British Literary Left in the 1930s

IAN A. BELL

It is clear that the 1930s, however stigmatised for subsequent readers as a 'low dishonest decade', represented a major period of distinctive creativity in twentieth-century British writing, producing poetry and prose (and drama and film) of great power and innovativeness. Many of the major Modernist writers of the 1920s were still active throughout the subsequent decade, including T. S. Eliot, W. B. Yeats, Ezra Pound, Virginia Woolf and James Joyce. At the same time, the period which also saw the emergence of W. H. Auden and Louis MacNeice as poets, of Lewis Grassic Gibbon and Graham Greene as novelists, of F. R. Leavis and Christopher Caudwell as critics, alongside the less individualised development of experimental theatre groups and the growth of an indigenous British cinema, is one which surely demands our attention and commentary. And indeed, there now exists a great wealth of scholarly and argumentative books and articles on various literary aspects of the period, the great majority of which still interpret events largely through what I will argue is the limiting and over-prescriptive perspective of 'the Auden generation'.

The purpose of this chapter is to offer a slightly different interpretation of the literary world of the time. By looking at the irreverent, erratic and at times even quixotic figure of the prolific Scottish poet and essayist 'Hugh MacDiarmid' (Christopher Murray Grieve), so often ignored nowadays by literary commentators on the 1930s, I hope to uncover a less familiar way of articulating the complex intersections of writing and politics in the 1930s. By focusing on one provocative understanding of the role of the poet in society, I seek to reconsider the available versions of the poet's responsibility towards the assumed audience. Although MacDiarmid's best-known work, the great poem *A Drunk Man Looks at the Thistle*, first appeared in 1926, I will argue that the poetry he wrote in the early 1930s has been improperly neglected in recent years, and that his two powerful *Hymns to Lenin* in particular offer an influential presentation of the politically-committed writer unavailable elsewhere in British writing at this time.[1]

There are always many different ways of defining the specific literary characteristics of something as vague as a decade, but on inspection it becomes apparent that one feature which distinguishes the world of letters in the 1930s from the periods immediately before and after is the unusual prominence of politics and political issues in the work of most writers of the time. Many of the most significant writers of 1930s Britain chose to offer relatively undisguised statements of their political alignments through their work, seeming unusually aware of the complex interventionist implications of their writing. The effect of a coincidence of intensely controversial and divisive public issues, notably the Spanish Civil War, the National Government's policy of appeasement towards Nazi Germany, and mass unemployment in Britain, was to create a context in which writers were encouraged to make comparatively open statements about contemporary public affairs and crises in their writing. In so doing, British writers of the 1930s were also encouraged to come clean about their own political affiliations, and, for many of them, a more or less rigorous and more or less substantial left-wing slant seemed to offer the most honourable response to the situation.

Of course, not all writers of the period aligned themselves with the left, however generously it might be defined. Some, like Dylan Thomas or William Empson, made few gestures of any significant kind towards the immediate and specific public world of political events. Others identified themselves with different points of the political spectrum. The examples of the variously inflected right-wing sentiments of T. S. Eliot, Ezra Pound, Wyndham Lewis, T. E. Lawrence, P. G. Wodehouse, Agatha Christie, Roy Campbell and Evelyn Waugh are too well known to invite a wholly uniform presentation of the espoused or implied politics of writers at this time. But while the voices of the British literary right were as shrill and loud in the 1930s as ever, the voices of the broad anti-fascist left were definitely increasing in volume and claiming the attention of many.[2] The pervasive leftist influence of W. H. Auden, Louis MacNeice, Stephen Spender, Cecil Day Lewis, Edgell Rickword,

Edward Upward, Rex Warner, Christopher Isherwood and others on the rhetoric of the times (and on our retrospective reconstruction of that rhetoric) cannot be denied. Indeed, for many contemporary and subsequent commentators, these engaged and self-conscious leftist writers were not only prominent, they were, as a collaborative group, the most powerful and influential of the time – 'the Auden generation' – setting a poetic style and constructing an orthodoxy of opinion which was often seen as dominant.

And as we might expect, by no means everyone welcomed the emergence of such a powerful left-wing literary grouping. It was not only the predictable opponents on the right, like the prolific polemicist Wyndham Lewis, who took issue with such apparent unanimity of political and literary feeling. More traditionally liberal commentators saw in this development the dangers of a contamination of subtle and evanescent literature by crude and clumsy materialist politics. To take one relatively familiar example, F. R. Leavis denounced what he saw as the 'Marxist' tendencies of 1930s writers in his editorial 'Retrospect of a Decade', published in *Scrutiny* in 1940. Recalling the widespread hostility to the opening issues of his influential critical journal in the early 1930s, he said:

> We remember as representative of the prevailing assumptions and indicative of the pressure of the environment at that time, this comment on our 'political attitude,' made with malicious intent by an eminent young intellectual: 'Well, of course, you're as little Communist as you dare to be.' The assumption that not to be Communist required courage was at that time a natural one. The pressure was certainly tremendous – to wear red, or some colour recognized as its opposite.[3]

Although one unattributed casual remark is perhaps not everyone's idea of tremendous pressure, Leavis goes on to assemble a philistine 'red menace' pressure group which he claimed had marauded through the previous decade, whose effects on the world of polite letters had been wholly negative and destructive. Discussing the absence (as he saw it) of significant new creative work in the decade past, he suggests that 'the prevalent Marxizing and the barrenness might well seem to be in obviously significant relation'.[4] For the self-styled defender of the 'humane tradition'[5] therefore, the red tide of the 1930s was a very important part of cultural demonology, even if it was not always so easily supported by demonstrable fact.

Other jaundiced liberals also saw the pernicious effects of the
left on 1930s British writing just as clearly. For some, it was the
coerciveness of fashion and orthodoxy, and the absence of individuality, which was most to be deplored. For instance, George
Orwell, recollecting his emotions in the tranquillity of 1948, said:

> at any given moment there is a dominant orthodoxy, to offend
> against which needs a thick skin and sometimes means cutting
> one's income in half for years on end. Obviously, for about fif-
> teen years past, the dominant orthodoxy, especially among the
> young, has been 'left'. The key words are 'progressive', 'demo-
> cratic' and 'revolutionary', while the labels which you must at all
> costs avoid having gummed upon you are 'bourgeois', 'reaction-
> ary' and 'Fascist'. Almost everyone nowadays, even the majority
> of Catholics and Conservatives, is 'progressive', or at least wishes
> to be thought so. No one, as far as I know, ever describes himself
> as 'bourgeois', just as no one literate enough to have heard the
> word ever admits to being guilty of antisemitism. We are all of
> us good democrats, anti-Fascist, anti-imperialist, contemptuous
> of class distinctions, impervious to colour prejudice, and so on
> and so forth.[6]

Although Orwell saw this leftist and progressivist orthodoxy as
more attractive than its possible conservative rivals, he still lamented
the unthinking conformity it seemed to entail. In Orwell, therefore,
as in Leavis, and in many other comparable liberal interpretations,
it is this notion of uniformity, of the need to conform to the authoritarian demands of the left, which 'obviously' (a key word in both
Leavis and Orwell) lies at the heart of the British intellectual mal-
aise of the 1930s.

On closer examination, however, the political commitments of
the self-styled left-wing writers of the period are nothing like as
homogeneous or as intense as these analyses would imply, and
their effectiveness is hard to discover. As Samuel Hynes puts it, 'in
the Myth of the Thirties . . . the Left plays a powerful role, but in
the actual period the role of the Left was not clear'.[7] The political
role of the left under the National Government was indeed unclear,
with insistent and enfeebling conflicts of interests between the Labour Party, the Independent Labour Party (ILP) and the Communist Party, leading to an embarrassing failure to produce a concerted

and powerful left-wing presence in British political life. As one commentator put it, 'it was a decade in which the impact of the entire British left on practical problems and immediate events was virtually nil'.[8] But at the same time as it was being so singularly ineffective in the world of national politics, if we are to believe Leavis and Orwell, the left was apparently taking over the world of literature and setting the style of British intellectual life.

But what was it about the left which attracted these upper-class and upper middle-class public-school educated English writers? At the risk of wholly belittling their commitment, it looks in retrospect as though, for most of the better-known poets at least, the left was a relatively comfortable haven. Through its very political impotence, its remoteness from the real operations of power, the left became a venue from which British writers could express a safely oppositional Romantic idealism, and strike their world-weary idealistic poses. Whereas the genuinely radical Shelley confidently saw poets as the unacknowledged legislators of the world, by the 1930s they had become no more than Auden's 'ironic points of light'.[9] That is to say, apart from the strongly-committed figures of Christopher Caudwell, Ralph Fox, John Cornford, Lewis Jones and a few others, most of the more prominent British writers of the 1930s used the left as a way of articulating a familiar bohemian or bourgeois dis-illusionment, as a way of rationalising (and sustaining) their distance from power.

For Auden, Spender and Day Lewis in particular, espousal of the causes of the left became a strategy of radical disaffection, a means of disaffiliation rather than a commitment or an alignment to genuine working-class movements. Rather than espousing a doctrinaire or programmatic activist Marxism, they gave voice to an emotionally-oriented utopian disenchantment, combining stirring cries on behalf of the 'masses' with personal pleas for a more relaxed attitude towards unorthodox sexual conduct. In a way which contrasts sharply with the contemporary 'agit-prop' of Bertolt Brecht, for instance, many of the British leftist writers of the time seem to have appropriated the left as a way of accommodating themselves to their society, claiming the authority of marginalisation, and offering powerful humanist slogans rather than a coherent Marxist opposition. Given their lofty disdain towards the world of working-class life, so strongly articulated in parts of Louis Mac-Neice's *Autumn Journal*, their left-wing politics remained gestural and insubstantial, a matter of rhetoric and style above all.

But at the same time there were notable and honourable exceptions. I have already mentioned Caudwell, Cornford, Jones and
Fox, and for the remainder of this chapter I want to look at an unorthodox figure whose politics fell outside the coercive coterie of
'MacSpaunday' (to use Roy Campbell's dismissive term for the literary *élite*): Hugh MacDiarmid. Always a self-consciously political
creature, MacDiarmid (then still Christopher Grieve) had joined the
ILP as early as 1908, when he was only sixteen, but in later years
he had gradually moved through Fabianism and the Nationalist
movement towards the harder left. By the 1930s, he was established
as a rather maverick member of the Communist Party of Great
Britain.

His harder line on political issues in the 1930s can be seen in his
response to the critical question of Spain, published in *Authors Take
Sides on the Spanish War*, a poll organised by the wealthy left-wing
socialite Nancy Cunard in 1937. Amid the often rather rhetorical
and self-advertising protestations of virtue from Auden, George
Barker, Samuel Beckett, Cyril Connolly, Havelock Ellis, Ford Madox
Ford, Victor Gollancz, Geoffrey Grigson, and many other leading
literary figures, MacDiarmid characteristically goes straight for the
jugular:

> I am a member of the Communist Party and wholly on the side
> of the legal Government and the People of Republican Spain – as
> are the vast majority of the people of Scotland, where at succes-
> sive General Elections a majority of the total poll has been cast
> for Socialism, and where – if we had had national independence
> – we too would have had a Socialist Republican Government
> long ago. Practically all the Scottish writers of any distinction to-
> day are of the same way of thinking. But for the connection with
> England, Fascism would never be able to raise its head in Scot-
> land itself. If we are subjected to a Fascist terror in Scotland, the
> London Government will be to blame, as it is mainly to blame for
> the horrible tragedy inflicted on our Spanish comrades – a trag-
> edy which must, and will, be turned yet into a glorious victory
> over the Principalities and Powers of Darkness, and end with the
> liquidation of Franco and all his fellow-murderers.[10]

This fiery combination of nationalism and internationalism, expressed through his own kind of militant and truculent Anglophobia,
is much stronger than any of the other responses, both more overtly

political in its content and more histrionic in its expression. The attempt to identify London as the source of all the problems is highly characteristic of Hugh MacDiarmid's accusatory style of argument. At times, MacDiarmid's internationalist politics were undeniably distorted by his intense distrust of England, which inevitably proved difficult for others on the left to take. After he had suggested in an article in the *Voice of Scotland* in 1938 that the Scottish, Irish and Welsh members of the International Brigade fighting in Spain had found it impossible to work alongside their English comrades, even the Communist Party was no longer able to accommodate him, and he was expelled.[11] With characteristic contrariety, he re-joined in 1957, just as so many English intellectuals were leaving in protest at the Soviet invasion of Hungary.

But although MacDiarmid's political position was inconsistent, deliberately pugnacious and combative in expression, and occasionally downright confused, he was, throughout the early 1930s, working on a body of poems which contain some of the most confident and committed political rhetoric of the period. His view of himself was always that of a poet committed to speaking to everyone, and in this idiosyncratic populism he saw himself as being radically at odds with the better-known English (and Irish) writers of the time:

> How many Communist or near-Communist poets in Great Britain can go to unlettered working-class people, and through their poetry give them comfort and strength, find common ground with them, and themselves derive strengthened faith and reinforced resolution from the experience? Can we imagine Auden or MacNeice or Spender doing anything of the sort? Can we even imagine them thinking of trying to do anything of the sort?[12]

Such a down-to-earth, common-sense attitude is not easy to find in all his poetry. I find it very hard to see how such a difficult and wilfully obscure poem like 'On a Raised Beach' (1934), for instance, could be offered as an exercise in comforting the unlettered. However, the desire to 'find common ground with them' clearly animates the movement and the rhetoric of fine pieces like 'The Seamless Garment' (1931), 'First Hymn to Lenin' (1931) and 'Second Hymn to Lenin' (1932).

MacDiarmid's sneering references to Auden and the others here are by no means isolated remarks. Whenever he mentions any of them in his letters or essays, he is largely unsympathetic to their work, and sceptical of their political authenticity. For him, the better-known poets of the time were no more than opportunist fellow-travellers of the left, whereas he himself represented a more genuine and radical socialist alignment. His attack is stated at its most forceful and least conciliatory in his 'Third Hymn to Lenin' (1957):

> Michael Roberts and All Angels! Auden, Spender, those bhoyos,
> All yellow twicers: not one of them
> With a tithe of Carlile's courage and integrity.
> Unlike the pseudos I am *of* – not *for* – the working class
> And like Carlile I know nothing of the so-called higher classes
> Save only that they are cheats and murderers,
> Battening like vampires on the masses.
>
> (*CP*, p. 900)

The world of contemporary writing is here compared with the earlier radical period of the 1830s, and Michael Roberts and the others are seen unfavourably in relation to Richard Carlile, Thomas Paine's publisher, who continued writing and editing even after imprisonment. For MacDiarmid, the so-called radicals of the 1930s seemed much lesser figures, striking attitudes rather than struggling. These are harsh accusations, but MacDiarmid was prepared to beat his contemporaries with any stick that came to hand. After all, as well as offering an inauthentic political position, Auden was inevitably tainted by his later religiosity. MacDiarmid was convinced that too many modern poets had been ruined by their rejection of the material and political world in favour of 'devitalising and injurious' religion, including, as he said, 'the recent deplorable cases of T. S. Eliot, Edwin Muir, and W. H. Auden.'[13]

In trying to find a voice which would be able to communicate complex ideas to everyone, MacDiarmid is of course rooted in the Scottish literary tradition of directness of address, which goes back at least as far as Burns and Robert Fergusson. And it is clear that he also drew strength from his familiarity with the political work of John Maclean and other recent prominent figures on the Scottish left, as he acknowledges in his outspoken poem 'John Maclean (1879–1923)', written around 1934, but not published until 1956. Such a tradition of demotic radicalism, unavailable to his English and Irish contemporaries, informs his poetry throughout this period. However, as well as respecting his native antecedents, he was also aware of comparable literary activities in the contemporary Soviet Union, citing the left-wing Futurist poet, illustrator and activist Vladimir Mayakovsky as someone who fulfilled the demands the modern world made on its poets.

MacDiarmid said unusually generous things about Mayakovsky in his two autobiographical sketches, *Lucky Poet* (1943) and *The Company I've Kept* (1966), and wrote a poem in memory of him after his suicide in 1930.[14] He saw in Mayakovsky a way of addressing political issues directly in poetry, and a way of communicating these very complex but profoundly important matters as simply as possible to an audience, without being patronising or obscurantist. As he puts it in *Lucky Poet*, it is of the utmost urgency that 1930s poets take on 'the practical activities – the capacity for using poetry as weapon in the day-to-day struggle of the workers, with no scruples in using extra-literary means, in organizing rows and literary scenes, in doing everything *pour épater les bourgeois* – of a Vladimir Mayakovsky' (*LP*, p. 357). His version of Mayakovsky may be something of a caricature, based on rather limited information, and there is surprisingly little sense that the Soviet poet might be a more challenging and difficult mentor than the intelligent practical joker invented by MacDiarmid for his own purposes.[15] At no point, for example, does MacDiarmid attempt to discuss the complexities of the debates between Futurism and Formalism in the Soviet Union, nor the importance of Trotsky's critique of the apolitical and regressive bohemianism of the literary avant-garde in his *Literature and Revolution* (1924).[16]

However, bearing these reservations in mind, it is still possible to see MacDiarmid exploiting Mayakovsky and Maclean to take on responsibilities unfamiliar to Auden or Spender or other comparable English poets, and at the same time using his progressivist commitments to sidestep the pervasive pessimistic inheritance of Eliot and Yeats. The issue which Mayakovsky most vigorously dramatises and articulates for MacDiarmid is the poet's relationship with his audience. In a 1928 essay called 'The Workers and Peasants Don't Understand You', Mayakovsky gives a startling account of the notion of 'art for the masses':

'We don't need books for the few or art for the few! Yes or No?'
Yes and no.

If a book is meant for the few, so as to be exclusively an object of consumption by those few, and if, outside that area of consumption, it has no function, then that book is unnecessary.

If a book is addressed to the few in a way that the energy of the Volkhovstroi power station is sent to a few transmission substations so that they will carry the transformed current to the electric light bulbs, then that book is necessary.

Such books are addressed to the few, to the producers, not to the consumers.

They are the seeds and framework of mass art.[17]

This startling comparison of the poet and the power station is reminiscent of MacDiarmid in both its technicality and its egotism. Mayakovsky's formulation allows the poet to be both ordinary and highly remarkable, combining utility and grandeur, the mundane and the spectacular. As MacDiarmid often put it, the poet must be *both* of and for the people. The contrast between this view of the poet's function and, say, Auden's needs little further commentary.

MacDiarmid may well not have known this particular essay (the depths of his knowledge of the figures he cites can often be safely doubted) but he was none the less fond of similarly flamboyant self-descriptions. In a 1964 letter to George Bruce, for instance, he claimed 'my job, as I see it, has never been to lay a tit's egg, but to erupt like a volcano, emitting not only flame, but a lot of rubbish'.[18] Such Whitmanesque plenitude certainly dominates many of his later poems, by no means always to their advantage, and the tensions between the poet as superman and the poet as common old working chap (as anyone here can see) are not always successfully negotiated. However, during the 1930s MacDiarmid confronted this problem directly, and wrote a series of pieces which offer much more disciplined and concentrated efforts to pursue these lines of thought about the poet's role in political society, encouraged by his acquaintance with at least one version of Mayakovsky's career.

In 'The Seamless Garment' (1931), for instance, a poem written in a fluent and easily flowing Scots, MacDiarmid compares the workings of a woollen mill to the creation of poetry, and relates both activities to the world of politics. Unlike Auden's 1933 poem on broadly similar themes, 'A Communist to Others', this piece avoids elaborate abstraction and bluster, and seems unusually humble and respectful in its handling of its parable. Confidently set in the workplace, MacDiarmind's poem starts with a familiar address to an intimate, emphasising both the poet's closeness to his subject and his distance from it:

> You are a cousin of mine
> Here in the mill.
> It's queer that born in the Langholm
> It's no' until
> Juist noo I see what it means
> To work in the mill like my freen's.
>
> (*CP*, p. 311)

From this moment of insight and discovery, this paradoxical recognition of magical ignorance, MacDiarmid explains to 'Wullie' just what makes the experience of weaving similar to the experience of writing poetry, and, more importantly, why both of these activities are smaller versions of the still greater enterprise of revolution and social transformation. Above all, the poem is driven by a desire to explain these connections 'In a way I can share it wi' you.'

As MacDiarmid sees it, the mill is chaotic to anyone uninitiated in its crafts and skills. Yet to the workers, it is only a noisy and hectic way of creating beauty, of producing 'the seamless garment'. They alone can see the organisation and discipline which lie behind the chaotic impression made on outsiders, and they alone have the creative skills necessary to turn noise into music. The skilled workers are then compared to the German poet, Rainer Maria Rilke, who created his own seamless garment of 'music and thought', and to Lenin, 'the best weaver Earth ever saw'. The movement of the poem involves, then, a tribute to the skills of the Dumfriesshire weavers, and commensurately greater tribute to the comparable master craftsmen of art and politics.

The choice of the two great figures for comparison is interesting. In *Lucky Poet*, MacDiarmid approvingly quotes Rilke's remark 'the poet must know everything' (*LP*, p. 67), which he also includes in his compendious poem *The Kind of Poetry I Want* (1947, *CP*, p. 1016). His praise of Rilke (who had died as recently as 1926), then, seems to introduce the notion of the poet as great-souled being, the repository of all that can be known and thought. Lenin, too, who died in 1924, turns into a superhuman figure within the poem, but this may be less surprising. Lenin was certainly the arch-ogre of the right, but for many on the left at this time, the Russian Revolution was created by the extraordinary political skill and acumen of Lenin virtually single-handed. Typical of this attitude is the following passage from a short biography by James Maxton, of the ILP, published around 1932:

> But standing out above all the scientific reasons, economic and historical, above the poets and writers, dwarfing everything and every one, is the man Lenin, interpreter of Russia, liberator of Russia, inspirer and initiator of the New Russia. To large masses of common people the world over he stands, not merely as the Russian liberator and the founder of a New Russia, but as the pioneer of a new world order which, having resolved the economic difficulties that confront the nations to-day, will usher in the age of plenty and give to all mankind that free and abundant life which has till now been only a dream.[19]

Within MacDiarmid's poem, it is this heroic liberating Lenin who stands supreme. Lenin, along with Rilke (and presumably Mac-Diarmid himself), seems to represent the possibility of re-making the world along more purposeful and intelligent lines, and as the poem goes on it combines its propagandist intensity with a more ruminative hymn to technological and social progress. The weaving of cloth, with its reliance on technology and on its metaphoric dialectical tensions between warp and woof, is a particularly apposite image for socialist renewal. Perhaps uncharacteristically, the poem does not labour its image, and with studied casualness, MacDiarmid draws attention to himself as a 'maker' of progressivist sentiment:

> Are you helpin'? Machinery's improved, but folk?
>   Is't no high time
> We were tryin' to come into line a' roon?
>   (I canna think o' a rhyme.)
> Machinery in a week mak's greater advances
> Than Man's nature twixt Adam and this.
>   (*CP*, p. 313)

By the end of the poem, our attention is concentrated on the poet's role, on MacDiarmid's conception of his own 'fricative work'. It becomes a plea for integrity, a demand that the poet be as skilled and dedicated as the weavers, or as Lenin himself, and as willing to put himself at the service of social transformation.

'The Seamless Garment' is certainly MacDiarmid's most integrated and cohesive political poem, with the direct address, the imagery of weaving, and the discussion of the disciplines of writing and politics interacting to great purpose. His 'First Hymn to Lenin' (1931) contains many of the same ideas, but is less metaphorically developed. Lenin is presented in this poem as the successful successor to Christ – 'You mark the greatest turnin'-point since him' (*CP*, p. 297) – in an optimistic and glorious riposte to Yeats's bitter apocalyptic vision of ten years earlier, 'The Second Coming'. But, in its immediate context, what makes this poem especially interesting is its uncompromising acceptance of the inevitability of violence:

> As necessary, and insignificant, as death
> Wi' a' its agonies in the cosmos still
> The Cheka's horrors are in their degree;
> And'll end suner! What maitters't wha we kill
> To lessen that foulest murder that deprives
> Maist men o' real lives?
>
> (*CP*, p. 298)

By 'the Cheka' MacDiarmid refers to the Bolshevik police force, notoriously vigorous and savage in suppressing counter-revolutionary elements.[20] His chilling acceptance of the need to kill without remorse is histrionic and maybe bombastic in its expression, sounding rather distant from the realities of the situation. But no apology is offered.

MacDiarmid's nonchalance here contrasts interestingly with the way W. H. Auden responded to criticism of the equally casual treatment of political violence in his poem 'Spain' (1937). There is a line in that poem which, on first publication, read, 'The conscious acceptance of guilt in the necessary murder', which clearly echoes the strain of MacDiarmid's hard-headed and unsentimental radicalism. However, in 'Inside the Whale' (1940), George Orwell took great exception to this statement. While acknowledging that the poem was 'one of the few decent things that have been written about the Spanish war', Orwell felt that it was still too glib and self-satisfied in its assumptions:

The second stanza is intended as a sort of thumbnail sketch of a day in the life of a 'good party man'. In the morning a couple of political murders, a ten-minutes' interlude to stifle 'bourgeois' remorse, and then a hurried luncheon and a busy afternoon and evening chalking walls and distributing leaflets. All very edifying.

But notice the phrase 'necessary murder'. It could only be written
by a person to whom murder is at most a *word*. Personally I would
not speak so lightly of murder. . . . Mr Auden's brand of amoralism
is only possible if you are the kind of person who is always
somewhere else when the trigger is pulled.[21]

Orwell catches something of the attitude-striking in Auden which
equally irritated MacDiarmid, and by the time the poem was published in a collected volume in 1940 it had been changed to 'The
conscious acceptance of guilt in the fact of murder'.[22] It seems to me
as though Orwell's criticisms, if they are valid at all, apply at least
as strongly to MacDiarmid as to Auden, but the 'First Hymn to
Lenin' remained as originally published each time it appeared.

The last poem I want to discuss is MacDiarmid's 'Second Hymn
to Lenin' (1932), in which the poet's political and literary roles are
most stirringly discussed. This piece takes the form of an epistle to
a fellow poet, with Lenin seen as a tolerant, literary man:

> Ah, Lenin, you were richt. But I'm a poet
> (And you c'ud mak allowances for that!)
>   (*CP*, p. 323)

MacDiarmid is trying to forge an alliance of purpose between the
poet and the social engineer, giving politics immediate priority
and urgency but retaining all the mystical prestige of poetry. In this
poem, the author moves away from the propagandist position of
Mayakovsky, and instead of seeing poetry as being at the service
of the revolution, he sees the revolution as being at the service of
poetry:

> The greatest poo'er amang men.
>   (*CP*, p. 326)

The poet thus becomes the ultimate repository of all human values,
and however much respect is accorded to politicians and revolu-
tionaries like Lenin, they are in the end subordinate to the greatest
writers.

How is this highly Romantic conception of the writer's social
position to be made consistent with MacDiarmid's avowed political
radicalism? At first sight, the two seem at odds. The idealist demands
of great writing seem incompatible with the need to transform

society, and within the poem these idealist claims are given respect
and status. But however much MacDiarmid might wish to get beyond material considerations, and contemplate instead the eternal
verities of art, politics still keeps getting in the way. Despite his
elevation of the poet, MacDiarmid retains in this poem a clear sense
of the specific and immediate need for political agitation:

> That breid-and-butter problems
> S'ud be in ony man's way.
>
> (*CP*, p. 325)

Exasperation at the political injustices of ordinary life is still prominent in this poem, even if the poet is no longer seen as the figure
who might help solve the problems. But the writer does not escape
from social commitments, and MacDiarmid demands that literature
adopt a more socially responsible role:

> Are my poems spoken in the factories and fields,
>   In the streets o' the toon?
> Gin they're no', then I'm failin' to dae
>   What I ocht to ha' dune.
>
> (*CP*, p. 323)

This is a more forceful and dogmatic version of the address to
'Wullie' in 'The Seamless Garment', and it makes the poet responsible
not only for having visions of wholeness denied to most people, but
for communicating them to everyone as well. While acknowledging
the difficulties involved in this populist position – recognising that
not even 'Shakespeare . . . Or Dante or Milton or Goethe or Burns'
satisfy its demands – MacDiarmid states and restates it in this poem
with characteristic certainty.

While few would claim that his own subsequent poetry lives
up to this stirring cry, the very fact of the collision between materialist politics and mystical poetry in his writing at this time creates
very provocative tensions. In moving away from a propagandist
notion of poetry to a much more exalted, almost Shelleyan defence,
MacDiarmid was trying to reconcile the claims of art and politics in
a way which was very different from either the leftist British writers of the time or the contemporary writers of the Soviet Union,
beset by rigid notions of 'correctness' and 'socialist realism'. Like
Lewis Grassic Gibbon, MacDiarmid was trying to maintain a strict

and progressivist ideological line, while never sacrificing the aesthetic integrity of his work.[23] In later poems, like 'On a Raised Beach' (1934) or 'In Memoriam James Joyce' (1955), the conflicts between the spiritual and the material are rephrased and confronted differently, without the confidence in readership or the desire to communicate witnessed here. By that time, MacDiarmid's poetry was less obviously activist, and the brief moment of clarity, humility and populism in the 'Second Hymn to Lenin' and 'The Seamless Garment' had passed.

Compared with Auden and the others, then, MacDiarmid's early-1930s verse is both more directly political and more Romantic. The tensions between these positions are never reconciled, and MacDiarmid seems content to confront us with contradictions. Other British writers of the time seemed largely ignorant of these poems, perhaps finding their use of Scots as difficult to cope with as their manifest delight in contrariety. Occasionally, though, the message got through, and MacDiarmid was seen as a harbinger of the better-known leftist poetry of the immediately subsequent period. As Cecil Day Lewis puts it in *A Hope for Poetry* (1934):

> The 'First Hymn to Lenin' was followed by a rush of poetry sympathetic to Communism or influenced by it. 'New Signatures' (1932) showed the beginning of this trend; 'New Country' (1933) contained definitely Communist poems by Auden, Charles Madge, R. E. Warner and others: Spender's 'Poems' and my own 'Magnetic Mountain,' both published in 1933, continued the movement.[24]

If there is a single reason why MacDiarmid's poetry changed its emphasis in the later 1930s, away from orthodox politics and populism, then perhaps it is to be found here. As ever, he sought to avoid being simply one of a group. He persistently tried to retain his individuality, his differences, and if the trend became leftist, then he either had to abandon the left, or find his own peculiar and idiosyncratic version of it. So by influencing these English writers, however unconsciously, he was, in a way, legislating for his own poetic demise. His hostility to Auden and the others was generated by a great many factors, but one of them was certainly his resentment at the way they had stolen his thunder. When it became fashionable to be a left-wing poet, MacDiarmid had no option but to become something else, even if that was to the detriment of his poetry.

For MacDiarmid, the 'hauf-way hoose' of the Auden generation was to prove uninhabitable, and he had to move on to the metaphysical extravagance of the next phase of his poetic career.

Notes

1. All poems are from *The Complete Poems of Hugh MacDiarmid* (London: Martin Brian & O'Keefe, 1978) p. 328. References to MacDiarmid's poems will be incorporated in the text, citing the abbreviation *CP*.
2. For an extended discussion of the voices of the right in the 1930s, see Richard Griffiths, *Fellow Travellers of the Right: British Enthusiasts for Nazi Germany 1933–39* (London: Constable, 1980). For a discussion of the more literary voices of the left, see Valentine Cunningham, *British Writers of the Thirties* (Oxford: Oxford University Press, 1988) pp. 26–35.
3. F. R. Leavis, 'Retrospect of a Decade', in *Scrutiny*, IX (1940) p. 70.
4. Ibid., p. 71.
5. Ibid., p. 70.
6. George Orwell, 'Writers and Leviathan', in *The Collected Essays, Journalism and Letters of George Orwell*, ed. Sonia Orwell and Ian Angus (Harmondsworth: Penguin Books, 1970) vol. IV, pp. 464–5.
7. Samuel Hynes, *The Auden Generation: Literature and Politics in England in the 1930s* (London: Faber & Faber, 1976) p. 12.
8. Ben Pimlott, *Labour and the Left in the 1930s* (Cambridge: Cambridge University Press, 1977) p. 1.
9. W. H. Auden, 'September 1, 1939', in *The English Auden: Poems, Essays, and Dramatic Writings, 1927–1939*, edited by Edward Mendelson (London: Faber & Faber, 1977) p. 247.
10. *Authors Take Sides on the Spanish War* (1937), in *Spanish Front: Writers on the Civil War*, ed. Valentine Cunningham (Oxford: Oxford University Press, 1986) pp. 54–5.
11. See Alan Bold, *MacDiarmid: A Critical Biography* (London: John Murray, 1988) p. 375.
12. Hugh MacDiarmid, *Lucky Poet: A Self-Study in Literature and Political Ideas* (London: Methuen, 1943) p. 156. Further references will be incorporated in the text, citing *LP*.
13. Hugh MacDiarmid, *The Company I've Kept* (London: Hutchinson, 1966) p. 174.
14. The connections between MacDiarmid and Mayakovsky are discussed in detail in Peter McCarey, *Hugh MacDiarmid and the Russians* (Edinburgh: Scottish Academic Press, 1987) pp. 129–61.
15. For a very interesting account of the peculiar appropriateness of

Mayakovsky for Scottish writers, see Edwin Morgan, *Wi the Haill Voice: 25 Poems by Vladimir Mayakovsky Translated into Scots* (Oxford: Carcanet Press, 1972).

16. See *The Futurists, the Formalists, and the Marxist Critique*, ed. Chris Pike (London: Ink Links Press, 1979).

17. 'The Workers and Peasants Don't Understand You', translated by Alex Miller, in *Vladimir Mayakosky: Selected Works in Three Volumes* (USSR: Raduga Publishers, 1987) vol. III, pp. 214–15.

18. *The Letters of Hugh MacDiarmid*, ed. Alan Bold (London: Hamish Hamilton, 1984) p. 531.

19. James Maxton, *Lenin* (London: Daily Express Publications, 1932?) p. 7.

20. For a discussion of the Cheka, see E. H. Carr, *The Bolshevik Revolution 1917–1923* (London: Macmillan, 1950) vol. I, pp. 158–70.

21. George Orwell, 'Inside the Whale' (1940), in *The Collected Essays, Journalism and Letters of George Orwell*, ed. Sonia Orwell and Ian Angus, vol. I, p. 566.

22. See the discussion of the revisions of this poem in Humphrey Carpenter, *W. H. Auden: A Biography* (London: George Allen & Unwin, 1981) p. 219.

23. See my article, 'Lewis Grassic Gibbon's Revolutionary Romanticism', in *Studies in Scottish Fiction: Twentieth Century*, ed. Joachim Schwend and Horst W. Drescher, Scottish Studies, 10 (Frankfurt, Bern, New York, Paris: Peter Lang, 1990) pp. 257–71.

24. Cecil Day Lewis, *A Hope for Poetry* (Oxford: Basil Blackwell, 1934) p. 53. MacDiarmid seizes on this passage for a piece of self-advertisement in *Lucky Poet*, pp. 157–8.

11

British Surrealist Poetry in the 1930s

STEVEN CONNOR

Hardly anything had been heard in Britain about surrealism and its impact by 1935, when the nineteen-year-old David Gascoyne published his *Short Survey of Surrealism*, an account of the beginnings of the movement in France and summary of the principal theoretical texts about surrealism by André Breton and others. In that work Gascoyne cagily suggests that 'it is within the bounds of possibility that a surrealist group will be founded shortly in London'.[1] Within a year, such a group had indeed been formed, and surrealism may be said to have taken a hold of literary and artistic London which it did not relinquish until the end of the decade. The International Surrealist Exhibition, held in London in 1936, acted as a focus for most of the energies of surrealist writers and artists in Britain. The writers included most notably David Gascoyne, Humphrey Jennings, Hugh Sykes Davies and Herbert Read, along with artists like Roland Penrose and Ithell Colquhoun, who also wrote and published surrealist texts.[2] The exhibition was followed by a volume of essays edited by Herbert Read, and entitled simply *Surrealism*.[3] Intended to consolidate the work of introducing and establishing surrealism in Britain, the volume contained essays by Read, Hugh Sykes Davies, André Breton and Georges Hugnet. Surrealist artistic activity was concentrated in a few places. Geoffrey Grigson's periodical *New Verse* published the work of many surrealist writers and, in particular David Gascoyne, up to and during 1936. Thereafter surrealist activity centred on a small number of periodical publications. These included most particularly *Contemporary Prose and Poetry*, edited by the communist surrealist Roger Roughton, which ran from 1936 to 1939, and the *London Gallery Bulletin* (which became the *London Bulletin* after its first number). This latter was edited by the Belgian poet and artist E. L. T. Mesens and for three years, from 1938 to 1940, acted as a focus for artists and writers alike. After the beginning of the war, surrealist activity flagged, though there were one or two landmarks, notably the appearance of the first (and only) number of a surrealist journal entitled *Arson: An Ardent Review*, and the surrealist section of a publication called *New Road 1943*, both edited by the incendiary propagandist for Trotskyist surrealism, Toni del Renzio.[4]

It was in the work of the young David Gascoyne that surrealism produced its most coherent and publicly-recognisable body of surrealist poetry, and, although Gascoyne had already moved decisively away from surrealism by 1937 (at the age of 21!), many have agreed with John Press that his are 'the only English poems of any merit inspired by the movement'.[5] Whatever the limitations of this judgement, and this style of judgement, Gascoyne's surrealist poems remain particularly interesting, not only for their exemplification of surrealist principles in action but also for their self-conscious thematisation of the surrealist aesthetic of disintegration, the way in which, as Michel Remy has remarked, Gascoyne's 'countless images of disintegration and destruction are in themselves images of the way we are asked to read'.[6]

'The Diabolical Principle' is only one of a number of poems from Gascoyne's surrealist period which enact such a vision of anguished but purifying disintegration. The first stanza evokes a scene of threatening unreality, the curtain of the poem lifting onto a landscape which seems from the beginning to be about to collapse into unreality:

The red dew of autumn clings to winter's curtains
And when the curtain rises the landscape is as empty as a board
Empty except for a broken bottle and a torso broken like a bottle
And when the curtain falls the palace of cards will fall
The card-castle on the table will topple without a sound[7]

A series of sinister, enigmatic images in the second stanza (an eye winking, a tumbled bed, a suicide with mittens stumbling out of a lake) gives way to a more grandiose, Eliotesque embodiment of cosmic disintegration, which mingles the fear of chaos with the possibility of some kind of religious revelation:

A sound drops into the water and the water boils
The sound of disastrous waves
Waves flood the room when the door opens

A white horse stamps upon the liquid floor
The sunlight is tiring to our opened eyes
And the sand is dead
Feet in the sand make patterns
Patterns flow like rivers to the distant sky
Rippling shells like careful signatures
A tangled skein of blood

(*CP*, p. 55)

But the poem ends without making it clear whether this means mere unredeemed desolation or the possibility of some new dispensation. There is only one moment when the relentless, strangely impassive present indicatives of the poem ('the storm falls across the bed like a thrice-doomed tree', 'waves flood the room when the door opens', 'a worm slithers from the earth and the shell opens') give way to anther grammatical mood, the anguished imperative of an unidentified voice crying 'Stop it tormentor stop the angry planet before it breaks the sky', and then the indicative mood returns for the final lines:

Having shattered the untapped barrel
Having given up hope for water
Having shaken the chosen words in a hat
History opened its head like a wallet
And folded itself inside

(*CP*, p. 55)

These lines may represent the surrender or submission of a personified history to the emergence of meaning in temporal contingency and becoming rather than Hegelian teleology (history shakes the chosen words in a hat, following Tristan Tzara's dadaist instructions for writing a poem), or they may suggest that history remains radically inattentive to the new surrealist dispensation, folding itself away as prudently as the bourgeois a spare banknote.

This Nietzschean theme of exposure to terrifying but potentially purifying chaos – what another poem calls 'the gross tumult of turbulent / Days bringing change without end' ('Yves Tanguy', *CP*, p. 46) – is to be found throughout Gascoyne's surrealist poetry, and perhaps most emphatically in a poem called 'Purified Disgust'. This poem begins with a sudden vision of terror breaking into the

close, contaminated atmosphere of bourgeois life, with its mixture
of carnality and violent abstraction:

> An impure sky
> A heartless and impure breathing
> The fevered breath of logic
> And a great bird broke loose
> Flapping into the silence with strident cries
> A great bird with cruel claws
>
> Beyond that savage pretence of knowledge
> Beyond that posture of oblivious dream
> Into the divided terrain of anguish
>   (*CP*, p. 44)

Gascoyne's 'divided terrain of anguish' has a number of recurring elements which build up, as it were, a grammar of disintegration. First of all there is the sea, its liquidity called upon frequently
to suggest terrifying formlessness (the 'circling seas / And foaming
oceans of disintegration / Where navigate our daylight vessels' in
'Unspoken', *CP*, p. 43). This is set against the recurring image of the
desert, presumably evolving emptiness of life of bourgeois life, so
routinely despised by the surrealists, the 'endless desert / Engrossed
in its tropical slumber' of 'Yves Tanguy' (*CP*, p. 46), and the waste
land whose 'sand is dead' in 'The Diabolical Principle' (*CP*, p. 55).
    Then there is the image of flight, as evoked in 'The Cage', which
sets against the 'ornate birdcage' of contained but expectant ordinary life, the 'feathered hour' of flight 'towards the forest'. Sometimes
this flight of release is signified by an eagle, or other annunciatory
bird, as in the eagle pinions which 'thunder through the darkness'
in 'The Diabolical Principle' (*CP*, p. 55), or, as we have just seen in
'Purified disgust', the great bird which 'broke loose / Flapping into
the silence with strident cries / A great bird with cruel claws' (*CP*,
p. 44). It may be that Gascoyne's interest in the eagle as a bird of
surrealist annunciation derives from, or at least has an analogy
with, the vision of the eagle which initiates the quest at the beginning
of Hugh Sykes Davies's surrealist narrative *Petron* (1935), which
Gascoyne in fact reviewed.[8] At the beginning of that narrative, the
hero, the semi-mythical Petron, 'chanced to look into the unbroken
azure above him, and had seen in the misty brilliance below the
sun a black speck slowly circling ... until his whole being had

become entangled in its silent distant motion, its remote and misty motion'.[9] He timidly retreats from this vision into the dark realm of the purblind mole, but is awakened by the descent from the air of 'an eagle's golden feather'.[10] But Davies's eagle has another surrealist predecessor, the eagle evoked by Georges Bataille in his essay 'La Vieille taupe et le préfixe *sur* dans les mots *surhomme* et *surréaliste*', written in the early 1930s as part of his long battle with André Breton.[11] In that essay, Bataille unfavourably compares the soaring, aquiline splendour of the values associated with Breton's surrealism with the baseness of the 'old mole' of communism in Marx's Communist Manifesto, grubbing in the bowels of the proletariat. Here, as elsewhere, Bataille resists the transformations of the Hegelian dialectic in surrealist aesthetics, but Gascoyne's sympathies seem to be with Breton in this matter, for the eagle seems in his work to signify quest, exploration, deliverance.

Recurrently associated with the eagle in Gascoyne's work is the image of an arrow. 'The Symptomatic World', a poem which describes something like an apprenticeship in psychic automatism in terms of 'following an arrow / To the boundaries of sense-confusion / Like the crooked flight of a bird' (*CP*, p. 58). The 'anxious arrow' appears in 'The Supposed Being' as well (*CP*, p. 62), and at the beginning of 'The Rites of Hysteria', where the 'cold mist of decayed psychologies' is pierced by 'An arrow hastening through the zone of basaltic honey / An arrow choked by suppressed fidgetings and smokey spasms / An arrow with lips of cheese' (*CP*, p. 56).

These various motifs can be overlayed and combined with each other, as in 'The Supposed Being', in which the 'turbulent sea approaching' itself becomes a predatory bird, 'Shivering ravenous venomous scarred / By the sharp-taloned claws of its waves' (*CP*, p. 62). Indeed, this overlayering enacts that very process of liquid dissolution which Gascoyne's surrealist poems are so often concerned to evoke and enact. Most notably, this will involve the violent conflation of opposites. If the eagle signifies the high aspiration to transcendence, then the feather signifies the reversion of spiritual height onto Bataillean baseness, rot and decomposition, the 'droppings of eagles' which are evoked at the end of 'And the Seventh Dream is the Dream of Isis' (*CP*, p. 27). 'Three Verbal Objects', for example, ends with the following description:

From the tower of a quietly blazing mansion whirled a flock of doves, and the smell of their half-scorched feathers became

confused with the scent of the countless damp and trampled plants
that lay a-rotting on the terraces. And the sky flung a column of
wind like a wide-flung scarf into the distance, where the earth
was turning on its never-ending hinge.

(CP, p. 66)

In 'The Symptomatic World', the steady and direct flight of the
arrow decomposes in a similar way into a confused swirl of feathers:

> The glass-lidded coffins are full of light
> They displace the earth like the weight of stones
> Eating and ravaging the earth like moths
> Which follow the arrow
> In a shower of freshly variegated sparkles
> Confusing the issue of the arrow's flight
> Till its feathers are all worn out
> And the trees are all on fire
> The pillow-case is bursting
> The feathers are blown across the roofs
> The room is falling from the window

(CP, p. 58)

Characteristically, in Gascoyne's surrealist poetry it is the body
which is subject to this kind of dissolution. As in many surrealist
paintings, the body suffers grotesque distortions of scale: 'My eye-
lashes are big as churches', we read in 'Automatic Album Leaves'
(*CP*, p. 34), while 'Future Reference' ends with an image of 'A colossal thigh covered with veins', which is 'the monument to be
raised on the seaswept shore / To all those who have lost their
lives in pursuit of a dream' (*CP*, p. 31). Often, the body's boundaries are transgressed, as it merges violently into its various envi-
ronments; ('The sun bursts through its skin', we read in 'Antennae'
(*CP*, p. 53), while 'Phantasmagoria' evokes 'faces like pillows wet
with tears and moulting feathers through the torn holes of their
eyes' (*CP*, p. 67). The topography of the body is subject to unpre-
dictable mutations; 'My eyes are on top of my head / To see all that
happens in the sky', declares 'The Symptomatic World', and 'My
ears grow out of my feet'. The first surrealist poem which Gascoyne
published, 'And the Seventh Dream Is the Dream of Isis', turns
upon the idea of the broken or scattered body. Isis was required to
gather the torn limbs of her brother–husband Osiris, that he might

be reborn; but here it is the scattering of the body, rather than its regathering, which promises new birth. The hallucinatory body evoked in the second section of the poem is simultaneously in decomposition and horrifyingly abundant growth:

there is an extremely unpleasant odour of decaying meat
arising from the depetalled flower growing out of her ear
her arms are like pieces of sandpaper
or wings of leprous birds in taxis
and when she sings her hair stands on end
and lights itself with a million little lamps like glow-worms
(*CP*, p. 25)

In 'The Supposed Being', Gascoyne evokes the body of a woman, phantasmatically dismembered into mouth, eyes, hands, breasts and sex, each of which is made to drift metaphorically away from unity and fixity:

Supposing the mouth
The hard lips crowned with bright flowers
A bursting foam of petals
And each gold stamen an anxious arrow
(*CP*, p. 62)

The effort to 'suppose' the desired body as something fixed and integral, 'the being entire / The tangible body standing / The visible limbs existing / And moving across the daylight', gives way to an acceptance that the body is unknowable except in its mobile contrariety:

Such a being escapes from the sight of my visible eyes
From the touch of my tangible hand
For she only exists
Where all contradictions exist
Where darkness is light and the real is unreal and the
World is a dream in a dream.
(*CP*, p. 63)

For many surrealists, it was the state of hysteria which summoned this shifting, changeable, grotesquely distorted body, a body whose woundings, eruptions and disseverings were a kind of language in themselves. Gascoyne's 'The Rites of Hysteria' concludes with his most extreme evocation of the violated, scattered body:

Now the beckoning nudity of diseases putrifies the saloon
The severed limbs of the galaxy wriggle like chambermaids
The sewing-machine on the pillar condenses the windmill's halo
Which poisoned the last infanta by placing a tooth in her ear
When the creeping groans of the cellar's anemone vanished
The nightmare spun on the roof a chain-armour of handcuffs
And the ashtray balanced a ribbon upon a syringe
An opaque whisper flies across the forest
Shaking its trailing sleeves like a steaming spook
Till the icicle stabs at the breast with the bleeding nipple
And bristling pot-hooks slit open the garden's fan
In the midst of the flickering sonorous hemlocks
A screen of hysteria blots out the folded hemlocks
And feathery eyelids conceal the volcano's mouth.

(*CP*, p. 56)

Here, the scattering of the phantasmal body is run together closely with the scattering of language or meaning themselves. This is how Michel Remy enthusiastically describes things:

In the space of this text, identities shatter and split. They tremble on the boundary between death and desire in the pulsive movement of a vision which constitutes itself through fragments seized beyond their reality as it is usually acknowledged, a vision which can never be complete. Here is the *drama* of meaning as it is celebrated by surrealism, the drama of transformation in the midst of self-making, of permanent decentring and derailing of every search after meaning. Violence, decay and monstrosity join together to contaminate the very constitution of meaning; the meeting of the subject with itself is thus deported and deferred in its insatiate meeting with what is always other.[12]

Gascoyne's surrealist poetry is recurrently concerned with the drifting mutability of language itself, especially of 'automatic' language freed from the bonds of grammar and logical connection. 'The Symptomatic World' concludes with an image which seems to run together the monstrosity of automatism in language with the

alternately exhilarating and fearful uncertainties of the 'lines of
the meridian' which 'resemble fish / That fly away', the heat that
'softens the equator', the 'rain that whispers in decrepit castles /
Great clots of clay and effigies falling to dust', in short, the collapse
of all forms of definition in general:

> Preserve us from the singing towers
> And the chapter which turns the page of its own accord
> For fear of reading its own history there.
>
> (*CP*, p. 61)

'Unspoken' makes more substantial this parallel between the
mutability of the world, 'All those formless vessels / Abandoned
palaces / Tottering under the strain of being' and the mutability of
language itself. Here the (normally) unspoken words of the unconscious allow a journey into

> man's enormous continent
> No two roads the same
> Nor ever the same names to places
> Migrating towns and fluid boundaries
>
> (*CP*, p. 42)

What seems to be occurring in this poem, as in others that deal
with the issue of language, or the derangement of meaning more
generally, is a self-designation of the processes of automatic writing
which lie at the heart of surrealist aesthetics. British surrealist aesthetics of the 1930s joins with French aesthetics in the praise of
process, performance and chance over product and predetermining
intention in poetry. In his *Short Survey of Surrealism*, Gascoyne
quoted with approval André Breton's famous definition of surrealism in his 1924 *Manifesto of Surrealism* as

> Pure psychic automatism, by which it is intended to express,
> verbally, in writing, or by other means, the real process of thought.
> Thought's dictation, in the absence of all control exercised by the
> reason and outside all moral and aesthetic preoccupations.[13]

Such a definition seems entirely negative – deriving from the
absence or annihilation of the customary restraints on the play of

free association in language. The whole point about such a definition is that, by itself, it tells us nothing in advance about the kind
of writing likely to ensue from it; indeed it would seem to deny the
possibility of identifiable style or form of any kind, in so far as these
things belong to the orders of discourse. As J. Gratton writes, 'to
participate in a surrealist poem is to consent to its movement, to
surrender one's totalizing impulse to the very spur of writing's
moment'.[14] Similarly, Hugh Sykes Davies warns his reader, at the
beginning of *Petron*, that 'all that my relation can give you is the
vertigo, the falling, the precipitate descent itself'.[15]

This obviously poses a problem for any kind of critical writing
about surrealist poetry which would wish to characterise that writing without inflicting the kind of violence of definition that such
characterisation might seem to necessitate. But this is not merely a
difficulty for the contemporary critic, for it was a concern just as
much to writers about surrealism in the 1930s (and in the 1930s,
most writers *of* surrealism were, at least occasionally, also writers
about surrealism). One example of a critic facing this difficulty is
George Hugnet's introductory and illustrative essay about French
surrealist poetry in Herbert Read's volume *Surrealism*.

Hugnet's essay, which is entitled simply '1870 to 1936', stresses
the dadaist origins of surrealism, in its 'abolition of poetic forms',
and emphasises that surrealism therefore has no narrow interest in
the technicalities of language as such or for its own sake. The efforts
of surrealism, he writes, 'are not directed towards technical reforms.
Surrealism puts the emphasis on the experimental power of poetry.
It is only interested in any form of writing to the extent that the
author *gives himself away*'.[16] And what does the author give himself
away *to*, if not to language itself, and a language become autonomous as well as automatic? Earlier, Hugnet has stressed the fact
that, in the pure destructiveness of dada, 'words become beings'.[17]
In automatic writing, consciousness surrenders itself to the pure
play of language, rather than attempting to fix and regulate that
play. But a curious contradiction emerges a little later in Hugnet's
text, when he writes that 'Since the idea of formal beauty plays no
part in surrealist writings, it is unnecessary to state that it is not by
its perfection . . . that the surrealist poem is distinguished, but by a
particular kind of consciousness or by a predetermined attitude.'[18]

Here, it seems, what matters most, what is needed to guarantee
or 'predetermine' the success of giving oneself away, is the accred-
iting decision in advance to do so. But how is one to apply this

intentional test, to determine the authenticity or not of any particular piece of poetic automatism? It seems that only a poem in which there is conscious control of the process of surrender to the unconscious can count as truly automatic. But, if this is so, what would it mean to *fake* a piece of automatic writing, that is, not to give oneself away to language, but to retain conscious control over it, or over the process of giving oneself away – since we have just seen that this is exactly the legitimating condition for all automatic writing? The difficulty of the question here is instanced nicely by David Gascoyne's own comments on his poem 'Phantasmagoria'. This poem, he says, was written at the insistence of a friend in 1939, after the period at which he had stopped writing poetry 'classifiable as surrealist'. Unable to produce a poem to order, he 'proceeded to employ the formula of quasi-automatism' (in other words, he produced a poem to order). However, Gascoyne acknowledges that the poem shows signs of its false origin, since 'the deliberate repetition of such a motif as a little black town on the edge of the sea is a device I would not formerly have allowed myself' (*CP*, p. xvii). The words are striking; the poem cannot be truly automatic, because the poet allows himself too much, gives himself away to a true randomness (in which repetition is as likely as not to occur) rather than to a consciously directed randomness, the retentive surrender of 'quasi-automatism'. Elsewhere, Gascoyne was concerned carefully to mark off authentic from inauthentic automatic writing in his own work. His collection *Man's Life Is This Meat* (1936) distinguishes surrealist poems from others, as do his prefatory remarks to his *Collected Poems* of 1988.[19] There, Gascoyne helpfully explains some of the more puzzling random associations. *Man's Life Is This Meat*, for example, derives from a chance encounter with a sample-book of printers' type-faces, which showed the words 'man's life is' in one type-face and 'this meat' in a different type-face on a facing page (*CP*, p. xv). The puzzlingly-named poem 'Gnu Opaque' is explained too; the title came about since 'Gnu Opaque' 'was the watermark faintly distinguishable in the paper on which it was written' (ibid.).

These are certainly examples of the inclusion of the random, though we might feel that Gascoyne's explanations rather complicate the matter, since they simultaneously guarantee randomness and annul it. What is more, these particular incursions of chance involve a certain, interesting circularity, or self-reflexiveness, since they have to do with encounters with instances of language itself.

To illustrate this, let us look at 'Gnu Opaque', which I give in full now.

No more resistance
  No letters this morning
  Tomorrow will be a fine day
Screeds of such blossomings
Should fill each lenten interval
Lobster-clawed love should diminish
On the roads leading to all countries
Famine veers away

They said maritime provinces
N or M
It isn't easy to see in this light
And night writes no replies

                              (*CP*, p. 27)

The clue offered by the attribution of the phrase 'Gnu Opaque' suggests that this fragmentary, opaque poem may be made coherent by organising it around the themes of language and writing themselves. The opacity of the 'faintly visible' watermark is the opacity of the surface rather than of depth – an opacity, should we say, of language in process, rather than a mystery of hidden meaning. The poem runs together the domestic ('No letters this morning') and the universal ('the roads leading to all countries') to suggest various kinds of (linguistic) expansion, abundance and abandon ('screeds of such blossomings') supervening upon the 'lenten intervals' of intellectual and affective deprivation. In the way of some of Gascoyne's less stagey poems of this period, there is a deliberate refusal of climax in the hesitant uncertainty of the ending – for if some glorious escape on to the roads is planned, then the destination is puzzlingly unclear. There is also a looping back to the opening words of the poem via the uncertainty about letters, here the letters 'N or M', rather than letters in the sense of written communications. If there were no letters this morning, there are some letters buried like the watermark behind and within the writing itself, or the paper on which it is inscribed. On one level the bizarre promise of the gnu of the title is redeemed, with the suggestion of a journey to be taken beyond the everyday. On another level, the gnu is acknowledged to be merely a collection of letters, barely visible, and anyway uncertain ('N or M?' perhaps it is, after all, GMU not GNU?).

For all its brevity, this poem richly and admirably balances the uncertainty or fragmentariness of a vision of release, abundance and escape – all of them named as opaque – and the promise held by the fact of opacity itself, opacity here connoting chance, the openness of metonymic drift in language. The opacity of the vision is the vision itself. To put it in more contemporary language – the uncertain enunciation of the liberated signifier is the very condition of its liberation.

Of course, this is only a way of reading the poem, a way of reading that allows the poem to 'give itself away' to chance and pure association, even as it construes the poem as a self-conscious exploration of the conditions of possibility of these things. A critical manoeuvre like this, which actually fixes and contains the play of language in the act of affirming it, is always in principle possible when encountering any example of free or aleatory writing. Two recent readings of Gascoyne's 'The Diabolical Principle' exemplify this. Writing in 1975, Rob Jackaman argued that the 'illogical welter of weird images' in the poem could be made to yield 'a meaning – indeed a *coherent* meaning'.[20] For Jackaman sees the poem not as an enactment of the breakdown of meaning, or crisis of consciousness, but rather a representation or portrayal of those things. Jackaman therefore sees the poem's value as lying in its '*calculated* (rather than accidental) richness and multiplicity'.[21] Replying to this reading in the same journal, Paul C. Ray suggests that to produce from this poem a coherent meaning and narrative line is a form of betrayal and violence, 'an attempt to put a brake on the free play of signi-fication, to reduce the mystery, tame the terror, domesticate the discomfort, to provide assurance by insisting on the "coherence" of the poem'.[22] Instead of a reading that attempts to substitute itself for the body of the text, reducing the complexity of its textual rela-tions, Ray insists on a 'logic of the surface',[23] which stays faithful to the play of signification in the poem. Oddly, however, Ray seems to resort to something very like Jackaman's reading to support his argument for textuality over coherent meaning. Reminding us that the title of the poem refers to Wyndham Lewis's *The Diabolical Principle and the Dithyrambic Spectator*,[24] and perhaps especially to Lewis's strictures in that book against the chaotic automatism of surrealism, Ray argues that it can thus be seen as the concrete demonstration of the victory of what Lewis called the Diabolical Principle, a principle that threatens the normal 'forms and perspectives as we know them,' a demonstration that the poem achieves by itself being its own subject; in other words, it is a mirror of both itself and its subject. It is not *about* the Diabolical Principle: it is the Diabolical Principle itself at work, wreaking the chaos that Lewis dreaded.[25]

In other words, this poem is about its own procedures, about the very indeterminacies of the automatic method and surrealism in general. If in one sense this is to free it, and surrealist poetry in general, from the totalising impulse of critical commentary determined to make it yield a meaning, in another sense this is always to restore coherence to surrealist automatism, which can always now be construed as an allegory of its own displacing processes. Read in this way, as it were, in the subjunctive rather than the indicative mood, surrealist writing is always a kind of demonstration, or exemplification, of what surrealist writing could be, and the effects that it might have. This kind of writing is never the thing in itself, but always precedes or self-consciously succeeds that thing, as anticipation or repetition.

This all represents a particular risk for contemporary criticism, especially poststructuralist criticism, which has sometimes turned to surrealist writing as an exemplification of its own preoccupations with linguistic indeterminacy. Michel Remy, in what is in fact the most extended treatment of British surrealist writing available, construes this writing as 'an endless transgression of the meaning of words . . . the real and the unreal become equally possible and the text becomes a journey through meaning and the making of meaning'.[26] The poems of David Gascoyne, he can write, 'accumulate instances of perfect deconstruction'.[27] But 'perfect' deconstruction, is like 'pure psychic automatism', in being impossible; the more perfect an example it is of the deconstruction of meaning, the more it holds in reserve against the threat of absolute lack of meaning (despite all the local indeterminacies of the text, its meaning as 'deconstruction', as 'automatism', is always stable). As Derrida writes, in criticism of Jacques Lacan's paradoxical promotion of the principle of castration to textual centrality in Edgar Allan Poe's *The Purloined Letter*: 'In this sense, castration-truth is the opposite of fragmentation, the very antidote for fragmentation: that which is missing from its place has in castration a fixed, central place, freed from all substitution. Something is missing from its place, but the lack is never missing from it [*Quelque chose manque à sa place, mais le manque n'y manque jamais*].'[28]

It seems as though the 'purity' of automatism must always be compromised, must always be subject to this risk of recruitment to some system of truth or ideology of meaning. This struggle between indefiniteness and definition represents more than just an error, or failure of nerve or tact, in contemporary criticism. For we may say that this issue – of the compromised openness of meaning – lies at the heart of surrealism itself, and especially at the heart of British surrealist poetry. Throughout the surrealist poetry and criticism of this period, there is a continuous, anxious need for self-definition and legitimation, which runs athwart, but is inextricably related to, the desire to escape the bonds of all semiotic and political authority. Of course, French surrealism is also characterised, like many other twentieth-century aesthetic movements, by the assiduity of its self-definitions; these centre on the two manifestos and associated pronouncements issued by André Breton, but radiate outwards through many other acts of definition, counterdefinition, diagnosis and, of course, denunciation. Surrealism everywhere announces, enunciates itself, predicting its effects, determining its scope and intentions. Along with this goes the tendency towards periodic self-purgations, in its splits, condemnations and expulsions of the alien within itself. But British surrealism, though less violent, and more gentlemanly, represents that self-consciousness, that anxiety of self-definition raised to a higher power. This is because surrealism is always already precedented for its British inheritors, always possessed of a history. British surrealist poetry has its particular interest precisely because of its self-consciousness, the struggle it illustrates between knowingness and unknowing, intention and performance.

The issue of definition is addressed nicely by Hugh Sykes Davies's 'Poem', published in the *London Bulletin*, which constantly offers negative definitions of the 'it' which is its subject, without ever giving it a name:

It does not look like a finger it looks like a feather of broken
    glass
It does not look like something to eat it looks like something
    eaten

It does not look like an empty chair it looks like an old woman searching in a heap of stones.[29]

Elsewhere, however, Davies displays an extraordinary, and apparently unironic, sense of the need for exact and authorised definitions of what surrealism is:

> There is going to be a surrealist exhibition in London in June. Of course it will be necessary to continue explaining what surrealism is; and of course this explanation will be given by the official leaders of the movement in Paris or by their accredited agents. This is very right. The leaders of the official movement have worked for many years with great industry, ability, and success; they are the only proper judges of what is surrealism, and who is surrealist.[30]

Here surrealism is poised on the hinge of definition and indefiniteness, coming into being in the interval between these two. Of course, the most important question of definition for surrealist writers in Britain, as in France, was the issue of political identification and commitment. Throughout British surrealist writing of the late 1930s there is an explicit and restated commitment to Marxist politics, a pledging of the surrealist project to the service of Marxist revolution. 'In a world of competing tyrannies,' wrote Herbert Read in 1936, 'the artist can have only one allegiance: to that dictatorship which claims to end all forms of tyranny and promises, however indefinitely, the complete liberation of man: the dictatorship of the proletariat.'[31] For Read, as for Hugh Sykes Davies, this was to be achieved by an unproblematic, if also mistily unspecific melding of Marx and Freud, where Freud was to supply the individual psychic dimension in a more generalised lifting of repression and entry into liberated life, all this to be achieved by an understanding of the 'laws' of dialectical materialism.[32] The most emphatic statement of the relationship between poetry and revolution, between the aesthetic and the political, is to be found in the work of Roger Roughton, a young poet and Communist Party member, who edited the journal *Contemporary Poetry and Prose*, in which most of the surrealist writers were represented, from 1936 to 1937. Roughton's editorials in the journal acknowledge that surrealism only has a small and particular part to play in revolutionary activity more generally, but he insists that this part is a revolutionary one, and calls repeatedly for loyalty to the Communist United Front, lest the 'revolutionary essence' of surrealism be adulterated by the anarchic intractability of individual artists.[33]

Roughton's own poems in *Contemporary Poetry and Prose* show a certain unwillingness to surrender to the semiotic perils of automatism. Most of his poems employ certain kinds of localised and contained dislocation to evoke, or explicitly to invoke, the excitement of imminent revolution. The Audenesque 'Watch this Space' concludes:

> For a message has removed the sun
> And a signal changed the season,
> While the land expectant for a reason
> Alters the anomalous design.[34]

In 'Animal Crackers In Your Croup', a kind of prophetic intensity 'Tomorrow the clocks will chime like voices / Tomorrow a train will set out for the sky / National papers please reprint' mingles with a certain note of self-conscious naughtiness – what one writer has called 'stink-bombs to embarrass the middle-class mind':[35]

> Tomorrow REVOLT will be written in human hair
> Tomorrow the hangman's rope will tie itself in a bow
> Tomorrow virginia creeper will strangle the clergy
> Tomorrow the witness will tickle the judge.[36]

The problem for Roughton is a simple one of how to reconcile the formlessness and undirected violence of surrealist aesthetics with a firm political programme. He is somewhat embarrassed by Ezra Pound's intemperate argument, published in *Contemporary Poetry and Prose*, that 'When it comes to "breaking down irrational" (or rational for that matter) "bourgeois prejudices" . . . the simple practice of using WORDS with clear and unequivocal meaning will blast all the London Schools of Economics'; for he is forced to argue that the surrealist dislocation of meaning is necessary, not because of any implicit link between rationality, clarity and political oppression, but merely as a tactic to convince those who remain unconvinced by such texts as the Communist Manifesto, even though it is 'a brilliant pamphlet using WORDS with clear and unequivocal meaning, containing nothing but true statements based on a rational and correct analysis of capitalism'.[37]

I think that Samuel Hynes is right in his judgement that, despite all the public declarations, surrealism and communism remain uneasily distant from each other in British surrealist writing.[38] However, this distance is in fact thematised within that writing, both explicitly in surrealist theory, and in the uneasy and only half-acknowledged consciousness of the overlapping of theory and practice in surrealist poetry. Surrealist poetry can then be said to take itself as its subject, not in any narrow, formalist self-mirroring, but in an anxious meditation on its own social function and destination: as it were, the social meaning of its meaninglessness.

In fact, most official surrealist pronouncements in Britain in the 1930s are concerned to try to harness the energies of pure psychic automatism, to turn it to some kind of profit, by predetermining its direction and outcome. In this sense, Herbert Read's argument, which tries to argue that surrealism is merely the continuation of romanticism, and English romanticism at that, is of a piece with Roger Roughton's attempt to press surrealism into a merely accessory role in the revolution, for both are attempts to retrieve, incorporate, or otherwise legitimate the anarchic threat of surrealism. This impulse is caustically identified in a remarkable review by Humphrey Jennings of Read's *Surrealism* collection. Jennings has no time for Read's comfortable assimilation of surrealism to native romanticism, or with Hugh Sykes Davies's confidence in the unfailing logic of the historical process. Devastatingly, he suggests that surrealism itself, by its very public success, may already be being incorporated, its energies captured and turned to account, not by the traditional centres of cultural power, but by a newly-emerging but ever more diversified mass culture industry:

> Is it possible that in place of a classical–military–capitalist–ecclesiastical racket there has come into being a romantic–cultural–*soi-disant* co-operative–new uplift racket ready and delighted to use the 'universal truths of romanticism – co-eval with the evolving consciousness of mankind' as symbols and tools for its own ends? Our 'advanced' poster designers, our educational propaganda film-makers, our 'young' professors and 'emancipated' business men – what a gift Surrealism is to them when it is presented in the auras of 'necessity,' 'culture' and 'truth' with which Read and Sykes Davies invest it.[39]

All this is given particular point by the fact that Jennings himself was closely associated with the surrealist group in Britain, published in the surrealist journals, translated French surrealist poetry, signed declarations and manifestos, exhibited in the London Gallery and was associated with the 1936 Surrealist Exhibition (which he mocks in his review of Read's book). Jennings argues powerfully against the precomprehension of intentions, performance and outcome in surrealism, the false systematisation of an aesthetics of the unprecedented. On this account, there is no point or purpose in looking for respectable English antecedents to surrealism. 'Creation is *not* the re-presentation of "the truth" however much it may at times look like it', Jennings writes, so that the significance of surrealist works is due not to their representation of eternal or absolute truths, but to 'their unquestioning acceptance of *all* the conditions of the moment: forgetting all "beliefs" preceding the picture, which would deny the promise of the unknown'.[40] Not the least of the forces of what Jennings calls 'the sleep of selectivity', in its paradoxically 'agile' capacity to categorise and differentiate among the promises of the unknown, is the character and function of the artist himself: 'to be *already* a "painter," a "writer," an "artist," a "surrealist," what a handicap'.[41]

Jennings is now remembered mostly for his work at the BBC as a film-maker, but in the late 1930s he also published a number of extremely interesting texts in *Contemporary Poetry and Prose* and the *London Bulletin*, sometimes called 'poems', sometimes called 'reports'. These are remarkable for their refusal of the official stylistics of automatism, with their routines of runaway accretion, and predictable surprises of image. Jennings's 'reports' are short quasi-anthropological accounts of events and social scenes, or fragments of narrative, sometimes historical. The most striking feature of these texts is the unspecifiability of their genre or context. We have no idea of the destination or addressee of these accounts and no continuing narrative or explanatory syntax of relations into which to insert them; and yet, rather than glamorously flaunting their indeterminacy, these texts appear to be plain and transparent. Rather than embracing nonsense, they are the uncanny phantom or disturbing double of sense. This may be seen in Jennings's 'Report on the Industrial Revolution', where a description of what might be a locomotive merges puzzlingly into a larger and less rational perspective:

The material transformer of the world had just been born. It was trotted out in its skeleton, to the music of a mineral train from the

black country, with heart and lungs and muscles exposed to view
in complex hideosity. It once ranged wild in the marshy forests
of the Netherlands, where the electrical phenomenon and the
pale blue eyes connected it with apparitions, demons, wizards
and divinities.[42]

Often these reports are published in short sequences, or stitch
together fragments of apparently variant provenance, but without offering any guidance as to how they are to be read together.
The 'Three Reports' which appeared in *Contemporary Poetry and
Prose* in June 1936 consist, first, of a brief extract apparently from a
biography of Salvator Rosa; secondly, there is a fragment of narrative describing the interior of a house of a Mr Kellerman, the floor
'covered with retorts, crucibles, alembics, bottles in various sizes,
intermingled with old books piled one upon another', as well as
two heads, which suggests to the narrator that Mr Kellerman 'was
engaged in remaking the brazen speaking head of Roger Bacon and
Albertus'; and, finally, this short text:

> When the horse is impassioned with love, desire, or appetite,
> he shows his teeth, twinkles his coloured eyes, and seems to
> laugh.
> He shows them also when he is angry and would bite; and
> volumes of smoke come from his ears.
> He sometimes puts out his tongue to lick. His mouth consists
> of the two rays of the eternal twins, cool as a sea-breeze.[43]

It is the undecidable ratio of connection and disconnection, presence and absence, determination and riddle, which makes this sequence so unnerving. The same may be said for Jennings's studies
for a report to be called 'From the Boyhood of Byron', which appeared in two versions in the late 1930s. Here, authentic-sounding
biography ('It is certain that one of the poet's feet was, either at
birth or at an early period, so seriously clubbed or twisted as to
affect his gait') is intercut with evocations of wild horses, specula-
tions about the effects of landscape on the Greek temperament, a
passage, or pastiche of a passage, from a treatise on light and photo-
graphy, and a narrative apparently describing a journey to Delphi
to view a huge locomotive.[44] One of the most striking things about
these texts is that it is hard to be sure if they really *are* surrealist;

but, paradoxically, that very categorial indeterminacy is what seems to make them more representative of the possibilities of the unprecedented opened up by surrealist theory than the more obedient and conventional floods of free association which typified surrealist writing in this period.

Suggestive though Jennings's poetry is in its own terms, however, it is even more so in the light of his involvement with the Mass Observation movement. Some time in the late 1930s, Jennings conceived with Charles Madge, then a journalist with the *Daily Mirror* and occasional poet, and Tom Harrisson, an anthropologist, the idea for a collective anthropology of the present, to be called 'Mass Observation'. According to Kathleen Raine's description of it, Mass Observation was to be a technique for recording the 'subliminal stirrings of the collective mind of the nation; through the images thrown up in such things as advertisements, popular songs, themes in the press, the objects with which people surround themselves (have on their mantelpiece for example)'.[45] In a letter–manifesto in the *New Statesman* of January 1937, Harrisson, Jennings and Madge gave a list of the proposed subjects for investigation:

Behaviour of people at war memorials
Shouts and gestures of motorists
The aspidistra cult
Bathroom behaviour
Beards, armpits, eyebrows
Anti-semitism
Distribution, diffusion and significance of the dirty joke
Funerals and undertakers
Female taboos about eating
The private lives of midwives[46]

Most importantly, Mass Observation was to be compiled from reports contributed by hundreds of non-professional observers. In its combination of wit and defamiliarising absurdity and its clear commitment to the ideal of a collective authorship, Mass Observation sought to forge a kind of social knowledge which would be free of the objectifying and totalising violence of social and anthropological theory. In seeking to merge social theory and action with a bizarre kind of poetry, Mass Observation is one of the points where British surrealism gives promise of a cultural politics which puts the aesthetics of surrealism to work, without reducing it to a formula, or compromising its difficult commitment to the open and the accidental, to '*all* the conditions of the moment'.

Notes

1. David Gascoyne, *A Short Survey of Surrealism* (London: Cobden Sanderson, 1935) p. 129.
2. See especially, Roland Penrose's *The Road is Wider than Long: An Image Diary from the Balkans July–August 1938* (London: London Gallery Editions, 1939). Ithell Colquhoun's interesting surrealist texts have never been collected, but a couple of them are reprinted in Mel Gooding, 'A Selection of British Texts on Surrealism 1930–1943', in Alexander Robertson, Michel Remy, Mel Gooding and Terry Friedman, *Angels of Anarchy and Machines for Making Clouds: Surrealism in Britain in the Thirties* (Leeds: Leeds City Art Galleries, 1986) pp. 82–3. This catalogue in fact reprints the widest range of surrealist writings from the 1930s in Britain currently available.
3. Herbert Read (ed.), *Surrealism* (London: Faber and Faber, 1936).
4. *Arson: An Ardent Review* (London, 1942); *New Road 1943: New Directions in European Art and Letters*, ed. Alex Comfort and John Bayliss, surrealist section ed. Toni del Renzio (Billericay: Grey Walls Press, 1943). This summary outline of the development of literary surrealism in Britain can be supplemented by J. H. Matthews, 'Surrealism and England', *Comparative Literature Studies*, 1 (1964) pp. 55–72 and Paul C. Ray, *The Surrealist Movement in England* (Ithaca and London: Cornell University Press, 1971).
5. John Press, *Rule and Energy: Trends in British Poetry since the Second World War* (London: Oxford University Press, 1963) p. 82.
6. Michel Remy, 'Surrealism's Vertiginous Descent on Britain', in *Angels of Anarchy and Machines for Making Clouds*, p. 35.
7. David Gascoyne, *Collected Poems 1988* (Oxford and New York: Oxford University Press, 1988) p. 54. All references to this edition, in the abbreviated form *CP*, will henceforth be incorporated in my text.
8. Hugh Sykes Davies, *Petron* (London: J. M. Dent, 1935), reviewed by Gascoyne in *New Verse*, 18 (December, 1935) p. 19.
9. Davies, *Petron*, p. 4.
10. *Ibid.*, p. 6.
11. Georges Bataille, *Oeuvres Complètes* (Paris: Gallimard, 1976) vol. II, pp. 93–109.
12. Michel Remy, *David Gascoyne: ou, L'urgence de l'inexprimé. Suivi de Notes sur les Collected Poems et du scénario inédit d'un film surréaliste* (Nancy: Presses Universitaires de Nancy, 1984) pp. 23–4 (my translation).
13. Quoted in Gascoyne, *Short Survey of Surrealism*, p. 61.

14. J. Gratton, 'Runaway: Textual Dynamics in the Surrealist Poetry of André Breton', in *Surrealism and Language: Seven Essays*, ed. Ian Higgins (Edinburgh: Scottish Academic Press, 1986) p. 31.
15. Davies, *Petron*, p. 4.
16. Read (ed.), *Surrealism*, p. 214
17. *Ibid.*, p. 206.
18. *Ibid.*, p. 215.
19. David Gascoyne, *Man's Life Is This Meat* (London: Parton Press, 1936).
20. Rob Jackaman, 'View from the White Cliffs: A Close Look at One Manifestation of English Surrealism', *Twentieth-Century Literature*, 21 (1975) p. 78.
21. *Ibid.*, p. 79.
22. Paul C. Ray, 'Meaning and Textuality: A Surrealist Example', *Twentieth-Century Literature*, 26 (1980) p. 321.
23. *Ibid.*, p. 317.
24. Wyndham Lewis, *The Diabolic Principle and the Dithyrambic Spectator* (London: Chatto and Windus, 1931).
25. Ray, 'Meaning and Textuality', p. 319.
26. Michel Remy, 'Surrealism's Vertiginous Descent on Britain', in *Angels of Anarchy and Machines for Making Clouds*, pp. 35, 37.
27. *Ibid.*, p. 35.
28. Jacques Derrida, *The Post Card: From Socrates to Freud and Beyond*, trans. Alan Bass (Chicago and London: University of Chicago Press, 1987) p. 441.
29. Rob Jackaman, *London Bulletin*, 2 (May 1938) p. 7.
30. Hugh Sykes Davies, 'Sympathies with Surrealism', *New Verse*, 20 (April–May 1936) p. 15.
31. Herbert Read, 'Introduction', *Surrealism*, ed. Herbert Read, pp. 89–90.
32. See Davies's 'Sympathies With Surrealism' of 1936.
33. Roger Roughton, 'Surrealism and Communism', *Contemporary Poetry and Prose*, 5 (August–September 1936) p. 74, and 'Eyewash, Do You?: A Reply to Mr Pound', *Contemporary Poetry and Prose*, 7 (November 1936) pp. 137–8.
34. Roger Roughton, *Contemporary Poetry and Prose*, 1 (May 1936) p. 7.
35. Roger Roughton, *The Freedom of Poetry: Studies in Contemporary Verse* (London: Falcon Press, 1937) p. 45.
36. Roger Roughton, *Contemporary Poetry and Prose*, 2–3 (June 1936) p. 55.
37. Ezra Pound, 'The Coward Surrealists' and Roger Roughton, 'Eyewash, Do You: A Reply to Mr. Ezra Pound', *Contemporary Poetry and Prose*, 7 (November 1936) pp. 136–7.
38. *The Auden Generation: Literature and Politics in the 1930s* (London: Bodley Head, 1976) pp. 217–27.
39. Humphrey Jennings, review of *Surrealism*, ed. Herbert Read, *Contemporary Poetry and Prose*, 8–9 (December 1936) p. 168.
40. *Ibid.*
41. *Ibid.*
42. Humphrey Jennings, *Contemporary Poetry and Prose*, 10 (Spring 1937) p. 41.

43. Humphrey Jennings, *Contemporary Poetry and Prose*, 2–3 (June 1936) pp. 94–5.
44. Humphrey Jennings, *Contemporary Poetry and Prose*, 8–9 (December 1936) pp. 146–7. A longer version of this 'Study for a long report' appeared in the *London Bulletin*, 12 (March 1939) pp. 7–8.
45. Kathleen Raine, *Defending Ancient Springs* (London: Oxford University Press, 1967) pp. 47–8.
46. Quoted in A. Robertson et al., *Angels of Anarchy and Machines for Making Clouds*, p. 57.

12

The Poetry of the Second World War

JOHN PIKOULIS

Three writers emerged with literary reputations during the Second World War: Keith Douglas, Alun Lewis and Sidney Keyes. Others who wrote well-known poems – among them Henry Reed and F. T. Prince – did not produce the same substantial body of work. Since then, Keyes has faded fast, leaving interest divided between Douglas, polished and theatrical, and Lewis, more anguished and complex.

I

Douglas's poetry is characterised above all by the theme of death. An early poem reads:

> Death has made up your face, his quiet hand
> Perfects your costume to impersonate
> The one who cannot enter this living land.
>
> And it is death who makes sure, and chances
> No tenderness in the recesses of your eyes.[1]

He is the pitiless theatrical producer of effects, self-possessed, formidable and imposing, like the poet himself. The subject of this poem, 'Poor Mary', Mary Oswin, was not dead at the time and received such treatment because she considered Douglas to be arrogant and snobbish, someone not easy to neglect but difficult to like, a judgement few would quarrel with.

Repeatedly, Douglas's poems confront death (or the idea of death) with lucid detachment. After the outbreak of war, he vowed: 'I shall never write a word to escape, / our life will take on a hard

193

shape' (*CP*, p. 26), and it is that 'shape' that his poems cling to, usually without effort.

> always to think, and always to indite
> of a good matter, while the black birds cry.
>   (*ibid.*)

The black birds of war add lustre to the self-regarding archaism of 'to indite / of a good matter', the foppish elegance of which is entirely characteristic.

Douglas's composure before death was as much forced on him as elected; how else, as he himself observed, could he 'harvest yet among the general dearth' (*CP*, p. 28)? Undoubtedly he was fascinated by the thought of death and personified it as 'the adept subtle amorist' (another dandy phrase), a 'rich man', 'wicked' (*CP*, p. 32). He must have felt as much flattered as threatened by his attentions.

Douglas grew up the only child of a mother plagued by ill-health and a father whose desertion condemned them to a life of genteel poverty. Rescued by successive scholarships to Christ's Hospital and Oxford, his close ties with his mother were not counterbalanced by other sources in the usual way, so that he remained guarded against a potentially hostile world, his heart and will being neither steady nor secure. The upshot, in 1939 and 1940, was his identification with Death the gentleman dandy, invulnerable, superior to the accidents of time, beyond both love and hate: he had found his ultimate identity. All delight in earthly things was 'God's impermanent bluff' (*CP*, p. 38), while fear filled his heart. As early as 1940 we find him saying that he was enjoying what he felt was his last summer. He was proving himself against the ultimate deception.

The romantic aggrandisement of death is evident in the poems from this period.

> Death says: 'If I don't get you,
> then Time aha will presently upset you – . . .
> rest you merry near your last breath.'

> In deference to his advice
> I look in maidens' faces after
> what men cannot but need the most.
>   (*CP*, p. 45)

Cool, calculating lines. Douglas had an automatic succession of girlfriends whom he won and lost, now as later, with the minimum of emotional fuss. Being trapped by Time and Death, he 'cadged careless hearts' because he was already possessed by death, the warrior–victim. In 'A Ballet' (*CP*, p. 52), he writes of a dance performed by a dead girl and a limbless boy:

> How horribly spry
> he is on his stumps:
> he bleeds, but he jumps
> ten feet at a prance.
> I don't like this dance.

Yet he writes about it unflinchingly and, in doing so, prefigures the many mutilated figures who appear in his poems and drawings (Douglas was a very good draughtsman). In 'John Anderson' (*CP*, p. 56), he describes the hero as being attended in death by Zeus, and his body being cleansed by Apollo before being taken to Lycia by Sleep and Death.

Douglas's elation on joining the army in 1940 is related to his sense of hurrying towards a desired climax. Social reasons meant that the son of a father who was a chicken farmer and cold-storage tank maker and a mother who was a lady's companion could not impersonate an army officer without taking Death as his model. No wonder the officers he actually met were uneasy in his presence; he was unconsciously mimicking them. As he explains in 'The House' (*CP*, p. 69), he felt transparent and humble, an attentive yet endangered being, fragile as glass though strong as a pillar, ghostly in the shadows of war and preoccupied by love and the imagination. A photograph of him at the time, reproduced in Desmond Graham's biography, *Keith Douglas 1920–1944*,[2] shows him standing in a cavalry officer's uniform, chin up, hands behind his back. He had embellished the photo with pillars, laurel wreaths and hearts and etched a halo round his head as well as providing a motto: 'Dulce et decorum est pro patria mori'. It is as offensive a gesture as could be imagined. When his training regiment was mechanised, he was thoroughly disconcerted; in the desert, however, he was to use the tank as if it were a horse.

Douglas enjoyed life and prepared to enjoy death with an equal zest. In 'Time Eating' (*CP*, p. 71), he notes that the lizard's tail and the snake's skin can be remade but not the boy-become-a-soldier.

Nevertheless, he imagines that his own undoing will share some of the same glitter. He was not a man to be discomposed by fate. From this complex arises one of his most famous poems, 'Simplify me When I'm Dead', which shows him presenting himself as a posed or arranged quality:

> Remember me when I am dead
> and simplify me when I'm dead.
>
> As the processes of earth
> strip off the colour and the skin
> take the brown hair and blue eye
>
> and leave me simpler than at birth, . . .
> (*CP*, p. 74)

This reduction to essence is also a curious ennoblement and it is accomplished in polished phrases like 'the processes of earth'. (Compare 'horribly spry' and 'cannot but need'.) After the pain comes purification; after death, hearts and laurels.

   Douglas's enchantment by death followed him to the Middle East. Not for nothing was he appointed Camouflage Officer. Everything now amazed him but he regarded it with either levity or indifference; war had made him careless. Like the beggar woman of 'Egypt' (*CP*, p. 89), he came to regard life and death as 'the difference of moving / and the nuisance of breath'; beauty was kin to 'disease, disease and apathy'. The dry and the fertile, the worthless and the valuable, good and evil – all meant the same to him.

> Here I am a stranger clothed
> in the separative glass cloak
> of strangeness.
> (*CP*, p. 85)

The 'glass cloak' reminds us of his portrait in 'The House', and, like the odd, self-regarding word 'separative', suggests the self-consciousness that set him apart from others while serving as a mirror for his reflections. He is proof against his own perceptions and remains intensely watchful.

> The dark eyes, the bright-mouthed
> smiles, glance on the glass and break

falling like fine strange insects.

(*ibid.*)

Thus Douglas picked his way through life. Yet, for all his 'separativeness', he was eventually poisoned by it. The glass could not prevent him from lapsing into humility. Still, the smooth lines and elegant diction remain firm: nothing, it seems, can penetrate them. They are abstract, allegorical, unemotional. This is certainly not how the poets of the First World War wrote. But then, as Douglas observed, 'hell cannot be let loose twice: it was let loose in the Great War and it is the same old hell now' (*KD*, p. 192). To write as if it could would be to commit a tautology and Douglas would never be guilty of a solecism.

Besides which, why protest against something he was enamoured of – death? Indeed, he was a connoisseur of misfortune and, in his glassy world, turned to 'kiss my swarthy mistress pain' (*CP*, p. 92). This sublimated sensuality is typical of one who regarded his misfortunes so enticingly.

For Douglas, then, winning or losing hardly mattered: 'after the death of many heroes /' he writes, 'evils remain' (*CP*, p. 94).

> The stars are people in a house of glass
> the heavenly representative of a class
> dead in their seats
> the sun officially goes round
> organising life: and all he's planned
> Time subtly eats.

A very great indifference is stirring here and it is not easy to contradict. 'Dead Men' shows him tranced in communication with moonlit ghosts, suspended in stillness and regarding their once-human virtue as no more than 'a vapour tasteless to a dog's chops'. Here is a 'simplification' which helps him outface the horror of dispensing with his humanity, clinically disinfecting death as fit for a dog's dinner.

Douglas's descriptions of North Africa, both in prose and verse,[3] repeatedly aestheticise the effects of random violence. Tanks and jeeps are 'sand vehicles' lying abandoned like stunned beetles or 'metal posies', their steel 'torn into fronds', while he gazes at them from afar like a 'pilot or angel' (*CP*, p. 103). Desert warfare is a stage whose 'decor' bears the 'terrible tracery / of iron' or 'maquillage'.

Later, the soldiers who return to England for the Normandy invasion of 1944 are described as 'waiting in the wings' while 'the colossal overture' strikes up (*CP*, p. 117).

The famous 'Vergissmeinicht' (Forget-me-not) (*CP*, p. 111) gives these qualities memorable definition. Here again is the cool stare and the aesthetic disposition of a scene (a reduction of the similar encounter between enemies in Owen's 'Strange Meeting', now rendered black comedy). The lover's message ('*Steffi Vergissmeinicht*') and her signature on the photo mock her but the dead man none the less achieves a kind of beauty: 'how on his skin the swart flies move'. Human feeling has been expelled from the portrait and is replaced by the embrace of death, which has 'the soldier singled'. The verb suggests both malice of forethought and the bestowal of a favour. Death grants the soldier his desired clarification beyond all mere accident.

Douglas's final achievement before his death in Normandy was the attempt to define his 'bête noire', the 'beast on his back' he felt had been harrying him for 'about' 11 years (i.e. since his schooldays). The beast is the 'monster' in his belly, a 'persuasive gentleman', both alter ego and harbinger of death (*CP*, pp. 118–19). Even now, however, he understands his 'black care' only imperfectly and prepares to embrace him by crashing through a window or breaking glass. The dandy faces his final unmaking, fear and compulsion robed as destiny.

II

Alun Lewis was also death-haunted but much less theatrically so. He certainly possessed the social identity that Douglas lacked and it came to him with the greatest intensity via the coal-mining valleys of South Wales during the Depression. Unfortunately, he forfeited it when he was sent by his parents to a quasi public school in the Vale of Glamorgan, an exclusion that filled him with a sense of guilt in later years. In one of his last short stories, 'Ward "O" 3 (b)', he describes how his protagonist watched 'the wheel of the pit spin round year after year . . . ; and then from 1926 on I watched it not turning round at all, and I can't ever get the wheel out of my mind. . . . I just missed the wheel sucking me down the shaft. I got a scholarship to the county school. I don't know when I started rebelling. Against the wheel in my head. . . .'[4] This identification of the year of his enrolment at Cowbridge Grammar School and his discovery of 'the wheel in my head' with the year of the miners' lock-out and General Strike is worth emphasising.

His poetry reached a new level of achievement when he enlisted in the Royal Engineers in May 1940. The outer disturbance of war mirrored the inner disturbance he felt. He volunteered for the Engineers in the hope that he could support the war effort without compromising his pacifist scruples. Even so, the tedium of technical training at Longmoor drove him to put in for an officers' training course and he joined the Sixth Battalion, the South Wales Borderers (an infantry unit) in December 1941.

Lewis's sense of waste at Longmoor recalled the attacks of depression he had first suffered as a student at Manchester University in 1935–6, when he confronted 'my living Mr Death'[5] or 'Doppelganger'.[6] In the poems he wrote in 1940, beauty is joined to death, as most famously in 'All day it has rained . . .'. The Longmoor poems are very varied in style and address, going from the sententious to the terse, from the lyrical to the dramatic, from novelistic resourcefulness to symbolic indirection, and the best of them are not necessarily those that are most unified or understated, though he was increasingly attracted to these qualities, for it is the very clash of registers that is significant, as it was in Owen, who saw himself very self-consciously taking Keats and Tennyson and Swinburne onto the battlefield, and who struggled mightily to reconcile them to its horrors.

Lewis first came to attention as one who could give the ordinary soldier's point of view, yet his gift encompasses more than the documentary. In him, the conflicting claims of lover, political idealist, admirer of beauty and childlike innocence were mediated through the figure of the First World War poet who meant most to him, Edward Thomas. By chance, his house lay only a few miles away from Longmoor and he visited it frequently. To Dylan Thomas, Lewis was the poet of social protest, most notably in 'The Mountain over Aberdare'.[7] To others, he was the lyric poet of poems like 'Post-script: for Gweno' (whom he married in 1941). For Robert Graves, he was the best of the new voices articulating a very different kind of war poetry from Owen and the rest. For them, war had been the subject of their imaginations; for Lewis's generation, it was that which came between them and their imagination.[8] In truth, it is possible to see elements of all these and still more in Lewis, for he was a complex man, both attracted to the war and repelled by it, as he was to life in general.

In 'The Mountain over Aberdare', Lewis appears on his mountain top surveying the scene below him: it is a classic of separation. For all the sympathy he feels for the valley folk, he cannot identify with them and describes their activities in a flat voice which contrasts with the symbolical language of his own thoughts, though his description contains a good deal of intricate verbal chiming and rhythmical play which relates their interests to his, the circumstantial to the poetic. The same subtle unifying tendency is displayed by 'All day it has rained . . .', where the tensions between the bored soldiers and innocent children gathering chestnuts and the fate of Edward Thomas (and, by implication, the poet, too) are held in suspension by an imaginative logic which converts tedium and waste into the same depressive crisis which drove Thomas to embrace the war as the solution to his difficulties, suicidal in character. The poem states boredom and lethargy but it enacts enchantment – see its heightened language and swaying rhythms.[9]

In 'The Soldier', another Longmoor poem, Lewis opens with an inflated account of a soldier's excited apprehension of death, and then modulates to a quiet close contemplating 'The flash and play of finches' (a deft tissuing of sounds). The meaning of the poem, however, rests neither with the opening, which none the less remains a truthful record of soldiers' responses to the war, nor with the serenity of the conclusion, but in their interaction, precisely judged by the poet through the introduction of his insouciant fellow-soldiers.

The complexity of Lewis's art and the many-sidedness of his character testify to the stirrings of potentially great writing. His repeated references to death eventually cohered into what he himself was conscious of forming, a journey through what he called 'the spirit's geography',[10] representing for him both conclusion and fulfilment. He explored the complex in his journals, part of which he fictionalised in the story 'Lance-Jack', first published in 1940.[11] In it, he ceases to identify with love and home and comes to appreciate instead the soldier's vagrant life, despite the many frustrations it occasioned him. This is the kind of existence Edward Thomas described in his poems, turning away from 'friendship, love, mutual knowledge, home, children, the rooted beauty of flowers' in favour of a casual 'regard to oneself and the preservation of self' (*TLI*, p. 78). It represents an artist's productive suffering.

This thralldom to death is lent sinister definition by 'The Sentry':

> I have left
> The lovely bodies of the boy and girl
> Deep in each other's placid arms;
> And I have left
> The beautiful lanes of sleep
> That barefooted lovers follow to this last
> Cold shore of thought I guard.[12]

Rhetorical phrases of considerable beauty in which danger is confounded with the appeal of love, the cold with the dark. It represents a kind of consummation and the opening lines of the poem point to it insidiously:

> I have begun to die.
> For now at last I know
> That there is no escape
> From Night. Not any dream
> Nor breathless images of sleep
> Touch my bat's eyes. I hang
> Leathery-arid from the hidden roof
> Of Night, and sleeplessly
> I watch within Sleep's province.

What ought to be a fearful transformation is greeted as if it were a strange metamorphosis. The composure is formidable and it is won with great effort, embodying as it does a ghastly chastening rather than the striking up of an attitude. We sense the pain beneath the fascination. Before he left England in the autumn of 1942, Lewis was to explore this complex memorably through the figure of T. E. Lawrence, for whom 'the only minds worth winning are the warm ones about us'. For Lewis, the artist 'has no vested interests in the warring elements. He is just so much an artist as he is disinterested' (*TLI*, p. 212).

Lewis's arrival in India in December 1942 inaugurated a new phase in his career and led to a poetry that was at once more austere, prosodically regular and searching. Interpretation, however, has been hampered by the veil of secrecy that, until recently, was drawn over what happened to him in India, in particular his love for Freda Aykroyd (wife of the Director of the Nutrition Research Laboratories), whom he met when he visited Coonoor, in the Nilgiri Hills, in July 1943, and his suicide in Burma in March 1944. Without knowledge of these, it has been impossible to understand the poems he wrote to Freda, in particular 'The Way Back', a poem of rare ebullience which, as ever, is complicated by its opposite quality, as its concluding lines show. Here, tragedy and triumph are thoroughly intermixed:

> And in the hardness of this world
> And in the brilliance of this pain
> I exult with such a passion
> To be squandered, to be hurled,
> To be joined to you again.[13]

The sexual consummation is also a 'squandering' and beyond this life. Lewis's letters to Freda, which remain unpublished, confirm his great gifts as a writer.

The official record of enquiry into Lewis's death states that it resulted from an accidental gunshot wound he received when he fell down a hillside used as latrines by the men. It has, however, been established that he in fact killed himself and this has obvious consequences for the interpretation of his poetry. Lewis's Indian poems were published posthumously in 1945 as *Ha! Ha! Among the Trumpets* (the title is drawn from Job) and develops attitudes that were first explored by E. M. Forster in *A Passage to India* and were to be employed again by Paul Scott in his *The Jewel in the Crown*, in particular the 'ou-boum' effect of the Marabar Caves, in which the loftiest of utterances are confounded with the most obscene by the same mocking sound: 'ou-boum'. The nihilism of India preyed on Lewis, offering him a vast panorama of purposelessness that was resistant to human effort, a reduction to essence which he responded to by trying to reduce himself to essence too, something Biblical, primitive. He identified the search, in his mind, with the pursuit of death, the 'IS' of complete identity or pure being that was inherent in the seductive power of the 'beautiful singing sexless angel' he describes at the end of a series of hospital poems written in early 1943 following a sporting accident (*HH*, p. 58). This tranquil–sinister figure appears again in 'Water Music', the best of a group of poems he wrote at a lakeside camp at Easter the same year.

> Cold is the lake water
> And dark is history.

Hurry not and fear not
This oldest mystery.

This strange voice singing,
This slow deep drag of the lake,
This yearning, yearning, this ending
Of the heart and its ache.

(*HH*, p. 49)

Suave rhetoric characterised by an increasingly grave rhythm that plays line-length off against phrase-length until, in the final enjambment, the emotion is finally released.

In 'The Maharatta Ghats', the Indian peasant is seen as participating in an ancient ritual which, with infinite pathos, is about to subsume the soldier. Lewis remains compassionate but daunted, overwhelmed by India's irresistible, beaten quality and defeated of all hope of social amelioration. Another poem, 'The Peasants', identifies a similar force in Indian cowherds and road-builders, including the pregnant women who break stones on the highway. In them Lewis sees 'Creation touching verminous straw beds' (*HH*, p. 56). The juxtaposition of 'Creation', with its rich Christian and other associations, with 'verminous' re-enacts the 'ou-boum' effect. Here is a world which brings the mind to the end of its tether, in which the sun is not the fertile principle but something arid, the 'universal evil eye'.[14]

The questions which had pursued Lewis for many years – what is life worth? what survives? – find their answer now. He had to put aside all his hopes for reconstruction and finally join the nomads about the earth, yielding up his image of the good life, 'the orange grove' (as described in the story of that title), an image of collective effort in adversity, both Jewish and Welsh, which the Arab soldier strays from. It is rather like the recoil from the 'horror' of the Congo that Conrad described in *Heart of Darkness*, an analogy that presented itself to Lewis in India when he contemplated the fate of the Portuguese settlers there.

His last poem, 'The Jungle', is also his finest. In the accents of Auden (as earlier he had employed the voice of Edward Thomas to contemplate the darkness that is in nature) he bids farewell to the hopes of the Thirties: 'The act alone sustains; there is no consequence' (*HH*, p. 67). Separated from 'the warm pacts of the flesh' (with which compare 'the warm ones about us'), he joins the eternal

round, holding on as long as he can to 'Instinctive truths and ele-
mental love' until they, too, are surrendered. The poem ends with
Lewis meditating on death: will it 'resound / With the imprisoned
music of the soul' or does it merely represent the end of 'the will's
long struggle', whether delivered by foe or friend? Put that way,
the friend who kills is a foe but does not stop being a friend for all
that. The bleakness of extinction is calmly contemplated. The poem
blends together public and personal concerns, high declamation
with sensitive lyric, and possesses an architectural structure: the
questions about death at the end return us to the opening, when the
soldiers come to the jungle pool to 'quench more than our thirst –
our selves', the word 'quench' playing on nourishment and extinction. It is a considerable achievement, attained in the most trying of
circumstances.

The issues Lewis deals with in his poems are not self-evidently
less searching than those described by the poets of the First World
War, and suggest that many of the complaints levelled against
him and other Second World War writers derive from prescriptive
notions of what their subject matter might be. To us, their poems
are the responses of men of great courage and imagination reacting to the situation that confronted them. The earlier recoil from the
slaughter of trench warfare has been widened into a general prevision of the anguish of life lived under the aegis of death.

III

Another poet who deserves to be considered a 'war poet', though
she saw no action and describes no battlefield, is Lynette Roberts.
She was born in Argentina of parents of Welsh extraction in 1909
and arrived in Llanybri, a small Carmarthenshire village, at the
outbreak of war in 1939 with her husband, the poet and editor
Keidrich Rhys; she stayed there for the duration. Her poems were
published by T. S. Eliot at Faber and Faber's, as *Poems* (1944) and
Gods with Stainless Ears (1951; despite the later date, this was written between 1941 and 1943; the last section appears in *Poems*). Roberts
continued writing poetry after the war, when she divorced her
husband, but by then the Muse had left her, and she appears to
have recognised as much, for she lapsed into a silence that has continued to this very day. As a consequence, she has been forgotten

by most readers, even those with feminist qualifications. This is unfortunate, for she is one of the period's most distinctive voices.

In the dust-jacket to *Poems*, Eliot wrote: 'She has, first, an unusual gift for observation of scenery and place, whether in Wales or in her native South America; second, a gift for verse construction, influenced by the Welsh tradition, which is evident in her freer verse as well as in stricter forms; and, third, an original idiom.' As a summary of her talents, it cannot be bettered.

Roberts's qualities are well-displayed by the poem she wrote to Alun Lewis called 'Poem from Llanybri':

> *If you come my way that is. . . .*
> Between now and then, I will offer you
> A fist full of rock cress fresh from the bank
> The valley tips of garlic red with dew
> Cooler than shallotts, a breath you can swank
>
> In the village when you come. . . .
>   The din
> Of children singing through the eyelet sheds
> Ringing smith hoops, chasing the butt of hens;
> Or I can offer you Cwmcelyn spread
>
> With quartz stones from the wild scratchings of men:[15]

Why 'valley tips'? Because the wild garlic reminded her of lilies of the valley. Why 'red with dew'? Because the dew on them reflected red light. Why 'eyelet sheds'? Because the windows of the sheds reminded her of little eyes. Why 'wild scratchings of men'? Because the cottages were built of quarried stone and were decorated with designs drawn on the whitewash with a dock leaf. In the same way, the pigeon she offers to cook for him is said to have a 'crop of green foil', thus reproving farmers, who thought of pigeons as pests because they fed on their crops; Roberts contended that they fed on 'green' grass, hence the emphasis. Then there is her friend, Rosie, who goes 'lace curtained in clogs', (*P*, p. 13), a reference to the villagers' custom of tucking bits of old lace curtains into their clogs to make them more comfortable. Many of the poems are thus intricate, riddling expressions of material that still has lyrical qualities.

In his sleeve-note for *Gods with Stainless Ears* (a good example of Roberts's punning style; the title refers to the soldiers' inability to hear what is said about them – they concentrate on their task), Eliot wrote:

> English poetry of our time, as in the first half of the seventeenth century, is greatly indebted to poets from Wales. Among the Welsh poets writing in English Miss Roberts has had a secure place ever since our publication of her *Poems* in 1944. In that volume she showed her skill in a variety of lyrical forms, and her command of a terse, economical idiom. *Gods with Stainless Ears* is a single poem – the author calls it an 'heroic poem'. It is therefore a more ambitious exercise, and a more difficult test of her ability to interest the reader. There are not many living poets who can hold the attention of even their warmest admirers with a volume which is not a collection, but one long poem. *Gods with Stainless Ears* is not an easy poem to grasp the meaning of. But it is astonishingly *readable*; having started it, we wanted to read to the end; and we found it had, even without the analytical 'argument' which the author has provided for each section, the quality of emotional communication, before it was understood.

This, of course, is what Eliot had said about his own poetry indirectly and, like Roberts, he had provided notes to clarify some of the many allusions.

Her long, continuous poem is presented in five parts and follows some of the events recorded in her diary of the time (another unpublished work of much interest, constituting virtually a kind of poetic source book, which, recording her life in Llanybri, is sometimes difficult but finally rewarding). It is evident that the war energised her imagination, too, for she is one of the most characteristic voices of the time, terse, elliptical, idiosyncratic, vivid, always moving and deeply poetical.

Notes

1. Keith Douglas, *Complete Poems*, ed. Desmond Graham (Oxford: Oxford University Press, 1979) p. 24. Hereinafter, all references to this edition are included in the text with the citation *CP*.
2. Desmond Graham, *Keith Douglas 1920–1944* (Oxford: Oxford University Press, 1974) p. 105. Hereinafter, all references to this volume are included in the text with the citation *KD*.

3. See *Alamein to Zem Zem*, ed. Desmond Graham (Oxford: Oxford University Press, first published 1966). For a critical evaluation of Douglas, see Ted Hughes, 'The Poetry of Keith Douglas', *Critical Quarterly*, Spring 1963, pp. 43–8.

4. John Pikoulis, *Alun Lewis, A Life* (Bridgend: Seren, second edition 1991) p. 154.

5. *Alun Lewis, Letters to My Wife*, ed. Gweno Lewis (Bridgend: Seren, 1989) p. 206.

6. Ibid., p. 410.

7. Dylan Thomas, *Quite Early One Morning* (London: Dent, 1954) p. 151.

8. *Alun Lewis, A Miscellany of his Writings*, ed. John Pikoulis (Bridgend: Poetry Wales Press, 1982) p. 132ff. Hereinafter *AMW*.

9. For a full account, see my 'Alun Lewis and Edward Thomas', *Critical Quarterly*, 23 (1981) pp. 25–44.

10. From an unpublished letter to his parents, 20 January 1943.

11. *Life and Letters Today*. Reprinted in *The Last Inspection* [and other stories] (London: Allen and Unwin, 1943) p. 75. Hereinafter, all references to this volume are included in the text with the citation *TLI*.

12. *Raider's Dawn and other poems* (London: Allen and Unwin, 1942) p. 20.

13. *Ha! Ha! Among the Trumpets* (London: Allen and Unwin, 1945) p. 40. Hereinafter, all references to this volume are included in the text with the citation *HH*.

14. 'Stones for Bread', an article printed in *The New Statesman* and reprinted in *AMW, above*.

15. *Poems* (London: Faber and Faber, 1944) p. 7. Hereinafter, all references to this volume are included in the text with the citation *P*.

13

Edwin Muir: Reading Eternity's Secret Script

ALASDAIR D. F. MACRAE

Remain seated as little as possible; trust no thought that is not born in the open, to the accompaniment of free bodily motion – nor one in which your very muscles do not celebrate a feast. All prejudices may be traced back to the intestines. A sedentary life . . . is the real sin against the Holy Ghost.[1]

This characteristically categorical assertion by Nietzsche is an aspect of the connection he saw between the thinker and the man of action, a connection Yeats often cherished:

> When I was young,
> I had not given a penny for a song
> Did not the poet sing it with such airs
> That one believed he had a sword upstairs
> ('All Things can Tempt me')

In Edwin Muir's poetry, and he was an admirer of Yeats and, for the first half of his career, Nietzsche, there is a curious lack of activity, an insistence on the static. In 'Childhood', the first poem included in his *Collected Poems*, we find:

> Over the sound a ship so slow would pass
> That in the black hill's gloom it seemed to lie.
> The evening sound was smooth as sunken glass,
> and time seemed finished ere the ship passed by.
> (*Collected Poems*, p. 19)

Half-way through his career, 'The Myth' opens with the lines:

> My childhood all a myth
> Enacted in a distant isle;

> Time with his hourglass and his scythe
> Stood dreaming on the dial,
> And did not move the whole day long
> That immobility might save
> Continually the dying song,
> The flower, the falling wave.
>
>   (*Collected Poems*, p. 144)

His final poem, in which he looks back across his life, again arrests any sense of progression:

> [I] Have drawn at last from time which takes away
> And taking leaves all things sin their right place
> An image of forever
> One and whole.
>
>   (*Collected Poems*, p. 302)

What is this condition of immobility to which he reverts so often?

There are three main positive forms of immobility which feature in Edwin Muir's work and they all relate primarily to time rather than to space. First, there is the still centre, or the moment out of time when motion is suspended or inoperative; this is a sense of timelessness described in many mystical writings and experienced, albeit fleetingly, by many of us in different circumstances. Secondly, there is a state of rest, when a sequence of events has run its course and come to a peaceful conclusion, the dialectic has achieved reconciliation in an eventual synthesis. This is connected with his teleological notion: 'Immortality is not an idea or a belief, but a state of being in which man keeps alive in himself his perception of that boundless union and freedom, which he can faintly apprehend in time, though its consummation lies beyond time.'[2] Thirdly, there is a starting point which, like Aristotle's acorn containing a full-grown oak tree, has a potential but remains at a prototypal stage. All three forms of immobility stand in a relationship to the mundane world of sequential time, but I wish to focus here on the third, prototypal form. The gravitational pull in Muir's poetry is not towards a millennarian vision but towards a prelapsarian nostalgia. What does this preference reveal of his view of his life and the world around him?

Some examples are needed with which to explore the tendency to move backwards. In 'The Fall', originally published in 1931 and very reminiscent of the earliest poem in *Collected Poems*, 'Ballad of the Soul' (originally 'Ballad of Eternal Life'), the opening stanza's question:

> What shape had I before the Fall?
> What hills and rivers did I seek?
> What were my thoughts then? And of what
> Forgotten histories did I speak
>
> To my companions? Did our eyes
> From their foredestined watching-place
> See Heaven and Earth one land, and range
> Therein through all of Time and Space?
> > (*Collected Poems*, pp. 68–9)

Much of the imagery in the poem derives from a dream experienced by the poet when he was undergoing analysis with the Jungian Maurice Nicholl in London in 1920, but the questions about beginnings were as persistent in Muir as queries about dying were for Emily Dickinson. 'The Ring' begins:

> Long since we were a family, a people,
> The legends say; an old kind-hearted king
> Was our foster father, and our life a fable.
> Nature in wrath broke through the grassy ring
> Where all our gathered treasures lay in sleep –
> Many a rich and many a childish thing.
> > (*Collected Poems*, p. 113)

Our world of time is presented as a usurpation of a good order of 'fable' and 'sleep'. The aptly named poem 'The Journey Back' (1948) may well have provided a model for the sequence-poems of self-exploration by Theodore Roethke in *The Far Field* (1964). Section 7 opens:

> Yet in this journey back
> If I should reach the end, if end there was Before
> the ever-running roads began
> And race and track and runner all were there
> Suddenly, always, the great revolving way
> Deep in its trance; – if there was ever a place

> Where one might say, 'Here is the starting-point,' . . .
>
> (*Collected Poems*, p. 174)

Of course, Muir presents his notion of a starting-point as a hypo-thesis, a question, introduced by 'if' or attributed to 'legends', but many commentators on his work have seen an opposition between an Eden where everything is 'permissible, all acceptable, / Clear and secure as in a limpid dream' and a labyrinth of 'deceiving streets / That meet and part and meet, and rooms that open / Into each other – and never a final room –' (*Collected Poems*, pp. 164–5). This opposition they find confirmed in *An Autobiography* in the move of Muir in 1901 from a blissful childhood on the Orkneys to a con-fusing and degrading life in industrial Glasgow. George Marshall's book *In a Distant Isle: The Orkney Background of Edwin Muir* (Edin-burgh: Scottish Academic Press, 1987) has been extremely helpful in dislodging the simplistic reading of *An Autobiography* as a straight, factual account and in demonstrating how Muir has selected and manipulated evidence to create a fictive situation of beginnings.

The earlier version of his autobiography, *The Story and the Fable*, was published in 1940 and, in a letter of May 1938, he describes what he is planning to write:

> I am taking notes for something like a description of myself, done in general outline, not in detail, not as a story, but as an attempt to find out what a human being is in this extraordinary age which depersonalises everything. . . . It may be that I have found at last a form that suits me; it may be that I haven't found a form at all, but merely a collection of fragments. . . . The problem is to discover what you are, and then what your relation is to other people: I am starting from that and it takes me in ever so many directions, inwards and outwards, backwards and forwards: into dreams on the one hand, and social observation on the other; into the past by a simple line, and over the present by countless lines.[3]

There is a curious mixture here of the personal and the impersonal, but the emphasis seems to be away from Muir's story in favour of himself as a typical case. His need was to find a counterbalance to the depersonalising forces of twentieth-century Europe. He had experienced Fascism at first hand, felt acutely the persecution of the Jews, and saw the whole movement as a dehumanising mad-ness. His own socialism was anti-Marxist and, for him, Stalinist

Communism, with its materialist determinism, was not an ideological opposition to Fascism but a similar denial of humanity. His
notion of humanity was centred on a belief in the immortality of
the soul, a belief from which all his poetry, according to himself,
'springs . . . in one form or another'.[4] In March 1939 this belief was
accommodated in an acceptance of Christianity (although Muir was
never to find a Church to which he could give his adherence). In his
poetry, certainly up to *The Labyrinth* (1949), the nature of immortality is more closely related to Wordsworth's '*Ode*' and 'the primal
sympathy / Which having been must ever be' than to any suggestions of heavenly mansions or Yeatsian Dreaming Back. The pro-
posal I am making is not so much that Muir's notion of Eden is
based on a happy rural childhood (which, by and large, he did
enjoy) but that the picture of his childhood on an island and his
notion of Eden inside its wall were both devised as, to use Frost's
phrase, stays against confusion.

Perhaps, however, the very reiteration of immobility, the resort-
ing to the enclosed moment, renders the whole enterprise somewhat suspect, as if a metaphor comes to be taken literally. A few
years before Muir wrote *The Story and the Fable*, Yeats, a fellow
mythographer, wrote in an introduction to the Second Edition of *A
Vision*:

> Some will ask whether I believe in the actual existence of my
> circuits of sun and moon. Those that include, now all recorded
> time in one circuit, now what Blake called 'the pulsation of an
> artery', are plainly symbolical, but what of those that . . . divide
> history into periods of equal length? . . . I can but answer that if
> sometimes, overwhelmed by miracle as all men must be when in
> the midst of it, I have taken such periods literally, my reason has
> soon recovered. . . . I regard them as stylistic arrangements of
> experience. . . . They have helped me to hold in a single thought
> reality and justice.[5]

My worry as regards Muir's poetry is that his desire for justice
constrains or warps his knowledge of reality. When adversity or
cruelty or deceit is oppressive he can retreat to where harmony and
understanding prevail:

> This is the Pattern, these are the Archetypes,[6]
> Sufficient, strong and peaceful. All outside

From end to end of the world is tumult.
('The Sufficient Place', *Collected Poems*, p. 87)

The reader may feel that, despite the poet's claims that such escape is difficult to gain, the solution is asserted and not won through struggle.

This suspicion is increased by the peculiar language in which the confrontation of pessimism and optimism is couched. Even Hardy and Housman, born long before Muir, can hardly match his archaic diction; can a poet writing in 1955 use the word 'sward' without apparent irony or self-mockery? Moreover, it is not just his rather fustian diction which jars or needs some special pleading; his terms of reference are remarkably unchanging and sound dated. For example, the title 'Scotland 1941' seems to intimate a very particular diagnosis, but the poet pulls back to locate Scotland's problems in the aftermath of John Knox's Reformation in the sixteenth century. Not only do we have to accept curiosities such as 'pelf' and 'lucre', not only is there not a single specifically contemporary reference in forty-one lines, but the poem hinges on a contrast between the 'iron text' of Calvinism and a romantic, picture-book view of medieval Scotland: 'A simple sky roofed in that rustic day'. In fact, the poem is intellectually tougher than this description suggests, but it contains an imbalance manifested in its diction. If the poem is placed alongside passages from Muir's *Scottish Journey* (1935) – a companion volume to J. B. Priestley's *English Journey* and Philip Gibbs's *European Journey* – the enormous difference between his prose and his poetry is immediately obvious. In *Scottish Journey*, his letters, large sections of *An Autobiography* and his books of criticism, he is a direct, informed and acute observer writing in a straightforward, lively manner. His poetry he saw as something specialised and more rarefied. It is significant that he chose not to include in his *Collected Poems* two poems in *Scottish Journey* which are direct and colloquial:

> A Scottish bullock has a look
> About him that you will not see
> In workless men shuffling their feet
> Outside some public W.C.[7]

And there are other examples of poems discarded because, it would seem, they were too topical. The material had to be aged and typified, the contemporary problem had to be presented as a costume drama. The period of the costume is not entirely specific but is a mixture of elements from classical myths, medieval pageants and legends or folk tales: arrows and helmets, kings and sacred groves, dragons and peasants all mingle as they do in Victorian illustrations to the Bible. The Bible itself, both Old and New Testaments, is the largest contributor to his image-hoard. His early admiration for the Border Ballads, William Morris's *The Earthly Paradise,* Tennyson's 'The Lady of Shalott' and Arnold's *Tristram and Iseult* not doubt had some effect on his style but, more important, they validated a tendency he found in himself when he began to write poetry. (He was thirty eight when his *First Poems* was published in 1925.)

It is possible in some cases to follow parts of the process by which a poem emerged and took shape. 'The Combat' is the most obvious example and has been adequately examined before now.[8] It is sufficient here to mention that the imagery of the eventual poem probably stems from an experience when he was five or six years old, incidents and dreams when he was nineteen in Glasgow added to the imagery and introduced drama, a dream in London when he was thirty-four developed the heraldic nature of the conflict, and the poem was written in Prague in 1947 when he was sixty and when he had come to understand more deeply the sufferings of people under absolute power. In 1955 in Harvard, in answer to a question on the meaning of the poem, he remained very tentative. A previously less discussed example is 'The Little General' from *The Narrow Place* (1943 but first printed in 1938):

> Early in spring the little General came
> Across the sound, bringing the island death,
> And suddenly a place without a name,
> And like the pious ritual of a faith,
>
> Hunter and quarry in the boundless trap,
> The white smoke curling from the silver gun,
> The feather curling in the hunter's cap,
> And clouds of feathers floating in the sun,
>
> While down the birds came in a deafening shower,
> Wing-hurricane, and the cattle fled in fear.
> Up on the hill a remnant of a tower
> Had watched that single scene for many a year,

Weaving a wordless tale where all were gathered
(Hunter and quarry and watcher and fabulous field),
A sylvan war half human and half feathered,
Perennial emblem painted on a shield

Held up to cow a never-conquered land
Fast in the little General's fragile hand.
(*Collected Poems*, pp. 110–11)

The poem is based on General Burroughs, a veteran of the Indian
Mutiny and landlord to Edwin Muir's father on the island of Wyre.
In *An Autobiography* Muir recalls the annual shooting visits of the
General and one particular occasion when he was about five years
old. The passage is too long to quote in its entirety but no physical
detail in the poem is missing in the prose description. The paragraph concludes:

> It was a mere picture; I did not feel angry with the General or
> sorry for the birds; I was entranced with the bright gun, the white
> smoke, and particularly with the soft brown tabs of leather on
> the shoulders of his jacket. My mother was standing at the end
> of the house with me; the General came over and spoke to her,
> then, calling me to him, gave me a sixpence. My father appeared
> from somewhere, but replied very distantly to the General's af-
> fable words. He was a bad landlord, and in a few years drove my
> father out of the farm by his exactions.[9]

It could be argued again that the poem and the passage, written
about the same time, are both constructs and are bound to have
similarities, but what is significant in the present discussion is not
the similarity between the poetry and the prose but the differences.
First, the venue is delocalised and the viewpoint is impersonalised.
Muir 'absents' himself from the poem and the description of the
little General is reduced drastically: he has no specific identity. Time
is both particular (line 1) and constant (line 12); the incident is part
of a recurring process ('ritual', 'boundless', 'perennial'). The syntax
thwarts a forward or narrative direction of sense and the two sentences roll back on themselves as if each lacks a crucial verb. Where
the sentences eddy is where the action is given an archetypal twist
in such pharses as 'pious ritual', 'fabulous field' and 'perennial
emblem'. Something fixed but unresolvable is maintained in the

paradoxes of the final couplet: 'cow . . . never-conquered'; 'fast . . .
fragile'. If the poem cannot be bound to its origins in late nineteenth-
century Orkney and predatory landlords, not can it be bound to the
late 1930s with its strutting generals. The terms 'hunter and quarry',
'wordless tale' and 'sylvan war' remove the struggle from any one
period. This despecifying, which is of a different but related sort
to Eliot's use of myth in *The Waste Land* and Edith Sitwell's parallelism in 'Still Falls the Rain', raises a large question: are menace
and cruelty and killing made palatable by being detached from an
immediate context and emblematised as aspects of a larger and
unchangeable pattern?

Muir was, or course, conscious of the question and tried to answer his doubting critics. His poem 'The Emblem', written in 1951,
concludes Part I of *One Foot in Eden* (1956):

> I who so carefully keep in such repair
> The six-inch king and the toy treasury,
> Prince, poet, realm shrivelled in time's black air,
> I am not, although I seem, an antiquary.
> For that scant-acre kingdom is not dead,
> Nor save in seeming shrunk. When at its gate,
> Which you pass daily, you incline your head,
> And enter (do not knock; it keeps no state)
>
> You will be with space and order magistral,
> And that contracted world so vast will grow
> That this will seem a little tangled field.
> For you will be in very truth with all
> In their due place and honour, row on row.
> For this I read the emblem on the shield.
>
> <div align="right">(<i>Collected Poems</i>, pp. 230–1)</div>

Despite his protestations and invitations, there remains something
suspect about the affirmation. The quaintness of 'scant-acre', the
poetical turn of phrase, even the grand Shakespearian gesture of
'You will be with space and order magistral' do not quite convince
me that he is not diverting himself with his toys. The very use of
the sonnet gives his attitude a pedigree. Order, tradition and authority summarised in 'the emblem on the shield' cause the world
around him to be dismissed as 'a little tangled field'.

Throughout his poems there is an emphasis on order. The world of Eden is the quintessential order and from its example derive various covenants, treaties, bargains and arrangements:

> The covenant of god and animal,
> The frieze of fabulous creatures winged and crowned,
> And in the midst the woman and the man –
> > (*Collected Poems*, p. 132)

Up to this point I have expressed some scepticism about the authority Muir grants to this fabulous domain. Are there more positive ways of assessing this element?

First, I offer a rather theoretical approach. Edwin Muir saw around him in the twentieth century a battle between two ideologies: one, he calls historical' (compare Popper's historicism) and the other he calls 'religious'. The struggles is not peculiar to this century but the confrontation has become more bitter and the historical side has been in the ascendant. Many of the essays in Part II of *Essays on Literature and Society* (originally published in 1949) return to this concern and his anxiety is most apparent when he writes on Oswald Spengler:

> To him the one operative factor in existence is not goodness, beauty or truth, but power, and so he praises the beast of prey and pours scorn on 'a human morality based on weakness'. The old view [the religious] of life sees endless variety and complexity in human existence, and yet makes certain fundamental distinctions: good and evil, truth and falsehood, guilt and innocence. The new historical view as expressed by Spengler sees no essential variety in human existence at all, but only the category of power, or, in other words, of necessity; and yet, in spite of its simplicity, it leads to no conclusion: it remains on the plane of pure relativity.[10]

Relativity has been a central concept in Modernist (and Post-Modernist) art, affecting both the content and the form of many works. Muir's opposition to it is very basic, primarily moral. His thoughtful analysis of 'The Politics of *King Lear*' (1948) identifies evil in the play precisely in the relativism of Goneril, Regan and Edmund and connects their thinking with twentieth-century Fascist *Realpolitik*. In the essay 'Natural Man and Political Man' he contrasts Pope and Wordsworth; Pope, by 'declaring that the proper study of mankind is man, enclosed man in an elegant vacuum, cut from nature in which his roots were fastened, and from God in whom he had his being', whereas Wordsworth, with a more complex and, according to Muir, a truer vision, saw the whole created world as

> workings of one mind, the features
> Of the same face, blossoms upon one tree;
> Characters of the great Apocalypse,
> The types and symbols of Eternity,
> Of first, and last, and midst, and without end –
> > *(The Prelude,* Book Six, II. 636–40)

Wordsworth's faith and the biblical tread of these lines anticipate Muir's absolutist doctrine. And, looking back across this century, we could argue that Muir is less singular than he was deemed by earlier critics: many poets who had espoused a relativist attitude in their earlier career gradually or suddenly give their allegiance to an extrapersonal order. Even William Carlos Williams, when he came to write *Paterson,* sought 'an image large enough to embody the whole knowable world about me'.[11] In what is probably his last poetic statement Muir affirms:

> And now that time grows shorter, I perceive
> That Plato's is the truest poetry,
> And that these shadows
> Are cast by the true.
> > *(Collected Poems,* p. 302)

'Plato'? 'the true'? Seven years later Derrida delivered his lecture 'Structure, sign and play in the discourse of the human sciences'.

Muir felt passionately about the struggle between the religious and the historical and was totally committed to the religious side and its fixities. There was another factor which caused him to cling to order; he was frightened of psychological disorder in himself. Like Tennyson, who was afraid that a family madness might overwhelm him at any moment, or like Frost, with his black depressions and guilts, he needed the solace of images of a good place, of sufficiency and security. From early childhood he suffered from ill health and the hyper-sensitivity which enabled him to perceive his world with such wonderful sharpness persisted to plague him as an adult in, as he experienced it, a hostile environment. Willa, his protective wife and loyal admirer, describes his condition in 1919: 'He shivered with apprehensions. Sometimes he felt that buildings were going to crash on his head as he passed them, sometimes he cowered beneath the conviction that he barely existed, being an anonymous unit in a crowd of anonymous units.'[12] Some pages later she writes of his desire for a supportive myth:

> In Nietzsche, especially in *Thus Spake Zarathustra*, he found the poetic content and wide cosmic sweep of story he wanted. Now [1920], although he was beginning to distrust Nietzsche's Super-Man, he still looked for some great story, some cosmic pattern that would assign a place to every experience in life, relating it to an inclusive whole and justifying it. He was looking for that in his visions, and he kept on looking for it as long as he lived, until he thought he had found it.[13]

(It is worth noting the fact that he never spent more than five years in any one house throughout his life and he was endlessly on the move back and fore across Europe and later America.) Writers on Muir have often presented him as a figure of benign and calm wisdom, but in the corpus of the poems, the autobiography and, most markedly, in the three novels, written between 1926 and 1932, a hectic, painful and baffled quality is apparent. In the poetry, there are figures locked in an obsession, for example, in 'Tristram's Journey', 'Holderlin's Journey' and Parts 1 and 2 of 'Effigies', figures unable to break a spell, whether of love or hate matters not. The person becomes the obsession in 'The Helmet':

> The helmet on his head
> Has melted flesh and bone
> And forged a mask instead
> That always is alone.
> (*Collected Poems*, p. 177)

Muir's poetry does have its ghouls and monsters; an interesting comparison could be made between 'The Bridge of Dread' and Browning's ' "Childe Roland to the Dark Tower Came" '. The heart of Muir's horror, however, is a comatose impotence, as, in 'The Enchanted Knight', the figure fails to respond:

> But if a withered leaf should drift
> Across his face and rest, the dread drops start

Chill on his forehead. Now he tries to lift
The insulting weight that stays and breaks his heart.
                                        (*Collected Poems*, p. 74)

The Knight's armour is rendered irrelevant, and across the poems
there are repeated instances of a mode of defence becoming part
of a trap. When the poet first read Kafka in 1929 he immediately
recognised a fellow-fear in him; the story, 'The Burrow', which the
Muirs later translated, could have been written by Muir himself.
Like Kafka, he had an inflamed sense of guilt and a consequent
hankering for release and exoneration. In poems such as *Variations
on a Time Theme*, IX, 'The Private Place', 'The Intercepter' and 'The
Charm', subversion takes place inside the speaker and any hope of
progress is subject to a cataleptic arrest.

THE RIDER VICTORY

The rider Victory reins his horse
Midway across the empty bridge
As if head-tall he had met a wall.
Yet there was nothing there at all,
No bodiless barrier, ghostly ridge
To check the charger in his course.
So suddenly, you'd think he'd fall.

Suspended, horse and rider stare
Leaping on air and legendary.
In front the waiting kingdom lies,
The bridge and all the roads are free;
But halted in implacable air
Rider and horse with stony eyes
Uprear their motionless statuary.
                                        (*Collected Poems*, p. 142)

The very immobility I discussed at the start of the chapter as something desirable comes to be seen as treacherous.
   Up to 1949 the majority of the poems doggedly point towards or
proclaim some position of salvation. The very reiteration of optimism causes us to doubt its efficacy and often a desperation is obvious in the assertiveness:

> That more is our salvation.
> Now let us seize it. Now we can.
> (*Collected Poems*, p. 99)

Muir himself heard the shrill desperation and he revised his original formulation of the final line; it had read 'Now let us seize it. Now we can, we can!'. In 1948, after the Communist take-over in Czechoslovakia, he returned to Britain and there suffered a major breakdown. In 1949 he went to Rome as Director of the British Council and his health improved. During his year and a half in Italy he found a realisation in people and places of what his earlier poems had pointed towards. Thematically and stylistically his later poems are continuous with the earlier ones, but in both respects a relaxation enters his poetry and a substantial development takes place. It is as if he no longer needs the protective shield of predictable endings and archaic verbal formulae. I have no wish to be disparaging about the earlier poetry but its repeated manoeuvres sometimes invoke Muir's own description of one of his favourite poets, Hölderlin, as manifesting 'a certain radiant monotony'.[14] There are excellent poems throughout his career, and his political ones of the 1940s are probably the only poems written in English which can bear the scrutiny of people who have lived under totalitarianism.

In *One Foot in Eden* (1956) and the poems written between then and his death in 1959, he even explores the completely new possibility of a nuclear holocaust destroying mankind:

> No place at all for bravery in that war
> Nor mark where one might make a stand,
> Nor use for eye or hand
> To discover and reach the enemy
> Hidden in boundless air.
> ('The Last War', *Collected Poems*, p. 282)

and

> If it could come to pass, and all kill all
> And in a day or a week we could destroy
> Ourselves ...
> Mechanical parody of the Judgement Day
> That does not judge but only deals damnation.
> ('The Day Before the Last Day', *Collected Poems*, p. 300)

In the much anthologised 'The Horses', highly praised by T. S. Eliot, Muir incorporates straight more items from the modern world than he previously managed to include in a whole collection: radios, a warship, a plane, tractors, kitchens. Previously he had manipulated emblems as a bulwark against the ordinary world, which he found frightening, and his identification of time as an enemy was because it was the element in which the ordinary world has its being and significance. His earlier heraldic menagerie could not have included such common specimens as 'The Late Wasp' and 'The Late Swallow' in *One Foot in Eden*. Curiously, despite his perpetual returning to the sources of his life, until the late poetry he seemed unable to accommodate the most obvious source, his parents and family. Between the opening poem, 'Childhood', in the *Collected Poems* and 'Day and Night' (p. 239) there is barely a reference to his mother and father. There are occasional hints of domesticity and workaday routines in such poems as 'The Wayside Station' and 'Suburban Dream' but they are notably rare until later. In the title poem 'One Foot in Eden', originally called 'Loss and Gain', he manifests a stronger acceptance of the world in which he finds himself and even some advantages in it over the Eden he had hankered for so avidly in his middle age:

> What had Eden ever to say
> Of hope and faith and pity and love
> Until was buried all its day
> And memory found its treasure trove?
> Strange blessings never in Paradise
> Fall from these beclouded skies.
>   (*Collected Poems*, p. 227)

With its singular lack of irony and wit, Muir's poetry offered meagre fare to the teeth of the New Critics and it was consequently ignored or embarrassedly discarded. It has tended to attract rather pious and solemnly Christian supporters although this situation is now changing.[15] For thoroughgoing Deconstructionists, he is surely too resolutely attached to presence, the meaning, the Fable, to merit much sophisticated unravelling, although his description of Penelope's delaying tactics with the suitors might find favour with such critics: 'endless undoing / Of endless doing, endless weaving, unweaving' (*Collected Poems*, p. 114). If, for Muir, meaning

exists in memory, in re-enactment of the original act, he puts himself beyond a current pale; on the other hand, he accepts the fallibility and deceitfulness of language as a means to discover meaning.
This chapter has tried to show how the poetic expression of asserted assurance raises many doubts and often reveals insecurity
rather than certainty. He would, I think, have seen the ludic manoeuvres of the Deconstructionists as trivialising and their attempts
to demolish the Mystery as, pace Nietzsche at the opening of this
chapter, the real sin against the Holy Ghost. In the end he would
like to emulate Kafka:

> But you, dear Franz, sad champion of the drab
> And half, would watch . . .
> > not aloof,
> But with a famishing passion quick to grab
> Meaning, and read on all the leaves of sin
> Eternity's secret script, the saving proof.
> > > > *(Collected Poems,* p. 233)

Notes

All quotations of Muir's poetry are, unless indicated otherwise, taken from
Edwin Muir, *Collected Poems* (London: Faber and Faber, 1960).

1. F. Nietzsche, *Ecce Homo* (1888), trans. C. P. Fadiman (New York:
    Modern Library, 1927) p. 25.
2. E. Muir, *An Autobiography* (London: The Hogarth Press, 1954) p. 170.
3. E. Muir, *Selected Letters,* ed. P. Butter (London: The Hogarth Press,
    1974) p. 100.
4. Ibid., p. 107.
5. W. B. Yeats, *A Vision and Related Writings,* ed. A. Norman Jeffares
    (London: Arrow Books, 1990) p. 86. I find that Seamus Heaney makes
    a similar point in a lecture, 'The Place of Edwin Muir', printed in
    Verse, vol. 6, no. 1 (March 1989) p. 27.
6. 'Archetypes' was given as 'Prototypes' in an earlier draft.
7. E. Muir, *Scottish Journey* (London: Heinemann/Gollancz, 1935) p. 100.
8. See, for example, C. Wiseman, *Beyond the Labyrinth* (Victoria,
    Canada: Sono Nis Press, 1978) pp. 87–90.
9. E. Muir, *An Autobiography,* p. 15.

10. E. Muir, *Essays on Literature and Society* (London: The Hogarth Press, 1949) p. 131.
11. W. C. Williams, *The Autobiography* (New York: New Directions, 1951) p. 391.
12. W. Muir, *Belonging* (London: The Hogarth Press, 1968) p. 36. See also pp. 244–50 for a description of his breakdown in 1948.
13. Ibid., pp. 45–6.
14. E. Muir, *Essays on Literature and Society*, p. 84.
15. See, for example, J. M. MacLachlen and D. S. Robb (eds), *Edwin Muir: Centenary Assessments* (Aberdeen Association for Scottish Literary Studies, 1990).

Index